ARCO

HOW TO BECOME A U.S. CITIZEN

3RD EDITION

Debra R. Shpigler, J.D.

ARCO
THOMSON LEARNING

Australia • Canada • Denmark • Japan • Mexico • New Zealand • Philippines
Puerto Rico • Singapore • South Africa • Spain • United Kingdom • United States

ARCO
THOMSON LEARNING

3rd Edition

An ARCO Book

ARCO is a registered trademark of Thomson Learning, Inc., and is used herein under license by Peterson's.

About Peterson's

Founded in 1966, Peterson's, a division of Thomson Learning, is the nation's largest and most respected provider of lifelong learning online resources, software, reference guides, and books. The Education Supersite℠ at petersons.com—the Web's most heavily traveled education resource—has searchable databases and interactive tools for contacting U.S.-accredited institutions and programs. CollegeQuest℠ (CollegeQuest.com) offers a complete solution for every step of the college decision-making process. GradAdvantage™ (GradAdvantage.org), developed with Educational Testing Service, is the only electronic admissions service capable of sending official graduate test score reports with a candidate's online application. Peterson's serves more than 55 million education consumers annually.

Thomson Learning is among the world's leading providers of lifelong learning, serving the needs of individuals, learning institutions, and corporations with products and services for both traditional classrooms and for online learning. For more information about the products and services offered by Thomson Learning, please visit www.thomsonlearning.com. Headquartered in Stamford, Connecticut, with offices worldwide, Thomson Learning is part of The Thomson Corporation (www.thomson.com), a leading e-information and solutions company in the business, professional, and education marketplaces. The Corporation's common shares are listed on the Toronto and London stock exchanges.

For more information, contact Peterson's, 2000 Lenox Drive, Lawrenceville, NJ 08648; 800-338-3282; or find us on the World Wide Web at: www.petersons.com/about

ISBN 0-7645-6097-2

Printed in the United States of America

10 9 8 7 6 5 4 3 2 1   02 01 00

ACKNOWLEDGMENTS

A few people helped make the writing of this book go smoothly. First, of course, is my editor, Roxane Stanfield. Her positive feedback and relaxed attitude helped make the process of writing an enjoyable one. I also want to thank my husband, Sorel, for always being there to offer advice, ideas, and, when all else failed, kind words and a good back rub! Finally, I'd like to acknowledge all of my immigration clients who taught me so much about immigration law and human nature over the years.

ABOUT THE AUTHOR

Debra R. Shpigler graduated with distinction from the University of Virginia in 1982, receiving a B.A. in economics and government (double major). After earning her J.D. at the University of Pennsylvania School of Law, she was admitted to the Ohio Bar in 1985. Ms. Shpigler served as a Trial Attorney for the U.S. Department of Justice in Cleveland, Ohio, until 1989, when she became a corporate attorney for Ulmer & Berne, a law firm based in Cleveland. Eventually, Ms. Shpigler began handling all of the immigration work for Ulmer & Berne's clients.

In 1993, Ms. Shpigler opened her own law firm in Cleveland in order to concentrate on providing immigration and naturalization legal services to individuals and corporations. In 1996, she moved the practice from Cleveland to Charleston, South Carolina. She is a member of the American Immigration Lawyers Association.

CONTENTS

INTRODUCTION

Here you are in the United States, and you think it is a great country. In fact, you like it so well that you would like to stay forever and become a citizen. Just wanting to become a citizen, however, is not sufficient. You must fulfill certain requirements, complete many forms, and follow detailed procedures. The process may be a complicated and lengthy one, but the goal of citizenship is worth the effort. This book will help you work your way step-by-step from the status of legal visitor or legal resident to that of a citizen of the United States of America.

You will notice the use of the word "legal." In a few special instances, a person who is in the United States without legal status can become a citizen, but this is very rare and is not addressed in this book. This book serves as a handbook for people who are already in the United States, who have entered by legal means, and who have maintained legal status.

If this is you:

A green card holder for 5 years, 18 years or older;

OR

A green card holder for 3 years who is and continues to be married to a U.S. Citizen for those 3 years.

OR

A green card holder who is a child of U.S. citizen parents.

OR

Someone with qualifying military service

AND

You meet the requirements for continuous presence, good moral character and time in district or state.

Then you can:

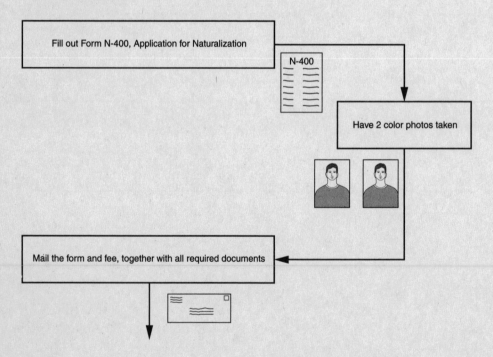

Fill out Form N-400, Application for Naturalization

N-400

Have 2 color photos taken

Mail the form and fee, together with all required documents

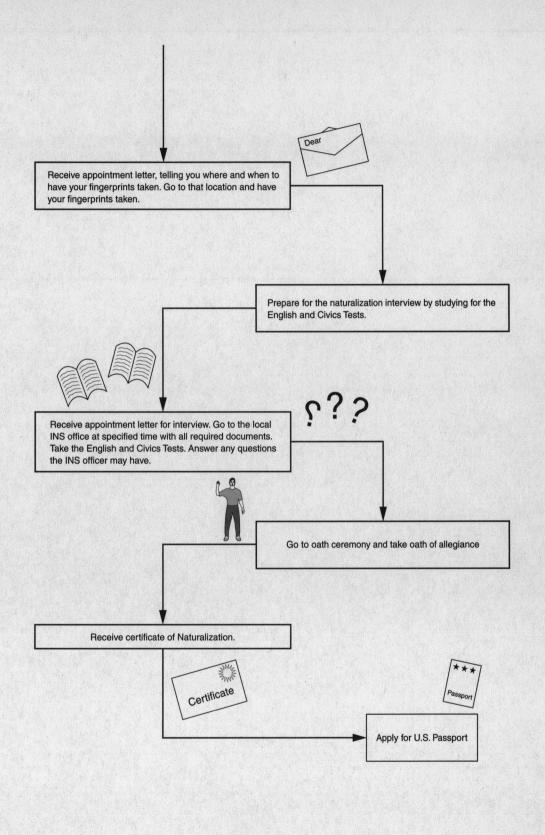

Receive appointment letter, telling you where and when to have your fingerprints taken. Go to that location and have your fingerprints taken.

Prepare for the naturalization interview by studying for the English and Civics Tests.

Receive appointment letter for interview. Go to the local INS office at specified time with all required documents. Take the English and Civics Tests. Answer any questions the INS officer may have.

Go to oath ceremony and take oath of allegiance

Receive certificate of Naturalization.

Apply for U.S. Passport

Part I
GETTING STARTED

Chapter 1

WHY YOU SHOULD WANT TO BECOME A CITIZEN

If asked why you want to remain in the United States, you could respond quickly with a large number of reasons. You might say that this a beautiful country or that many members of your family are here and that you would like to remain with them. You might mention the economic opportunities open to you and your hopes for a better quality of life than was possible in your home country. You might speak of war, famine, or political oppression in your home country. It is easy to think of really good reasons for wanting to stay in this country. Can you just as easily state your reasons for wanting to become a U.S. citizen?

- Citizens have the privilege of participating in the governments of their school districts, localities, cities, states, and of the nation. This means that you can work to nominate candidates, vote for candidates, and even hold office. (A naturalized citizen may hold any elected office except those of President and Vice President.)

- When you become a U.S. citizen, you are entitled to carry a U.S. passport. Many countries will admit someone with a U.S. passport for tourism or business purposes without requiring a visa. Residents of the United States who have maintained foreign citizenship must regularly renew their foreign passports and must apply for visas to visit many countries. Applying for visas is usually inconvenient, time-consuming, and costly. U.S. citizenship can simplify travel.

- A U.S. citizen is free to live outside of the United States for an unlimited period of time. A legal permanent resident—a *green card* holder—may not remain outside of the United States for more than one year, except under special circumstances and with special permission. Life is less complicated and less restricted after you become a United States citizen.

- As a U.S. citizen, you can enjoy the services of U.S. Embassies and Consulates. Emergencies can occur abroad, and it is reassuring to come under the protection of U.S. officials.

- Most jobs in the U.S. Civil Service are reserved for U.S. citizens. Civil Service employment offers security, good wages, excellent growth opportunities, and many other benefits. You might think of your U.S. citizenship as a passport to economic success. Citizenship is also required for employment in state and local law enforcement. For example, if you would like to serve as a police officer or correction officer, you must first become a citizen.

- U.S. citizens are entitled to bring members of their immediate families into the United States as permanent residents without regard to any quota or preference requirements. Your immediate family members include your parents (if you are over 21), your spouse, and any children you have who are under 21. Individuals who have green cards but who are not U.S. citizens must usually wait much longer if they want to bring these same family members into the country.

- Recent legislation has made many law-abiding, permanent-resident, noncitizens ineligible for food stamps and for certain health and welfare benefits. Unfortunately, even the hardest working people can have bad luck or be the victims of unforeseen illnesses and accidents. Of course, you hope to never need government health and welfare benefits, but you might want to protect yourself by becoming a U.S. citizen.

- U.S. citizens also are immune from deportation. Recent legislation has dramatically limited the possibility of obtaining relief from deportation for long-time, permanent residents who have criminal records. Even green card holders who have committed certain nonviolent crimes such as shoplifting are considered "aggravated felons" and are, therefore, deportable. This is true even if they committed those crimes years ago and even if they served their sentences or had no sentences imposed. We sincerely hope that you will be a law-abiding citizen, but should you commit a crime as a naturalized citizen, your penalty will not be deportation. The only U.S. citizen who is subject to deportation is an individual who achieved citizenship through fraudulent statements.

Along with the rights and privileges of citizenship come certain responsibilities. Citizens have a duty to inform themselves about social issues and political candidates. They should read, listen, and involve themselves in their communities by speaking up and voting regularly. All citizens should obey all laws, pay their taxes, and behave responsibly with respect to the environment. When called upon to sit on juries, citizens should serve willingly and thoughtfully, and, in times of national emergency, citizens should be willing to serve in the armed forces or some appropriate alternative.

An immigration examiner may ask you about the duties that accompany U.S. citizenship and may ask you whether you willingly accept these duties. The examiner may also ask you why you want to be a citizen. Be sure that you understand the benefits and responsibilities of citizenship before your interview. Reread this chapter before you go for your final interview. Think about what citizenship means to you so that you will be prepared to answer these questions.

Part II
THE IMMIGRATION SYSTEM

Chapter 2
OVERVIEW OF THE IMMIGRATION SYSTEM

PURPOSES AND GOALS OF THE IMMIGRATION SYSTEM

The immigration laws of the United States have a dual purpose. First, they are intended to facilitate the entry of persons who are legally admissible as visitors, temporary workers, and immigrants. This includes granting benefits, including temporary and permanent residence and naturalization (citizenship). Second, the immigration laws are intended to prevent unlawful entry, employment, or the receipt of benefits (visas, citizenship, and so on) by those who are not entitled to them.

The U.S. immigration system has three primary goals:

- The first goal is family reunification; our immigration laws are intended to encourage families to stay together. As a result, the immigration laws make it relatively easy for family members who are already in the United States to bring immediate family members (parents, children, and siblings) into the country.

- The second aim of our immigration system is to enable employers to hire a citizen of another country when no qualified U.S. citizen can fill the position.

- The third main goal of the current system is to provide refuge for individuals who are fleeing political, religious, or social persecution.

The Immigration and Naturalization Service (INS), an agency of the U.S. Department of Justice, is responsible for enforcing immigration laws. The Department of Labor gets involved in immigration matters when employment issues are involved, and the State Department issues visas abroad.

IMMIGRANT AND NONIMMIGRANT VISAS

As a foreign national (sometimes called an *alien*), you may not enter the United States unless you have permission in the form of a visa. Some limited exceptions to this rule exist for tourists from certain countries who plan to stay in the United States for three months or less and for certain other individuals, but most people need a visa.

Visas are stamps issued by consular officers in embassies and consulates around the world. Visas permit aliens to enter the United States. When you get a visa stamped in your passport, it means that the consular officer who authorized the stamp was satisfied, at the time of the stamp's issuance, that you were coming to the United States for the stated purpose and that you were not excludable from the United States for any reason.

Visas may be divided into two types: nonimmigrant (temporary) and immigrant (permanent). Nonimmigrant visas are issued in a wide variety of categories. For example, tourists are usually issued B-1 or B-2 visas; students are usually issued F-1 or M-1 visas; and temporary workers may be issued any one of several visas (H-1B, H-2B, L-1, and so on), depending upon the nature of their job offers and qualifications. Nonimmigrant visas are usually valid for a limited time. Some nonimmigrant visas are valid for less than one year, and others are indefinitely renewable.

Immigrant visas enable individuals to stay in the United States permanently. The so-called green card is an identification card issued only to lawful permanent residents (although it hasn't been green for years).

Upon entering the United States on a visa (immigrant or nonimmigrant), you receive an I-94 card. The I-94 card governs the terms of your stay in the country. This card lists your visa status (that is, the visa category in which you have been admitted), the date and place where you entered the United States, and the date by which you must depart. If you stay longer than the time printed on your I-94 card, you are considered an illegal alien; don't do it!

What if you are already present in the United States and you would like to stay longer? Depending upon the circumstances, you might be able to file an application to extend your stay in the same status or to change your status and, thereby, extend your stay. For example, if you have been admitted as a visitor in the B-1 or B-2 category for a period of six months and you would like to extend your stay, you might file an application to extend your B-1 or B-2 status for up to six more months. You will need to obtain the proper form from the INS, submit it with the correct filing fee and supporting documentation, and wait to receive an approval notice from the INS.

We recommend that you consult with a knowledgeable immigration attorney to make sure that you understand when you can extend your stay and/or change your status, when you can't, which documents you must submit, and how long you may remain in the United States while you are waiting for an answer from the INS. Indeed, we recommend that you consult with an immigration attorney whenever you are dealing with the immigration system!

Chapter 3

NONIMMIGRANT VISAS

There are various categories of aliens that may obtain nonimmigrant (temporary) visas. Nonimmigrant visas are usually identified by a letter and a number. For example, B-1 and B-2 indicate visitors' visas; H-1B indicates visas for workers in specialty (professional) occupations; F-1 indicates a student visa; and TN indicates visas for certain Canadian and Mexican professionals. We will discuss many of the more commonly used nonimmigrant visas in this chapter.

As we mentioned previously, some nonimmigrant visas are valid for as short as three months (visitors coming to the United States on the Visa Waiver Pilot Program, discussed later in this chapter), while others may be renewable indefinitely (TN visas, certain E visas, and others).

Let's discuss some of the more common nonimmigrant visas. Notice that many of these nonimmigrant visas must be obtained by an employer on behalf of an employee. In these cases, the employer is called the *petitioner*, and the employee is called the *beneficiary*. Some nonimmigrant visas may be obtained directly by an alien. We will discuss some of these visas as well.

You should understand that most nonimmigrant visas are issued for a limited initial period, but many can be extended for an additional period of months or years.

You also should know that when you are issued a nonimmigrant visa, your dependents may get corresponding visas. However, in most cases, even if your visa authorizes you to work, your dependents' visas do not authorize your dependents to work. A dependent may obtain his own work visa if an employer is willing to sponsor him.

Now let's take a look at those nonimmigrant visas.

B-1 AND B-2 VISITORS

B visas are commonly referred to as *visitor's visas*. The B-1 category is for *visitors for business*, and the B-2 category applies to *visitors for pleasure*. Generally, the B-1 visa is used for the purpose of engaging in business but not for the purpose of being employed. Thus, an alien may qualify for a B-1 visa if he is coming to the United States temporarily to

- Engage in commercial transactions that do not involve gainful employment in the United States.

- Negotiate contracts.

- Consult with business associates.

- Litigate.

- Participate in a convention or seminar.

- Undertake research.

This list is not exhaustive. *The key, however, is that the alien must not accept employment from a U.S. employer.*

The B-2 visa is primarily for tourists. People in this category are usually coming to the United States to visit with friends or family, to see the country, or to attend activities of a social, fraternal, or service nature. As is the case with B-1 visa holders, however, individuals holding B-2 visas may not accept employment from a U.S. employer while in the United States.

B-1 and B-2 visitors may be admitted for periods of up to one year, although most are admitted for periods of six months or less. If you have entered the United States on a B visa, check your I-94 card to see when your authorized period of stay expires.

THE VISA WAIVER PILOT PROGRAM

Individuals from certain countries (mostly those in Western Europe) are eligible for the Visa Waiver Pilot Program (VWPP). Individuals who qualify for the VWPP do not have to obtain a visitor's visa before coming to the United States. Instead, they simply come to the United States with a valid passport for a period not to exceed 90 days. Individuals visiting the United States under the VWPP may not accept employment from a U.S. employer.

Before coming to the United States on the VWPP, you must consider its disadvantages. For one thing, if you are admitted under the VWPP, you may not extend your stay or change your status. Generally, you can do either one if you arrive on a standard B visa.

F-1 STUDENTS

Many people come to the United States to go to school. Most of these people come on F-1 student visas. An F-1 student is an alien who has been accepted by an approved academic institution for full-time study and who has presented evidence of sufficient financial support for the period of the academic program in order for the school to issue a Form I-20. After the school issues a Form I-20, the prospective student must apply to the U.S. Consulate abroad for an F-1 visa to enter the United States. If the prospective student is in the United States in another status, he must file an application with the INS for a change of status. It is important to note, however, that the INS may deny an application for a change to student status (or a change to any other status, for that matter), if it appears that the individual entered the United States in one capacity (say, as a visitor) with a preconceived intent to change to student status. Therefore, if an alien does not have clear evidence that he did not have a preconceived intent to attend school, he should wait between 60 and 90 days before filing an application to change status.

F-1 students are granted a period of stay, which is called *duration of status* (this is noted as "D/S" on the alien's I-94 card). This period is defined as the time required to complete the program of study, plus any authorized period of post-academic practical training. During the program of study phase, the F-1 visa holder is required to be a full-time student. For undergraduates, this usually means that the student must register for at least 12 academic credit hours. For graduate students, the full-time requirement is more flexible.

The rules regarding F-1 status for elementary, middle, and high school students have gotten rather complicated, and we recommend that you consult with an immigration attorney if you are looking into this option.

In certain cases, F-1 students may be authorized to work, either on or off campus. Most schools have a foreign student advisor who assists the school's F-1 students with their applications for employment authorization (among other things).

The dependents of F-1 students are admitted in the F-2 category, and they are not authorized to work.

Another category for *nonacademic* students exists: the M-1 category. M-1 visas are available to full-time students who are attending approved vocational or nonacademic institutions, other than language training schools.

J-1 EXCHANGE VISITORS

J-1 visas are for individuals coming to the United States to participate in an approved exchange program. J-1 visas are obtained through sponsors of J visa programs. Some of the people who obtain J-1 visas include

- Students (although most students have F-1 student visas).

- Trainees.

- Teachers.

- Professors and research scholars.

- Foreign medical graduates.

- International visitors.

- Government visitors.

- Camp counselors.

- Au pairs.

The period of admission for a J-1 visa holder depends upon his program. For example, J-1 teachers may stay up to three years, but trainees are admitted for 18 months.

Dependents of J-1 visa holders are given J-2 visas. Unlike most dependents, J-2s may apply to the INS for employment authorization.

H-1B SPECIALTY OCCUPATION WORKERS

People working in *specialty* (meaning professional) occupations, as well as fashion models, may be eligible for H-1B visas. Generally, an employer can obtain an H-1B visa for a prospective employee if

- The prospective employee has the equivalent of a bachelor's degree or higher

- The job is one that ordinarily requires the degree that the prospective employee possesses

and:

- The employer can show that it will pay the prospective employee at least the prevailing wage for the position

Engineers, accountants, teachers, and many software professionals are typical H-1B workers.

An H-1B visa is valid for an initial period of up to three years. The visa may be extended for up to three more years. Spouses and children are given H-4 status and are not authorized to work.

THE H-1B CAP

Under current law (as of Spring, 2000), there is a cap on the number of new H-1B visas that can be issued. For fiscal year 2000 (beginning October 1, 1999), the cap is 115,000; in fiscal year 2001, the cap will be 107,500; and in fiscal year 2002, the cap will revert back to the old number of 65,000. A number of proposals currently in Congress are designed to raise or eliminate the cap, but they have not yet been signed into law as of this writing.

H-2B TEMPORARY WORKERS

Employers who want to hire skilled or unskilled aliens in nonagricultural positions, for which the employer has a temporary need and for which U.S. workers are not available, may use the H-2B category. Both the job itself and the employer's need for the specific alien must be temporary.

An employer must file an application for temporary labor certification with the Department of Labor before they may apply for an H-2B visa on behalf of an alien. The temporary labor certification process is a short version of the permanent labor certification process discussed in Chapter 4, "Immigrant Visas: Becoming a Lawful Permanent Resident." The temporary labor certification process, which usually takes several months, is used to determine whether there are U.S. workers who can perform the job for which the employer is seeking to fill.

An H-2B visa is valid for an initial period of up to one year. An employer may file up to two applications to extend an alien's H-2B visa, but the employer must go through the entire temporary labor certification process again if filing for an extension.

Dependents of H-2B aliens are given H-4 status, and they are not authorized to work.

L-1 INTRACOMPANY TRANSFEREES

The L-1 *intracompany transferee* visa is for individuals who have worked abroad for a company for one continuous year within the past three years in an executive, managerial, or *specialized knowledge* capacity and who are being transferred temporarily to work in an executive, managerial, or specialized knowledge capacity for a qualifying, related business entity (consult with an immigration lawyer to get an understandable translation of these terms!). Large companies and companies that have obtained approvals for at least ten L-1 petitions during the previous 12 months may file an L-1 *blanket petition* for several aliens at one time. Special rules apply for people who are being transferred to open new offices in the United States.

Individual L-1 petitions may be granted for an initial period of up to three years. All L visa holders may extend their visas for up to two years, and managers and executives may extend their visas for still another two years. Family members are given L-2 status and are not authorized to work.

E-1 AND E-2 TREATY TRADERS AND INVESTORS

E visas are for investors and traders who want to carry on their trade or business in the United States, if their home country has a treaty of commerce and navigation with the United States. According to the statute, an E-1 treaty trader comes to the United States "solely to carry on trade of a substantial nature, which is international in scope, either on the alien's behalf or as an employee of a foreign person or organization engaged in trade principally between the United States and the foreign state of which the alien is a national. . . ." Thus, among other things, the alien and the alien's employer must be the nationality of the country with which the United States has a treaty of commerce and navigation.

The statute says that an E-2 Treaty Investor is an alien who has invested or is in the process of investing "a substantial amount of capital in a bona fide enterprise in the United States . . . and is seeking entry solely to develop and direct the enterprise."

An employee of an E-1 or E-2 visa holder may be classified as E-1 or E-2 if he will be engaged in duties of an executive, managerial, or supervisory nature or if the employee has special qualifications that make his services essential to the efficient operation of the enterprise.

In most cases, E visas are issued for five years. Spouses and children are given the same classification as the principal alien, but they are not authorized to work.

TN VISAS FOR CANADIAN AND
MEXICAN PROFESSIONALS

Under the North American Free Trade Agreement (NAFTA), Canadians and Mexicans working in certain designated professions qualify for TN visas. Canadians who are part of this designated group of professionals can be admitted to the United States for indefinitely renewable one-year periods without having to obtain prior INS approval. A Canadian professional must simply come to the border, present documentation that he has a job offer in one of the designated fields and that he possesses the qualifications required for that field. The border official will then stamp a TN visa in the Canadian's passport, and the alien may enter the United States.

The process is somewhat different for Mexican professionals. The alien's employer must apply for TN status on the alien's behalf in much the same way that an employer would apply for an H-1B visa. The advantage, however, is that there is no limit on the period that the alien may remain with TN status.

Dependents of TN aliens are given TD status. They are not authorized to work.

K-1 FIANCE(E)S

The K-1 visa is for fiance(e)s of U.S. citizens. An alien and his minor children may enter the United States on a K-1 visa if the couple can show that

- They have previously met in person within two years of the date of filing the petition (in most cases)

- They have a bona fide intention to marry

and:

- They are legally able and actually willing to marry within 90 days after the alien's arrival

The K-1 visa is unique in that it is the only nonimmigrant status where the applicant must clearly show his intention to stay in the United States rather than return abroad after the authorized stay expires.

OTHER NONIMMIGRANT VISAS

Many other nonimmigrant visas exist. For example, there are R-1 visas for religious workers; O-1 and O-2 visas for aliens of extraordinary ability; P-1, P-2, and P-3 visas for artists, entertainers, athletes, and others. If you think you may qualify for one of these nonimmigrant visas, we suggest that you talk to an immigration lawyer to discuss your options.

WHAT TO DO IF YOU ARE CURRENTLY A NONIMMIGRANT

If you are here in the United States on a nonimmigrant visa, you should keep certain things in mind.

STAY LEGAL

Whatever your current status is, do not let it expire. The person who has allowed his legal permission to lapse is at a disadvantage as an applicant for permanent status and later for citizenship. Be careful to fulfill all the conditions of your current visa and do not violate any of its restrictions.

WATCH DATES

Until you become a citizen of the United States, you are the citizen of some other country. Your passport is the passport of the country of your citizenship. Your passport must remain up-to-date. This means that you must take steps to renew your passport regularly. Because you are not physically in the country that issued the passport, you must deal with that country's consulate in the United States. The process may take considerably longer than you expect. Six months before your passport's expiration date, you should contact your country's consulate, make inquiries, and begin the renewal application process.

Remember that the I-94 card that you received when you entered the United States is stamped with the date of arrival and with the date by which you must leave. Keep track of that date and do not let it pass.

You will lose your legal status if you overstay the date on your I-94. If you extend your visa or change your nonimmigrant status to a visa that permits you to remain for a longer period of time, you have to turn in your I-94 card to the INS for updating. When you get your I-94 card back from the INS, check to make certain that the new date has been entered accurately. Follow-through is your responsibility. Be alert and insistent.

If you are in the United States on a temporary visa of any kind, you must be careful not to let that visa expire.

DO NOT VIOLATE THE TERMS OF YOUR VISA

As we discussed, some of these visas are designed for the purpose of permitting their holders to work in the United States. Others specifically prohibit the holder from working. In fact, some temporary visas are issued only to applicants who submit proof that they have access to adequate funds to support themselves while in this country so that they will not need to work. Most student visas and tourist visas fall into this category.

If your visa restricts you from working, but you find and accept a job, you are violating the terms of your visa. In effect, you are endangering your legal status. Don't do it! You may be seriously endangering your chances for citizenship. If circumstances have changed and you must earn money to cover living expenses while in school, for example, you may make special application for permission to work. Your school can help you by filing Form I-538, Certification by Designated School Official. If you are in the United States legally, find that you must work, and are not a student, consult with a qualified immigration attorney to determine whether you qualify for a valid work visa. For example, if you have the equivalent of a bachelor's degree (or better) and you have been offered a job in your field, you may qualify for an H-1B visa. If so, talk to the company that offered you the job to see whether the employer is willing to sponsor you for an H-1B visa. *Remember, however, that you may not start working for the company until the INS has approved the petition for the visa.*

TRY NOT TO MAKE CHANGES BEFORE THE FIRST THREE MONTHS

Even though it is relatively easy to extend the authorized stay of a visa or to change your status from, for example, a tourist visa to a student visa, you should try not to make any changes in the first three months of your stay in the United States. Regardless of your total honesty in originally applying for a six-month visitor's visa, if you attempt to extend your stay or change your status too quickly, the INS may misinterpret your intentions. The INS is likely to assume that you really intended to stay in this country for a much longer period. If the INS suspects that you misstated your intentions, it may not believe other statements you make when you apply for immigrant status, which may make the whole process more difficult for you.

After you have been in the United States for three months, you can apply for a visa extension or change without arousing suspicion. It is assumed that three months is a long enough period in which you might reasonably change your mind or discover legitimate reasons to remain in another capacity.

You may find the whole process easier to understand by following an example. Your own situation will be different, of course, but Carla's story in this example is not an unusual one.

> At the age of 16, Carla Rojas was an Argentine citizen with an Argentine passport. Carla's mother received a grant from the Argentine government to come to the United States as an exchange student for special training to make her a more effective English teacher in Argentina. As an exchange visitor, Carla's mother was issued a J-1 visa, which would be valid for the two-year duration of her course of study. (All J visa holders are issued visas for the period of time necessary to complete their programs. This period is referred to as *duration of status* and is noted as "D/S" on their I-94 cards.) The terms of the grant included both tuition and living expenses, so there was no need for her to seek permission to work. As a dependent child, Carla accompanied her mother. Carla was issued a J-2 visa. While her mother attended college classes as provided in her grant, Carla attended the local public high school in the same town in which the university was located and earned a high school diploma.

> At the end of the two-year period, Carla's mother prepared to return to Argentina, but Carla wanted to stay in the United States. Carla applied to another local university that offered a program in her field of interest, preschool education, and was accepted into the freshman class. Carla's mother agreed to pay for her tuition, but she could not afford to pay for her room and board as well. Luckily, Dr. and Mrs. Turner offered to let Carla live in their home. Dr. and Mrs. Turner had come to know and respect Carla and her mother over the previous two years and were delighted at the prospect of having Carla with them and their children.

Carla called the INS forms line at 1-800-870-3676 and asked for the following forms:

- I-539 Application to Extend/Change Nonimmigrant Status (Carla's completed Form I-539 begins on the next page.)

- I-134 Affidavit of Support (Dr. Turner's completed Form I-134 begins on page 18; her mother probably filled one out, too.)

Carla then made photocopies of the completed Forms I-539 and I-134 and a copy (front and back) of the I-94 card she had received from the INS officers at the airport when she first arrived in the United States. The I-94 card, stamped with her date of entry, date of intended departure, and nonimmigrant status category, would serve as proof that Carla had entered and remained in the United States legally. Carla hated to let that card out of her possession, but she had to send it along with her request for change of status so that it could be updated by the INS. The INS would send her a new card to reflect her new status as holder of an F-1 visa and would print a new date showing that a change of status had been granted. She also photocopied her passport, including its expiration date, her birth certificate, her high school diploma, and her admissions letter. Carla gathered the originals of Forms I-539 and I-134 and her I-94 card, photocopies of the supporting documents and of her copy of Form I-20, and the required filing fee and sent them by certified mail, return receipt requested, to the appropriate INS office as directed on the Form I-539 for individuals changing to F status.

You will note that Carla mailed photocopies of documents that might prove impossible or very difficult to replace while mailing originals of the forms that she, her mother, and Dr. Turner had completed. The INS always wants originals with *live,* handwritten signatures on its own forms; all other documents should be submitted as photocopies unless the original is specifically requested, as is the case with the I-94 card. Carla filed a photocopy of her student copy of her I-20 in order to submit a complete package; the college should have filed an original document directly with the INS. Carla also went to the expense of mailing the package by certified mail with return receipt requested. Mail sometimes does go astray. The mailing receipt proves the fact and date of mailing. The delivery receipt proves the fact and date that the packet was received by the INS. Establishing these dates can save your application in situations governed by a deadline. Papers do get lost in transit and in government offices. Keep copies of every paper that passes through your hands and staple to each a packet of copies and official proofs of mailing and receipt.

U.S. Department of Justice
Immigration and Naturalization Service

Application to Extend/ChangeNonimmigrant Status

OMB No.1115-0093

START HERE - Please Type or Print

Part 1. Information about you.

Family Name ROJAS	Given Name Carla	Middle Initial A

Address - In Care of:

Street # and Name 1504 High Street	Apt. # 4-D

City Madison	State New Jersey

Zip Code 07941

Date of Birth (month/day/year) 6/7/79	Country of Birth Argentina
Social Security # (if any) 246-80-1234	A# (if any) N/A
Date of Last Arrival Into the U.S. 8/20/95	I-94# 998567880 05
Current Nonimmigrant Status J-2	Expires on (month/day/year) D/S

Part 2. Application Type.   (See Instructions for fee.)

1. **I am applying for:** (check one)
   a. ☐ an extension of stay in my current status
   b. ☑ a change of status. The new status I am requesting is: **F-1**
2. **Number of people included in this application:** (check one)
   a. ☑ I am the only applicant
   b. ☐ Members of my family are filing this application with me.
      The Total number of people included in this application is
      (complete the supplement for each co-applicant)

Part 3. Processing Information.

1. I/We request that my/our current or requested
   status be extended until (month/day/year)   **D/S**
2. Is this application based on an extension or change of status already granted to your spouse, child or parent?
   ☑ No   ☐ Yes (receipt #_____)
3. Is this application being filed based on a separate petition or application to give your spouse, child or parent an extension or change of status?
   ☑ No   ☐ Yes, filed with this application ☐ Yes, filed previously and pending with INS
4. If you answered yes to question 3, give the petitioner or applicant name:

   |_____|

   If the application is pending with INS, also give the following information.

   | Office filed at_____ Filed on_____ (date) |

Part 4. Additional Information.

1. For applicant #1, provide passport information:

Country of issuance Argentina	Valid to: (month/day/year) 1/20/04

2. Foreign address:

Street # and Name 16 Camino Cruz Blanca	Apt# 1060

City or Town Buenos Aires	State or Province Provincia Buenos Aires

Country Argentina	Zip or Postal Code N/A

Continued on back.

FOR INS USE ONLY

Returned	Receipt
Date	
_____	
Resubmitted	
Date	
_____	
Reloc Sent	
Date	
_____	
Reloc Rec'd	
Date	
_____	
Date	
☐ Applicant Interviewed	

☐ *Extension Granted*
   to (date):_____

☐ *Change of Status/Extension Granted*
New Class:_____ To (date):_____

If denied:
☐ Still within period of stay
☐ V/D to: _____
☐ S/D to:_____
☐ Place under docket control

Remarks

Action Block

To Be Completed by
Attorney or Representative, If any
☐ Fill in box if G-28 is attached to represent the applicant
VOLAG#

ATTY State License #

Form I-539 (Rev. 11/03/98)N

Part 4.   Additional Information. *(continued)*

3. Answer the following questions. If you answer yes to any question, explain on separate paper.	Yes	No
a. Are you, or any other person included in this application, an applicant for an immigrant visa or adjustment of status to permanent residence?		✔
b. Has an immigrant petition ever been filed for you, or for any other person included in this application?		✔
c. Have you, or any other person included in this application ever been arrested or convicted of any criminal offense since last entering the U.S.?		✔
d. Have you, or any other person included in this application done anything which violated the terms of the nonimmigrant status you now hold?		✔
e. Are you, or any other person included in this application, now in exclusion or deportation proceedings?		✔
f. Have you, or any other person included in this application, been employed in the U.S. since last admitted or granted an extension or change of status?		✔

If you answered YES to question 3f, give the following information on a separate paper: Name of person, name of employer, address of employer, weekly income, and whether specifically authorized by INS.

If you answered NO to question 3f, fully describe how you are supporting yourself on a separate paper. Include the source and the amount and basis for any income.

Part 5.   Signature.   *Read the information on penalties in the instructions before completing this section. You must file this application while in the United States.*

I certify under penalty of perjury under the laws of the United States of America that this application, and the evidence submitted with it, is all true and correct. I authorize the release of any information from my records which the Immigration and Naturalization Service needs to determine eligibility for the benefit I am seeking.

Signature *Carla A. Rojas*	Print your name Carla A. Rojas	Date 5/7/97

Please Note: *If you do not completely fill out this form, or fail to submit required documents listed in the instructions, you cannot be found eligible for the requested document and this application will have to be denied.*

Part 6.   Signature of person preparing form if other than above. *(Sign below)*

I declare that I prepared this application at the request of the above person and it is based on all information of which I have knowledge.

Signature	Print Your Name	Date

Firm Name
and Address

(Please remember to enclose the mailing label with your application)

Form I-539 (Rev. 04/01/98)N

This is how Dr. Turner completed Form I-134:

OMB No. 1115-0062

U. S. Department of Justice
Immigration and Naturalization Service

Affidavit of Support

(ANSWER ALL ITEMS: FILL IN WITH TYPEWRITER OR PRINT IN BLOCK LETTERS IN INK.)

I, Robert L. Turner, M.D. , residing at 19 Maple Lane
(Name)   (Street and Number)

Madison   New Jersey   07941   USA
(City)   (State)   (ZIP Code if in U.S.) (Country)

BEING DULY SWORN DEPOSE AND SAY:

1. I was born on January 24, 1950 at Trenton, NJ   USA
(Date)   (City)   (Country)

    If you are *not* a native born United States citizen, answer the following as appropriate:

    a. If a United States citizen through naturalization, give certificate of naturalization number _____

    b. If a United States citizen through parent(s) or marriage, give citizenship certificate number _____

    c. If United States citizenship was derived by some other method, attach a statement of explanation.

    d. If a lawfully admitted permanent resident of the United States, give "A" number _____

2. That I am 47 years of age and have resided in the United States since (date) January 24, 1950

3. That this affidavit is executed in behalf of the following person:

Name		Sex	Age
Carla A. Rojas		F	18

Citizen of—(Country)	Marital Status	Relationship to Deponent
Argentina	single	none

Presently resides at—(Street and Number)   (City)   (State)   (Country)
1504 High Street, Madison, NJ 07941

Name of spouse and children accompanying or following to join person:

Spouse	Sex	Age	Child	Sex	Age
N/A					
Child	Sex	Age	Child	Sex	Age
Child	Sex	Age	Child	Sex	Age

4. That this affidavit is made by me for the purpose of assuring the United States Government that the person(s) named in item 3 will not become a public charge in the United States.

5. That I am willing and able to receive, maintain and support the person(s) named in item 3. That I am ready and willing to deposit a bond, if necessary, to guarantee that such person(s) will not become a public charge during his or her stay in the United States, or to guarantee that the above named will maintain his or her nonimmigrant status if admitted temporarily and will depart prior to the expiration of his or her authorized stay in the United States.

6. That I understand this affidavit will be binding upon me for a period of three (3) years after entry of the person(s) named in item 3 and that the information and documentation provided by me may be made available to the Secretary of Health and Human Services and the Secretary of Agriculture, who may make it available to a public assistance agency.

7. That I am employed as, or engaged in the business of medical practice   with N.J. Medical Assoc.
(Type of Business)   (Name of concern)

at 210 Main Street   Madison   NJ   07941
(Street and Number)   (City)   (State)   (Zip Code)

I derive an annual income of *(if self-employed, I have attached a copy of my last income tax return or report of commercial rating concern which I certify to be true and correct to the best of my knowledge and belief. See instruction for nature of evidence of net worth to be submitted.)* $ 150,000

I have on deposit in savings banks in the United States $ 50,000
I have other personal property, the reasonable value of which is $ 25,000

Form I-134 (Rev. 12-1-84) Y   OVER

I have stocks and bonds with the following market value, as indicated on the attached list
which I certify to be true and correct to the best of my knowledge and belief. $ _____ 85,000
I have life insurance in the sum of $ _____ 250,000
With a cash surrender value of $ _____ none
I own real estate valued at $ _____ 200,000
With mortgages or other encumbrances thereon amounting to $ _____ 100,000

Which is located at _19 Maple Lane_____ Madison_____ NJ_____ 07941_____
            (Street and Number)   (City)   (State)   (Zip Code)

8. That the following persons are dependent upon me for support: *(Place an "X" in the appropriate column to indicate whether the person named is wholly or partially dependent upon you for support.)*

Name of Person	Wholly Dependent	Partially Dependent	Age	Relationship to Me
Barbara Turner		X	47	spouse
Stacy Turner	X		12	child
Michael Turner	X		10	child

9. That I have previously submitted affidavit(s) of support for the following person(s). If none, state *"None"*

Name	Date submitted
None	

10. That I have submitted visa petition(s) to the Immigration and Naturalization Service on behalf of the following person(s). If none, state none.

Name	Relationship	Date submitted
None		

11.*(Complete this block only if the person named in item 3 will be in the United States temporarily.)*
That I ☑ do intend ☐ do not intend, to make specific contributions to the support of the person named in item 3. *(If you check "do intend", indicate the exact nature and duration of the contributions. For example, if you intend to furnish room and board, state for how long and, if money, state the amount in United States dollars and state whether it is to be given in a lump sum, weekly, or monthly, or for how long.)*

Room and board for four years.

OATH OR AFFIRMATION OF DEPONENT

I acknowledge at that I have read Part III of the Instructions, Sponsor and Alien Liability, and am aware of my responsibilities as an immigrant sponsor under the Social Security Act, as amended, and the Food Stamp Act, as amended.

I swear (affirm) that I know the contents of this affidavit signed by me and the statements are true and correct.

Signature of deponent _Robert L. Turner_____

Subscribed and sworn to (affirmed) before me this _____ day of _____ ,19_____

at _____ .My commission expires on _____

Signature of Officer Administering Oath _____ Title _____
If affidavit prepared by other than deponent, please complete the following: I declare that this document was prepared by me at the request of the deponent and is based on all information of which I have knowledge.

_____
(Signature)   *(Address)*   *(Date)*

Carla also requested that the college file Form I-20 with the INS on her behalf. The college sent Carla the student copy of Form I-20. It looked like this:

U.S. Department of Justice
Immigration and Naturalization Service
Please Read Instructions on Page 2

Certificate of Eligibility for Nonimmigrant (F-1) Student Status - For Academic and Language Students

OMB No. 1115-0051

Page 3

This page must be completed and signed in the U.S. by a designated school official.

1. Family Name (surname)
    ROJAS

    First (given) name (do not enter middle name)
    Carla

Country of birth	Date of birth (mo./day/year)
Argentina	6/7/79

Country of citizenship	Admission number (Complete if known)
Argentina	N/A

    For Immigration Official Use

Visa issuing post	Date Visa issued

    Reinstated, extension granted to:

2. School (school district) name
    Friendly Town University

    School official to be notified of student's arrival in U.S. (Name and Title)
    John Doe, International Student Advisor

    School address (include zip code)
    852 Madison Ave., Madison, NJ 07940

    School code (including 3-digit suffix, if any) and approval date
    NJ _____ 214F **000 000** _____ approved on _____ **5/1/83**

3. This certificate is issued to the student named above for:
    (Check and fill out as appropriate)
    a. ☑ Initial attendance at this school
    b. ☐ Continued attendance at this school
    c. ☐ School transfer.
       Transferred from _____
    d. ☐ Use by dependents for entering the United States.
    e. ☐ Other _____

4. Level of education the student is pursuing or will pursue in the United States:
    (check only one)
    a. ☐ Primary   e. ☐ Master's
    b. ☐ Secondary   f. ☐ Doctorate
    c. ☐ Associate   g. ☐ Language training
    d. ☑ Bachelor's   h. ☐ Other

5. The student named above has been accepted for a full course of study at this school, majoring in **pre-school education** _____

    The student is expected to report to the school no later than (date) **8/20/97** and complete studies not later than (date) **5/30/01**
    The normal length of study is **4 years** _____

6. ☑ English proficiency is required:
    ☑ The student has the required English proficiency
    ☐ The student is not yet proficient, English instructions will be given at the school.
    ☐ English proficiency is not required because _____

7. This school estimates the student's average costs for an academic term of
    9 (up to 12) months to be:
    a. Tuition and fees $ **10,000**
    b. Living expenses $ **5,000**
    c. Expenses of dependents $ **none**
    d. Other(specify): books $ **500**

    Total $ **15,500**

8. This school has information showing the following as the students means of support, estimated for an academic term of **9** months (Use the same number of months given in item 7).
    a. Student's personal funds $ **10,500**
    b. Funds from this school $ **none**
       (specify type)
    c. Funds from another source $ **5,000**
       (specify type and source)   **Dr. Turner:room&bd**
    d. On-campus employment (if any) $ _____

    Total $ **15,500**

9. Remarks: _____
    _____
    _____
    _____
    _____
    _____

10. School Certification: I certify under penalty of perjury that all information provided above in items 1 through 8 was completed before I signed this form and is true and correct; I executed this form in the United States after review and evaluation in the United States by me or other officials of the school of the student's application, transcripts or other records of courses taken and proof of financial responsibility, which were received at the school prior to the execution of this form; the school has determined that the above named student's qualifications meet all standards for admission to the school; the student will be required to pursue a full course of study as defined by 8 CFR 214.2(f)(6); I am a designated official of the above named school and I am authorized to issue this form.

    John Doe | John Doe | Int'l Student Advisor | 6/1/97 | Madison, NJ
    Signature of designated school official | Name of school official (print or type) | Title | Date issued | Place issued (city and state)

11. Student Certification: I have read and agreed to comply with the terms and conditions of my admission and those of any extension of stay as specified on page 2. I certify that all information provided on this form refers specifically to me and is true and correct to the best of my knowledge. I certify that I seek to enter or remain in the United States temporarily, and solely for the purpose of pursuing a full course of study at the school named on page 1 of this form. I also authorize the named school to release any information from my records which is needed by the INS pursuant to 8 CFR 214.3(g) to determine my nonimmigrant status.

    Carla A. Rojas | Carla A. Rojas | | 5/10/97
    Signature of student | Name of student | | Date

    | Martina delCampo | 1504 High St Madison NJ | | USA
    Signature of parent or guardian if student is under 18 | Name of parent/guardian (Print or type) | Address(city) | (State or province) | (Country) | (Date)

    Form I20 A-B/I20ID(Rev 04-27-88)N

    For official use only
    Microfilm Index Number

Chapter 4

IMMIGRANT VISAS: BECOMING A LAWFUL PERMANENT RESIDENT

WHAT IS AN IMMIGRANT VISA?

An immigrant visa enables a person to stay in the United States permanently. The green card is an identification card issued only to lawful permanent residents, or *LPRs*. The green card is officially referred to as Form I-551, Alien Registration Receipt Card. Many years ago, green cards were in fact green. Over the years, their color has been changed a number of times, but they are still called green cards.

WHY OBTAIN A GREEN CARD?

There are many advantages to having a green card (as opposed to a simple nonimmigrant visa). For one thing, if you have a green card, you are free to take virtually any job. In contrast, if you have, for example, an H-1B visa, you may not work for anyone except the employer that sponsored you for the H-1B visa.

Second, individuals who have green cards may sponsor family members for green cards (although their family members probably will have to wait much longer for their green cards than the family members of U.S. citizens).

Third, traveling with a green card is much easier than with a nonimmigrant visa. Green card holders can make their way through the immigration line at the airport much faster than people who have nonimmigrant visas (although U.S. citizens have the easiest time of all!).

HOW DO I OBTAIN A GREEN CARD?

You can obtain a green card in several ways:

- Family-based immigration.
- Employment-based immigration.
- Filing an application for refugee status or for asylum.
- Winning the Diversity Visa (DV) lottery.

Remember that this is only a *summary* of the immigrant visa process. We suggest that you consult with an experienced immigration lawyer before beginning the process for yourself.

FAMILY-BASED IMMIGRATION

If you are an alien with a "qualifying family relationship," you might be able to obtain a green card. Two basic categories of family-sponsored immigrants exist: immediate relatives and preference immigrants.

Immediate Relatives

Immediate relatives include spouses of U.S. citizens, unmarried minor children (under 21) of U.S. citizens (including step-children), parents of U.S. citizens, provided that the citizen petitioner is at least 21 years old, and certain spouses of deceased U.S. citizens. There are no numerical limits on the number of visas that can be issued to immediate relatives. In addition, aliens who qualify as immediate relatives usually get their green cards faster than aliens in any other family-based category.

If you marry a U.S. citizen and he sponsors you for a green card, you should know that the INS will scrutinize your marriage closely. The INS will look for *proof* that your marriage is legitimate and that you didn't get married just to get a green card. In INS parlance, they are looking for "evidence of your life together." Among other things, you should submit photographs of your wedding, photographs of any vacations that you took together, statements showing that you have joint bank accounts, copies of your life insurance policies showing that you are each other's beneficiaries, copies of any property leases that list you both on the lease, copies of the deeds to any property that you own that shows joint ownership of the property, and the like.

Preference Immigrants

Preference immigrants are those aliens who are not immediate relatives but who do have qualifying family relationships. These qualifying relationships fall into four categories, which the INS refers to as "preference categories." The preference categories are part of a larger preference system, which is the system that the government uses to allocate available visas to nonimmediate relatives. Under current law, at least 226,000 family preference visas are issued each year. You can find the exact number of visas allocated to each preference category in the *Visa Bulletin*, which is published each month by the State Department. The State Department posts this information (and lots of other useful information) on its Web site at http://travel.state.gov.

The preference categories are as follows:

- **First Preference:** Unmarried adult sons or daughters of U.S. citizens, including those over 21 (in immigration lingo, a *child* is a person under 21; a *son* or *daughter* may be any age).

- **Second Preference:** This category is divided into two parts:

  - Spouses and minor children of LPRs (green card holders)

  - Unmarried adult sons or daughters of LPRs

- **Third Preference:** Married sons or daughters of U.S. citizens

- **Fourth Preference:** Sisters and brothers of adult U.S. citizens

Unlike immediate relatives, who are eligible to receive green cards fairly quickly, preference immigrants usually have to wait a long time to get green cards. In some categories, the waiting period can be as long as 12 years!

Derivative Beneficiaries

One nice thing about the immigration laws is that they generally permit an entire family to obtain their green cards at the same time. Thus, if Frank, a U.S. citizen, marries Maria, an alien with three kids, Maria and her children are all deemed immediate relatives, and all are eligible to receive green cards (the kids are Frank's step-children). In immigration lingo, Maria is the *principal alien,* and her kids are *derivative beneficiaries*.

EMPLOYMENT-BASED IMMIGRATION

You may also obtain a green card through employment. If you find an employer willing to sponsor you (or if you fit into certain narrow categories in which you can sponsor yourself), you may be able to become a permanent resident. Under current law, only 140,000 people may obtain green cards through employment-based immigration each year.

Like family-based immigration, employment-based immigration uses a preference system. The preference categories for employment-based immigration are as follows:

- **First Preference**: There are three groups of first preference workers:

  - Workers of extraordinary ability in the arts, sciences, education, business, or athletics (these individuals can self-petition—that is, sponsor themselves).

  - Outstanding professors and researchers.

  - Certain multinational executives and managers.

- **Second Preference**: There are two groups of second preference workers:

  - Members of the professions holding advanced degrees.

  - Workers of exceptional ability in the sciences, arts, or business.

- **Third Preference**: There are three groups of third preference workers:

  - Professionals.

  - Skilled workers.

  - Unskilled workers.

- **Fourth Preference:** Special immigrants (religious workers, persons seeking reacquisition of citizenship, certain U.S. employees abroad, persons who served honorably for 12 years in the armed services on active duty, and others).

- **Fifth Preference:** People who invest at least $1 million in a new commercial enterprise employing at least 10 full-time U.S. workers. If the investment is made in a target area of high unemployment, the alien must invest only $500,000.

The vast majority of people seeking employment-based immigrant visas are covered by the first three preference categories. Very few people fit into the fourth and fifth preference categories.

Remember that in most cases, an employer must sponsor an employee for an employment-based immigrant visa; if you are an employee, you cannot obtain this kind of visa on your own. A few types of individuals may self-petition; these include first-preference workers of "extraordinary ability" and second-preference workers who can prove that they are serving the "national interest" of the United States.

In addition, an employer who sponsors an individual for a green card in either the second and third preference category must (with a few exceptions) complete the Labor Certification process before filing a petition for a green card on behalf of that individual. The Application for Labor Certification is filed with the Department of Labor and is used to prove that the employer's hiring needs cannot be met by U.S. workers. Unfortunately, the Labor Certification process is extremely slow and cumbersome.

As you can see, the process of obtaining a green card through employment is very complicated. For that reason, we recommend that you consult an immigration attorney before starting the process.

REFUGEES AND PEOPLE SEEKING ASYLUM

A refugee is someone who is outside the country of his or her nationality and who is unable or unwilling to return to or avail himself of the protection of that country, because of persecution or a well-founded fear of persecution on account of race, religion, nationality, membership in a particular social group, or political opinion. Refugees are eligible for green cards.

An asylee is someone who is physically present or arriving in the United States and who otherwise meets the definition of a refugee.

The United States accepts a limited number of refugees each year. There is no limit on the number of people who may be granted asylum each year, but only 10,000 may become LPRs each year.

THE DIVERSITY VISA (DV) LOTTERY

Since the early 1990s, the government has held a green card lottery. The government allocates 55,000 immigrant visas each year to provide immigration opportunities for people from countries *other* than the principal sources of immigration to the United States. Thus, the lottery is the government's attempt to put some diversity into the immigration system.

The DV lottery program divides the world into six geographical regions: Africa, Asia, Europe, North America, Oceania, and South America/Central America/Caribbean.

The greatest number of visas are allotted to regions with lower rates of immigration. No one country can receive more than 3,850 diversity visas in any one year, and people from countries that have sent more than 50,000 immigrants to the United States in the past five years are not eligible to enter the lottery. A computer selects lottery winners. In general, the country from which you enter the lottery is the country in which you were born, but you may be able to enter from the eligible country of your spouse's birth if your own country is ineligible. In addition, there is a literacy requirement. You must also have the equivalent of a high school education or work experience in an occupation for which you received two years of training.

During a short period each year, lottery applications may be filed, and the filing period is likely to change from year to year. The lottery is administered by the Department of State rather than by the INS. You can call the Department of State at 1-202-663-1225 to get information about eligibility, filing dates, and procedures.

If you have already applied for an immigrant visa in a preference category and want to know how soon your number will be reached, you can call 1-202-663-1541. You may also consult the State Department's Web site at http://travel.state.gov. If you learn that you are in for a long wait, you may consider entering the lottery as well. You have nothing to lose by entering the green card lottery, so follow instructions and do so. If you are not selected, try again next year. Remember, though, that this is a lottery. You are competing with many other entrants; winning a green card is by no means guaranteed. Still, there is no harm in trying. You may enter only **once** in each lottery year.

No fee is charged for entering the green card lottery, and no official form must be filled out. However, you must include all of the following information, typed or printed in English, on a plain piece of paper:

1. Your full name. Underline your family name.

2. The day, month, and year you were born.

3. The place in which you were born—city or town; district, county, or province; and country. In naming the country in which you were born, use the current name of that place. (Bosnia rather than Yugoslavia, for instance.)

4. The country you are claiming as your native country for purposes of this lottery if your own birthplace is not eligible. You should state that this is the birthplace of your spouse or of one of your parents, if neither of them was born in or is a resident of the country in which you were born.

5. Names, dates of birth, and places of birth of your spouse and children if you have any.

6. Your full mailing address.

7. A recent photograph of yourself, 1.5 inches (37mm) square, with your name printed on the back. Tape this (do not staple or clip it) onto the application paper.

8. Your signature written in the alphabet of your native country.

If you fail to provide all of the information listed, your application will be disqualified. Submit your lottery entry in a plain envelope by ordinary mail or airmail. The envelope must be between 6 and 10 inches long and $3^1/_2$ and $4^1/_2$ inches wide. Do not use an express or messenger service. Above your return address in the upper-left corner, note the country that you are claiming as your native country for lottery purposes. All entries go to the same address except for the ZIP code. Use the ZIP code that applies to the region from which you are applying. If you are not certain of which region your country belongs to, a call to the State Department at the phone number listed previously should give you that information. Mail your lottery entry to

DV (year) Program
National Visa Center
Portsmouth, NH (see ZIP code list that follows)
U.S.A.

Use the ZIP code appropriate to the region from which you are applying:

Asia—00210

South America/Central America/Caribbean—00211

Europe—00212

Africa—00213

Oceania—00214

North America—00215

EXAMPLE: An applicant who was born in Australia and now lives in Spain may submit
one entry to the appropriate Zip (postal) code for Oceania; the envelope should look like this:

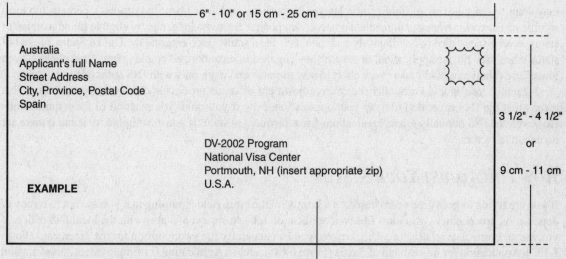

(If, for instance, the applicant's country is Australia (in Oceania), the Zip (postal)
code for Australia would be used, that is, 00214.)

ADJUSTMENT OF STATUS

Before 1952, aliens had to obtain their immigrant visas at a U.S. Consulate abroad. Usually, this was done in their home country. Since 1952, however, aliens who qualify may adjust their status to that of a permanent resident without leaving the United States. The term, *adjustment of status* refers only to the process of becoming a legal permanent resident *within* the U.S. by filing an application with the INS. It does not apply to a situation in which an alien changes her status from one nonimmigrant category to another or to a situation in which an alien obtains her immigrant visa at a U.S. Consulate abroad.

Most people who are in the United States see many advantages to using the adjustment of status process. Foremost among these is the fact that they can save the time and expense of returning home to obtain their green cards.

Let's briefly discuss the adjustment of status process.

WHEN YOU ADJUST YOUR STATUS

Generally, an alien who entered the United States legally may adjust her status to that of a permanent resident if (1) she applies for adjustment of status, (2) she is eligible to receive an immigrant visa and is admissible to the United States for permanent residence, and (3) an immigrant visa is immediately available to her at the time she files her application for adjustment of status. This means that, in most cases, an alien who is not in legal immigration status on the date she files the application, an alien who has failed to maintain continuous legal status (other than through no fault of her own) since entering the United States and an alien who has worked illegally in the United States may **not** adjust her status. Certain other groups of people are also ineligible for adjustment of status (e.g., crewmen, people who entered the United States on the Visa Waiver Pilot Program, and others).

In addition, spouses and fiance(e)s of U.S. citizens seeking permanent residence as immediate relatives obtain only "conditional permanent residence" status if their marriage is less than two years old at the time their application is processed. The Conditional Resident Alien (CRA) and his or her U.S. citizen spouse must file another form two years after the original application is adjudicated to remove the conditions on permanent residence. This form is generally accompanied by evidence showing that the parties entered into the marriage in good faith and are still married to each other. The CRA process is designed to prevent marriage fraud (getting married just to get a green card).

There are several exceptions to the general rules outlined here. Without going through all of them (you may want to consult with an immigration lawyer if you have questions about the process), perhaps the most significant exception relates to immediate relatives. Immediate relatives are generally eligible for adjustment of status, even if they failed to continuously maintain their legal status since entering the United States, are out of status when they file the application, or even if they engaged in unauthorized employment. Nevertheless, even immediate relatives should make every effort to stay in status and work only with INS authorization.

Finally, you should know that the entire adjustment of status process is discretionary in nature. That means that the INS is entitled to deny your application, even if you think you meet all of the requirements. However, the INS normally grants applications for adjustment of status if you are eligible for it and if there are no negative factors.

HOW YOU ADJUST YOUR STATUS

If you are trying to get a green card based on a family relationship (and assuming that you are not in removal/ deportation proceedings), you must file your application for adjustment of status with the local INS office. If you are an immediate relative of a U.S. citizen, you can generally file your petition for the green card (Form I-130), Application for Adjustment of Status (Form I-485), and an Application for Employment Authorization (Form I-765) at the same time.

If you have applied for an employment-based green card, you (or your employer) should file the application with the appropriate INS Regional Service Center.

Whatever category you use as the basis of your application, you may be surprised at the number of documents that you must file. Among other things, you must submit

- Form I-485.

- Form G-325A, Biographic Information Form.

- Form I-94, Departure Record (or other evidence that you entered the United States legally).

- Form 9003, Additional Questions.

- Results of your medical examination, recorded on Form I-693.

- Birth certificate/other proof of birth.

- Photographs.

- Marriage certificate (if required).

- Proof of immediate eligibility for visa.

- Form I-864, Affidavit of Support, and supporting documents (three years of federal tax returns, letter from employer, and so on) if you are applying on the basis of a family relationship; if your application is based on employment or on winning the DV Lottery, you must file Form I-134, Affidavit of Support, and supporting documents.

- Filing fee.

WHAT YOU SHOULD DO WHILE YOUR APPLICATION IS PENDING

When you file your adjustment of status documents, you will receive a receipt (if you file locally) or a receipt notice (if you file by mail at a regional service center). Don't lose this document! It is your proof that you filed for adjustment of status.

If you leave the United States without INS permission while your application for Adjustment of Status is pending, you may be denied permission to return. The INS requires that you file a Form I-131, Application for Travel Document, before you leave. On the form, you must list the dates that you plan to travel and the reason for your travel. You should then wait to receive INS approval before leaving the country.

THE FINAL INTERVIEW

Eventually, you will be summoned to the local office of the INS for the final stage of the process: the interview. At the interview, you will be placed under oath by an INS examiner. The examiner will review all of the documents that you filed with the INS (and with the Department of Labor, if it is an employment-based case). He will ask you a number of questions. Among other things, the examiner will review the biographical information on Form I-485 with you and correct any errors. He will also ask you the questions on page 5 of Form I-485 that relate to various bases for exclusion from the United States (e.g., "Have you ever been deported? Do you intend to engage in espionage?"). If yours is an employment-based case, the examiner may ask you questions about your job. If you have not been employed but you have been present in the United States for a long time, the examiner is sure to ask you questions designed to see whether you have engaged in unauthorized employment (this is not an issue for immediate relatives). He will also review the results of your medical examination.

If you are applying for permanent residence and adjustment of status at the same time based on your marriage to a U.S. citizen, the officer will probably ask to see evidence of your life together. He may then ask you and your spouse several questions that are supposed to help determine whether you really live together. The officer may question you as a couple or individually.

If all goes well at the interview, the examiner will usually give you the good news. Sometimes, he will tell you that you must provide additional evidence. Eventually, assuming that you have satisfied the examiner that your case is a good one, he will issue an approval, and you will return to the INS to get a stamp in your passport that states that you are a permanent resident (or conditional permanent resident, as the case may be). Several months later, the INS will mail you the green card itself.

As we told you previously, you may find it worthwhile to speak with a knowledgeable immigration attorney about your case. Even if your situation does not present any special problems, the immigration laws are so complicated and the procedures change so often that it makes sense to talk to a professional before you start the process.

Call the bar association (lawyers' professional organization) of your city, county, or state for the names of lawyers who specialize in this field and who offer their services at reasonable fees. You can also ask a friend or relative who went through the process for the name of a good immigration lawyer, but be sure to interview any lawyer that he recommends. Although each case is slightly different, following one person's story can help you to sort out the steps. Let us return now to Carla, the case study example used in Chapter 3.

> With the permission granted by her F-1 visa, Carla entered college and proceeded through her course of study. She kept track of the expiration date of her Argentine passport and renewed it months before it expired. Then, as she began her last year of schooling, she met David. Carla and David dated through most of the year, deepening their love. They announced their engagement and gave themselves a big party to celebrate. Friends had alerted them to the INS requirement for documentation, so they had their engagement announced in the newspaper and took lots of photos at the party. As their wedding date approached, they hired a hall and contracted for all the services that go with a wedding. They labeled a folder, "Our Wedding," and kept copies of contracts and receipts in it. The folder also held a copy of the invitation list and, eventually, a photocopy of the marriage license and marriage certificate. A friend videotaped the wedding as his wedding gift.

> Carla was moving from the Turner residence, and David's apartment was tiny, so they rented a new apartment and had both their names entered upon the lease as husband and wife. Then they began filling out forms.

David completed Form I-130, Petition for Alien Relative. Here is how the completed form looked:

U.S. Department of Justice
Immigration and Naturalization Service (INS)

Petition for Alien Relative

OMB #1115-0054

DO NOT WRITE IN THIS BLOCK - FOR EXAMINING OFFICE ONLY

Case ID#	Action Stamp	Fee Stamp
A#		
G-28 or Volag #		

Section of Law:
- [ ] 201 (b) spouse
- [ ] 201 (b) child
- [ ] 201 (b) parent
- [ ] 203 (a)(1)
- [ ] 203 (a)(2)
- [ ] 203 (a)(4)
- [ ] 203 (a)(5)

AM CON: _____

Petition was filed on: _____ (priority date)
- [ ] Personal Interview
- [ ] Pet. [ ] Ben. "A" File Reviewed
- [ ] Field Investigations
- [ ] 204 (a)(2)(A) Resolved
- [ ] Previously Forwarded
- [ ] Stateside Criteria
- [ ] 1-485 Simultaneously
- [ ] 204 (h) Resolved

Remarks:

A. Relationship

1. The alien relative is my
[✓] Husband/Wife [ ] Parent [ ] Brother/Sister [ ] Child

2. Are you related by adoption?
[ ] Yes [✓] No

3. Did you gain permanent residence through adoption?
[ ] Yes [✓] No

B. Information about you

1. Name (Family name in CAPS) (First) (Middle)
STONE, David B.

2. Address (Number and Street) (Apartment Number)
46 Chester Street, Apt. 3-L
(Town or City) (State/Country) (ZIP/Postal Code)
Madison, New Jersey 07941

3. Place of Birth (Town or City) (State/Country)
Philadelphia, Pennsylvania

4. Date of Birth (Mo/Day/Yr) 3/2/75
5. Sex [✓] Male [ ] Female
6. Marital Status [✓] Married [ ] Single [ ] Widowed [ ] Divorced

7. Other Names Used (including maiden name)
none

8. Date and Place of Present Marriage (if married)
August 2, 2001, Madison, NJ

9. Social Security Number
083-22-1111
10. Alien Registration Number (if any)
N/A

11. Names of Prior Husbands/Wives
none
12. Date(s) Marriages(s) Ended
none

13. If you are a U.S. citizen, complete the following:
My citizenship was acquired through (check one)
[✓] Birth in the U.S.
[ ] Naturalization (Give number of certificate, date and place it was issued)

[ ] Parents
Have you obtained a certificate of citizenship in your own name?
[ ] Yes [ ] No
If "Yes", give number of certificate, date and place it was issued

14a. If you are a lawful permanent resident alien, complete the following:
Date and place of admission for, or adjustment to, lawful permanent residence, and class of admission:

14b. Did you gain permanent resident status through marriage to a United States citizen or lawful permanent resident? [ ] Yes [ ] No

C. Information about your alien relative

1. Name (Family name in CAPS) (First) (Middle)
STONE, Carla Rojas

2. Address (Number and Street) (Apartment Number)
46 Chester Street, Apt. 3-L
(Town or City) (State/Country) (ZIP/Postal Code)
Madison, New Jersey 07941

3. Place of Birth (Town or City) (State/Country)
Buenos Aires, Argentina

4. Date of Birth (Mo/Day/Yr) 6/7/79
5. Sex [ ] Male [✓] Female
6. Marital Status [✓] Married [ ] Single [ ] Widowed [ ] Divorced

7. Other Names Used (including maiden name)
Carla A. Rojas (maiden)

8. Date and Place of Present Marriage (if married)
August 2, 2001, Madison, NJ

9. Social Security Number
246-80-1234
10. Alien Registration Number (if any)
none

11. Names of Prior Husbands/Wives
none
12. Date(s) Marriages(s) Ended
none

13. Has your relative ever been in the U.S.?
[✓] Yes [ ] No

14. If your relative is currently in the U.S., complete the following: He or she last arrived as a (visitor, student, stowaway, without inspection, etc.)
J2 (dependent of mother, who arrived

Arrival/Departure Record (I-94) Number
998-567880051
Date arrived (Month/Day/Year)
8/20/95
Date authorized stay expired, or will expire, as shown on Form I-94 or I-95
D/S

15. Name and address of present employer (if any)
none
Date this employment began (Month/Day/Year)
N/A

16. Has your relative ever been under immigration proceedings?
[ ] Yes [✓] No Where _____ When _____
[ ] Exclusion [ ] Deportation [ ] Recission [ ] Judicial Proceedings

INITIAL RECEIPT	RESUBMITTED	RELOCATED		COMPLETED		
		Rec'd	Sent	Approved	Denied	Returned

Form I-130 (Rev. 10/13/98)N

C. (continued) Information about your alien relative

16. List husband/wife and all children of your relative (if your relative is your husband/wife, list only his or her children).

(Name)	(Relationship)	(Date of Birth)	(Country of Birth)

N/A

17. Address in the United States where your relative intends to live

(Number and Street)   (Town or City)   (State)

46 Chester Street, Apt. 3-L   Madison   NJ

18. Your relative's address abroad

(Number and Street)   (Town or City)   (Province)   (Country)   (Phone Number)

16 Camino Cruz Blanca, Apt. 1060   Buenos Aires   Buenos Aires   Argentina   54-1-555-6785

19. If your relative's native alphabet is other than Roman letters, write his or her name and address abroad in the native alphabet:

(Name)   (Number and Street)   Town or City)   (Province)   (Country)

N/A

20. If filing for your husband/wife, give last address at which you both lived together:

(Name)	(Number and Street)	(Town or City)	(Province)	(Country)	From (Month)	(Year)	To (Month)	(Year)
	46 Chester St	Madison, NJ		USA	8	2001	pres.	

21. Check the appropriate box below and give the information required for the box you checked:

☐ Your relative will apply for a visa abroad at the American Consulate in _____

(City)   (Country)

☑ Your relative is in the United States and will apply for adjustment of status to that of a lawful permanent resident in the office of the Immigration and Naturalization Service at   Newark   NJ   . If your relative is not eligible for adjustment of status, he or she will

(City)   (State)

apply for a visa abroad at the American Consulate in _____ ,

(City)   (Country)

(Designation of a consulate outside the country of your relative's last residence does not guarantee acceptance for processing by that consulate. Acceptance is at the discretion of the designated consulate.)

D. Other Information

1. If separate petitions are also being submitted for other relatives, give names of each and relationship.

N/A

2. Have you ever filed a petition for this or any other alien before?   ☐ Yes   ☑ No
If "Yes," give name, place and date of filing, and result.

Warning: The INS investigates claimed relationships and verifies the validity of documents. The INS seeks criminal prosecutions when family relationships are falsified to obtain visas.

Penalties: You may, by law be imprisoned for not more than five years, or fined $250,000, or both, for entering into a marriage contract for the purpose of evading any provision of the immigration laws and you may be fined up to $10,000 or imprisoned up to five years or both, for knowingly and willfully falsifying or concealing a material fact or using any false document in submitting this petition.

Your Certification: I certify, under penalty of perjury under the laws of the United States of America, that the foregoing is true and correct. Furthermore, I authorize the release of any information from my records which the Immigration and Naturalization Service needs to determine eligibility for the benefit that I am seeking.

Signature   *David B. Stone*   Date   9/1/2001   Phone Number (201) 123-4567

Signature of Person Preparing Form if Other than Above

I declare that I prepared this document at the request of the person above and that it is based on all information of which I have any knowledge.

Print Name _____ (Address)_____ (Signature)_____ (Date)_____

G-28 ID Number _____

Volag Number _____

Form I-130 (Rev. 10/13/98)N

Carla completed this Form I-485, Application to Register Permanent Resident or Adjust Status:

OMB No. 1115-0053

U.S. Department of Justice
Immigration and Naturalization Service

Form I-485, Application to Register Permanent Resident or Adjust Status

---

START HERE - Please Type or Print

FOR INS USE ONLY	
Returned	Receipt

Part 1. Information About You.

Family Name STONE	Given Name Carla	Middle Initial R

Address - C/O

Street Number and Name 46 Chester Street	Apt. # 3-L

City Madison

State New Jersey	Zip Code 07941
Date of Birth (month/day/year) 6/7/79	Country of Birth Argentina
Social Security # 246-80-1234	A # (if any) N/A
Date of Last Arrival (month/day/year) 8/20/95	I-94 # 998567880 05
Current INS Status F-1	Expires on (month/day/year) D/S

Resubmitted

Reloc Sent

Reloc Rec'd

Applicant Interviewed

Part 2. Application Type. *(check one)*

I am applying for an adjustment to permanent resident status because:

a. ☑ an immigrant petition giving me an immediately available immigrant visa number has been approved. (Atttach a copy of the approval notice-- or a relative, special immigrant juvenile or special immigrant military visa petition filed with this application that will give you an immediately available visa number, if approved.)

b. ☐ my spouse or parent applied for adjustment of status or was granted lawful permanent residence in an immigrant visa category that allows derivative status for spouses and children.

c. ☐ I entered as a K-1 fiance(e) of a U.S. citizen whom I married within 90 days of entry, or I am the K-2 child of such a fiance(e). [Attach a copy of the fiance(e) petition approval notice and the marriage certificate.]

d. ☐ I was granted asylum or derivative asylum status as the spouse or child of a person granted asylum and am eligible for adjustment.

e. ☐ I am a native or citizen of Cuba admitted or paroled into the U.S. after January 1, 1959, and thereafter have been physically present in the U.S. for at least one year.

f. ☐ I am the husband, wife or minor unmarried child of a Cuban described in (e) and am residing with that person, and was admitted or paroled into the U.S. after January 1, 1959, and thereafter have been physically present in the U.S. for at least one year.

g. ☐ I have continuously resided in the U.S. since before January 1, 1972.

h. ☐ Other basis of eligibility. Explain. (If additional space is needed, use a separate piece of paper.)

I am already a permanent resident and am applying to have the date I was granted permanent residence adjusted to the date I originally arrived in the U.S. as a nonimmigrant or parolee, or as of May 2,1964, whichever date is later, and: *(Check one)*

i. ☐ I am a native or citizen of Cuba and meet the description in (e), above.

j. ☐ I am the husband, wife or minor unmarried child of a Cuban, and meet the description in (f), above.

Section of Law
☐ Sec. 209(b), INA
☐ Sec. 13, Act of 9/11/57
☐ Sec. 245, INA
☐ Sec. 249, INA
☐ Sec. 2 Act of 11/2/66
☐ Sec. 2 Act of 11/2/66
☐ Other _____

Country Chargeable

Eligibility Under Sec. 245
☐ Approved Visa Petition
☐ Dependent of Principal Alien
☐ Special Immigrant
☐ Other _____

Preference

Action Block

To be Completed by
Attorney or Representative, **if any**
☐ Fill in box if G-28 is attached to represent the applicant.
VOLAG #

ATTY State License #

Continued on back

Form I-485 (Rev. 02/07/00)N Page 1

Part 3. Processing Information.

A. City/Town/Village of Birth Buenos Aires	Current Occupation none
Your Mother's First Name Martina	Your Father's First Name Simon

Give your name exactly how it appears on your Arrival /Departure Record (Form I-94)

Carla A. Rojas

Place of Last Entry Into the U.S. (City/State) Newark, NJ	In what status did you last enter? *(Visitor, student, exchange alien, crewman, temporary worker, without inspection, etc.)*
Were you inspected by a U.S. Immigration Officer? ☑ Yes ☐ No	J-2
Nonimmigrant Visa Number 98765	Consulate Where Visa Was Issued Buenos Aires, Argentina
Date Visa Was Issued (month/day/year) 7/1/95	Sex: ☐ Male ☑ Female	Marital Status ☑ Married ☐ Single ☐ Divorced ☐ Widowed

Have you ever before applied for permanent resident status in the U.S.? ☑ No ☐ Yes If you checked "Yes," give date and place of filing and final disposition.

B. List your present husband/wife and all your sons and daughters. (If you have none, write "none." If additional space is needed, use a separate piece of paper.)

Family Name Stone	Given Name David	Middle Initial B	Date of Birth (month/day/year) 3/2/79
Country of Birth USA	Relationship Husband	A # N/A	Applying with You? ☐ Yes ☑ No
Family Name	Given Name	Middle Initial	Date of Birth (month/day/year)
Country of Birth	Relationship	A #	Applying with You? ☐ Yes ☐ No
Family Name	Given Name	Middle Initial	Date of Birth (month/day/year)
Country of Birth	Relationship	A #	Applying with You? ☐ Yes ☐ No
Family Name	Given Name	Middle Initial	Date of Birth (month/day/year)
Country of Birth	Relationship	A #	Applying with You? ☐ Yes ☐ No
Family Name	Given Name	Middle Initial	Date of Birth (month/day/year)
Country of Birth	Relationship	A #	Applying with You? ☐ Yes ☐ No

C. List your present and past membership in or affiliation with every political organization, association, fund, foundation, party, club, society or similar group in the United States or in other places since your 16th birthday. Include any foreign military service in this part. If none, write "none." Include the name(s) of the organization(s), location(s), dates of membership from and to, and the nature of the organization (s). If additional space is needed, use a separate piece of paper.

None

Part 3. Processing Information. *(Continued)*

Please answer the following questions. (If your answer is "Yes" to any one of these questions, explain on a separate piece of paper. Answering "Yes" does not necessarily mean that you are not entitled to adjust your status or register for permanent residence.)

1. Have you ever, in or outside the U. S.:
   a. knowingly committed any crime of moral turpitude or a drug-related offense for which you have not been arrested? ☐ Yes ☑ No
   b. been arrested, cited, charged, indicted, fined or imprisoned for breaking or violating any law or ordinance, excluding traffic violations? ☐ Yes ☑ No
   c. been the beneficiary of a pardon, amnesty, rehabilitation decree, other act of clemency or similar action? ☐ Yes ☑ No
   d. exercised diplomatic immunity to avoid prosecution for a criminal offense in the U. S.? ☐ Yes ☑ No

2. Have you received public assistance in the U.S. from any source, including the U.S. government or any state, county, city or municipality (other than emergency medical treatment), or are you likely to receive public assistance in the future? ☐ Yes ☑ No

3. Have you ever:
   a. within the past ten years been a prostitute or procured anyone for prostitution, or intend to engage in such activities in the future? ☐ Yes ☑ No
   b. engaged in any unlawful commercialized vice, including, but not limited to, illegal gambling? ☐ Yes ☑ No
   c. knowingly encouraged, induced, assisted, abetted or aided any alien to try to enter the U.S. illegally? ☐ Yes ☑ No
   d. illicitly trafficked in any controlled substance, or knowingly assisted, abetted or colluded in the illicit trafficking of any controlled substance? ☐ Yes ☑ No

4. Have you ever engaged in, conspired to engage in, or do you intend to engage in, or have you ever solicited membership or funds for, or have you through any means ever assisted or provided any type of material support to, any person or organization that has ever engaged or conspired to engage, in sabotage, kidnapping, political assassination, hijacking or any other form of terrorist activity? ☐ Yes ☑ No

5. Do you intend to engage in the U.S. in:
   a. espionage? ☐ Yes ☑ No
   b. any activity a purpose of which is opposition to, or the control or overthrow of, the government of the United States, by force, violence or other unlawful means? ☐ Yes ☑ No
   c. any activity to violate or evade any law prohibiting the export from the United States of goods, technology or sensitive information? ☐ Yes ☑ No

6. Have you ever been a member of, or in any way affiliated with, the Communist Party or any other totalitarian party? ☐ Yes ☑ No

7. Did you, during the period from March 23, 1933 to May 8, 1945, in association with either the Nazi Government of Germany or any organization or government associated or allied with the Nazi Government of Germany, ever order, incite, assist or otherwise participate in the persecution of any person because of race, religion, national origin or political opinion? ☐ Yes ☑ No

8. Have you ever engaged in genocide, or otherwise ordered, incited, assisted or otherwise participated in the killing of any person because of race, religion, nationality, ethnic origin or political opinion? ☐ Yes ☑ No

9. Have you ever been deported from the U.S., or removed from the U.S. at government expense, excluded within the past year, or are you now in exclusion or deportation proceedings? ☐ Yes ☑ No

10. Are you under a final order of civil penalty for violating section 274C of the Immigration and Nationality Act for use of fradulent documents or have you, by fraud or willful misrepresentation of a material fact, ever sought to procure, or procured, a visa, other documentation, entry into the U.S. or any immigration benefit? ☐ Yes ☑ No

11. Have you ever left the U.S. to avoid being drafted into the U.S. Armed Forces? ☐ Yes ☑ No

12. Have you ever been a J nonimmigrant exchange visitor who was subject to the two-year foreign residence requirement and not yet complied with that requirement or obtained a waiver? ☐ Yes ☑ No

13. Are you now withholding custody of a U.S. citizen child outside the U.S. from a person granted custody of the child? ☐ Yes ☑ No

14. Do you plan to practice polygamy in the U.S.? ☐ Yes ☑ No

Part 4.   Signature.   *(Read the information on penalties in the instructions before completing this section. You must file this application while in the United States.)*

I certify, under penalty of perjury under the laws of the United States of America, that this application and the evidence submitted with it is all true and correct. I authorize the release of any information from my records which the INS needs to determine eligibility for the benefit I am seeking.

Selective Service Registration. The following applies to you if you are a man at least 18 years old, but not yet 26 years old, who is required to register with the Selective Service System: I understand that my filing this adjustment of status application with the Immigration and Naturalization Service authorizes the INS to provide certain registration information to the Selective Service System in accordance with the Military Selective Service Act. Upon INS acceptance of my application, I authorize INS to transmit to the Selective Service System my name, current address, Social Security number, date of birth and the date I filed the application for the purpose of recording my Selective Service registration as of the filing date. If, however, the INS does not accept my application, I further understand that, if so required, I am responsible for registering with the Selective Service by other means, provided I have not yet reached age 26.

Signature	*Print Your Name*	*Date*	*Daytime Phone Number*
Carla R. Stone Carla R. Stone		9/1/2001	(201) 123-4567

Please Note: *If you do not completely fill out this form or fail to submit required documents listed in the instructions, you may not be found eligible for the requested benefit and this application may be denied.*

Part 5.   Signature of Person Preparing Form, If Other Than Above. *(Sign Below)*

I declare that I prepared this application at the request of the above person and it is based on all information of which I have knowledge.

Signature	*Print Your Name*	*Date*	*Daytime Phone Number*

**Firm Name
and Address**

Form I-485 (Rev. 02/07/00)N Page 4

Both David and Carla filled out these Forms G-325A:

U.S. Department of Justice	FORM G-325A	OMB No. 1115-0066
Immigration and Naturalization Service	**BIOGRAPHIC INFORMATION**	Approval expires 4-30-85

(Family name) STONE	(First name) Carla	(Middle name) Rojas	☐MALE ☑FEMALE	BIRTHDATE (Mo.-Day-Yr.) 6-7-79	NATIONALITY Argentine	FILE NUMBER A. N/A

ALL OTHER NAMES USED (Including names by previous marriages) Carla A. Rojas (maiden)		CITY AND COUNTRY OF BIRTH Buenos Aires, Argentina	SOCIAL SECURITY NO. (If any) 246-80-1234

	FAMILY NAME	FIRST NAME	DATE, CITY AND COUNTRY OF BIRTH (If known)	CITY AND COUNTRY OF RESIDENCE
FATHER	Rojas	Simon	2-8-49, Buenos Aires, Argentina	Rosario, Argentina
MOTHER (Maiden name)	delCampo	Martina	9-21-50, Buenos Aires, Argentina	Buenos Aires, Argentina

HUSBAND(If none, so state) OR WIFE	FAMILY NAME (For wife, give maiden name)	FIRST NAME	BIRTHDATE	CITY & COUNTRY OF BIRTH	DATE OF MARRIAGE	PLACE OF MARRIAGE
	STONE	David	3-2-79	Philadelphia, PA	8-2-01	Madison, NJ

FORMER HUSBANDS OR WIVES (If none, so state) FAMILY NAME (For wife, give maiden name)	FIRST NAME	BIRTHDATE	DATE & PLACE OF MARRIAGE	DATE AND PLACE OF TERMINATION OF MARRIAGE
None				

APPLICANT'S RESIDENCE LAST FIVE YEARS, LIST PRESENT ADDRESS FIRST

STREET AND NUMBER	CITY	PROVINCE OR STATE	COUNTRY	FROM MONTH	FROM YEAR	TO MONTH	TO YEAR
46 Chester Street	Madison	New Jersey	USA	8	01	PRESENT TIME	
19 Maple Lane	Madison	New Jersey	USA	8	97	7	01
1504 High Street	Madison	New Jersey	USA	8	95	8	97

APPLICANT'S LAST ADDRESS OUTSIDE THE UNITED STATES OF MORE THAN ONE YEAR

STREET AND NUMBER	CITY	PROVINCE OR STATE	COUNTRY	FROM MONTH	FROM YEAR	TO MONTH	TO YEAR
16 Camino Cruz Blanca, #1060	Buenos Aires		Argentina	3	79	8	95

APPLICANT'S EMPLOYMENT LAST FIVE YEARS. (IF NONE, SO STATE.) LIST PRESENT EMPLOYMENT FIRST

FULL NAME AND ADDRESS OF EMPLOYER	OCCUPATION (SPECIFY)	FROM MONTH	FROM YEAR	TO MONTH	TO YEAR
None				PRESENT TIME	

Show below last occupation abroad if not shown above. (Include all information requested above.)

N/A					

THIS FORM IS SUBMITTED IN CONNECTION WITH APPLICATION FOR: ☐ NATURALIZATION ☑ STATUS AS PERMANENT RESIDENT ☐ OTHER (SPECIFY):	SIGNATURE OF APPLICANT *Carla R. Stone*	DATE 9/1/2001

If your native alphabet is other than roman letters, write your name in your native alphabet here:

Are all copies legible? ☒ Yes

PENALTIES: SEVERE PENALTIES ARE PROVIDED BY LAW FOR KNOWINGLY AND WILLFULLY FALSIFYING OR CONCEALING A MATERIAL FACT.

APPLICANT: BE SURE TO PUT YOUR NAME AND ALIEN REGISTRATION NUMBER IN THE BOX OUTLINED BY HEAVY BORDER BELOW.

COMPLETE THIS BOX (Family Name) STONE	(Given name) Carla	(Middle name) Rojas	(Alien registration number)

Form G-325 A (Rev. 10-1-82)   **(1) Ident.**

U.S. Department of Justice

Immigration and Naturalization Service

FORM G-325A

BIOGRAPHIC INFORMATION

OMB No. 1115-0066

Approval expires 4-30-85

(Family name)	(First name)	(Middle name)	☑MALE ☐FEMALE	BIRTHDATE (Mo.-Day-Yr.)	NATIONALITY	FILE NUMBER
STONE	David	B.		3-2-75	USA	A. N/A

ALL OTHER NAMES USED (Including names by previous marriages)	CITY AND COUNTRY OF BIRTH	SOCIAL SECURITY NO. (If any)
None	Philadelphia, PA USA	083-22-1111

	FAMILY NAME	FIRST NAME	DATE, CITY AND COUNTRY OF BIRTH (If known)	CITY AND COUNTRY OF RESIDENCE
FATHER	Stone	Howard	6-22-49, Miami, FL, USA	Philadelphia, PA, USA
MOTHER (Maiden name)	Lee	Linda	1-5-49, Canton, OH, USA	Philadelphia, PA, USA

HUSBAND(If none, so state) OR WIFE	FAMILY NAME (For wife, give maiden name)	FIRST NAME	BIRTHDATE	CITY & COUNTRY OF BIRTH	DATE OF MARRIAGE	PLACE OF MARRIAGE
	ROJAS	Carla	6-7-79	Buenos Aires, Argentina	8-2-01	Madison, NJ

FORMER HUSBANDS OR WIVES (If none, so state)

FAMILY NAME (For wife, give maiden name)	FIRST NAME	BIRTHDATE	DATE & PLACE OF MARRIAGE	DATE AND PLACE OF TERMINATION OF MARRIAGE
None				

APPLICANT'S RESIDENCE LAST FIVE YEARS. LIST PRESENT ADDRESS FIRST

STREET AND NUMBER	CITY	PROVINCE OR STATE	COUNTRY	FROM MONTH	FROM YEAR	TO MONTH	TO YEAR
46 Chester Street	Madison	New Jersey	USA	8	01	PRESENT TIME	
71 Third Avenue	Madison	New Jersey	USA	6	97	7	01
276 Market Street	Madison	New Jersey	USA	8	93	5	97
13860 Lancaster Pike	Philadelphia	Pennsylvania	USA	3	79	8	93

APPLICANT'S LAST ADDRESS OUTSIDE THE UNITED STATES OF MORE THAN ONE YEAR

STREET AND NUMBER	CITY	PROVINCE OR STATE	COUNTRY	FROM MONTH	FROM YEAR	TO MONTH	TO YEAR
N/A							

APPLICANT'S EMPLOYMENT LAST FIVE YEARS. (IF NONE, SO STATE.) LIST PRESENT EMPLOYMENT FIRST

FULL NAME AND ADDRESS OF EMPLOYER	OCCUPATION (SPECIFY)	FROM MONTH	FROM YEAR	TO MONTH	TO YEAR
Barton Mfg Co. 410 Front Street, Madison, NJ	software engineer	6	97	PRESENT TIME	

Show below last occupation abroad if not shown above. (Include all information requested above.)

N/A					

THIS FORM IS SUBMITTED IN CONNECTION WITH APPLICATION FOR:	SIGNATURE OF APPLICANT	DATE
☐ NATURALIZATION ☑ STATUS AS PERMANENT RESIDENT ☐ OTHER (SPECIFY)(for spouse)	*David B. Stone*	9/1/2001

If your native alphabet is other than roman letters, write your name in your native alphabet here:

Are all copies legible?   [X] Yes

PENALTIES: SEVERE PENALTIES ARE PROVIDED BY LAW FOR KNOWINGLY AND WILLFULLY FALSIFYING OR CONCEALING A MATERIAL FACT.

APPLICANT: BE SURE TO PUT YOUR NAME AND ALIEN REGISTRATION NUMBER IN THE BOX OUTLINED BY HEAVY BORDER BELOW.

COMPLETE THIS BOX (Family Name)	(Given name)	(Middle name)	(Alien registration number)
STONE	David	B.	

Form G-325 A (Rev. 10-1-82)   **(1) Ident.**

Carla went to a doctor on the INS list and had a complete physical examination. The doctor filled out a Form I-693, Medical Exam of Aliens Seeking Adjustment of Status (see the Forms Appendix for a sample) and placed it in a sealed envelope (the envelope was to be opened by the INS examiner, at her interview).

David completed an I-864, Affidavit of Support. David also enclosed a letter from his employer stating his current salary, copies of his last three federal tax returns, copies of his most recent bank statements, and photocopies of all his stock certificates and U.S. Savings Bonds. Carla also filled out Form 9003, Additional Questions to be Completed by All Applicants for Permanent Residence in the United States. Carla's form looked like this:

Form **9003** (October 1994)	Department of the Treasury — Internal Revenue Service	OMB Clearance No. 1545-1065
	Additional Questions to be Completed by All Applicants for Permanent Residence in the United States	

This form must accompany your application for permanent residence in the United States

Privacy Act Notice: Your responses to the following questions will be provided to the Internal Revenue Service pursuant to Section 6039E of the Internal Revenue Code of 1986. Use of this information is limited to that needed for tax administration purposes. Failure to provide this information may result in a $500 penalty unless failure is due to reasonable cause.

On the date of issuance of the Alien Registration Receipt Card, the Immigration and Naturalization Service will send the following information to the Internal Revenue Service: your name, social security number, address, date of birth, alien identification number, occupation, class of admission, and answers to IRS Form 9003.

Name *(Last—Surname—Family)*   *(First—Given)*   *(Middle Initial)*

STONE   Carla   R.

Taxpayer Identification Number . . . . |2 | 4 | 6 |8 |0 |1 |2 |3 |4

Enter your Social Security Number (SSN) if you have one. If you do not have an SSN but have used a Taxpayer Identification Number issued to you by the Internal Revenue Service, enter that number. Otherwise, write "NONE" in the space provided; i.e., "⌐ ⌐ ⌐ ⌐ N·O·N·E·".

	Mark appropriate column	
	Yes	**No**
1. Are you self-employed? Mark "yes" if you own and actively operate a business in which you share in the profits other than as an investor.		X
2. Have you been in the United States for 183 days or more during any one of the three calendar years immediately preceding the current calendar year? Mark "yes" if you spent 183 days or more (not necessarily consecutive) in the United States during any **one of the three prior** calendar years **whether or not you worked** in the United States.	X	
3. During the last three years did you receive income from sources in the United States? Mark "yes" if you received income paid by individuals or institutions located in the United States. Income includes, but is not limited to, compensation for services provided by you, interest, dividends, rents, and royalties.		X
4. Did you file a United States Individual Income Tax Return (Forms 1040, 1040A, 1040EZ or 1040NR) in any of the last three years?		X

If you answered yes to question 4, for which tax year was the last return filed? . . . . 19 ___ ___

Paperwork Reduction Act Notice—We ask for the information on this form to carry out the Internal Revenue laws of the United States. You are required to give us the information. We need it to ensure that you are complying with these laws and to allow us to figure and collect the right amount of tax.

The time needed to complete and file this form will vary depending on individual circumstances. The estimated average time is 5 minutes. If you have comments concerning the accuracy of this time estimate or suggestions for making this form more simple, we would be happy to hear from you. You can write to both the **Internal Revenue Service**, Attention: Reports Clearance Officer, PC:FP, Washington, DC 20224, and the **Office of Management and Budget**, Paperwork Reduction Project (1545-1065), Washington, DC 20503. **DO NOT send this form to either of these offices. Instead, return it to the appropriate office of the Department of State or the Immigration and Naturalization Service.**

Remarks

Cat. No. 10126D   1. FILE COPY   Form **9003** (Rev. 10-94)

Carla and David worked together to complete the application package. They included a photocopy of Carla's I-94 card, a photocopy of Carla's passport, a photocopy of her current visa, a photocopy of her birth certificate, and a translation of her birth certificate prepared by a friend fluent in both Spanish and English. At the end of the translation, Carla's friend wrote and signed the following statement:

I hereby certify that I translated this document from Spanish to English. This translation is accurate and complete. I further certify that I am fully competent to translate from Spanish to English.

Carla's friend then had her translation notarized.

They also enclosed three photographs of Carla and three photographs of David, all complying with the required specifications.

U. S. IMMIGRATION & NATURALIZATION SERVICE

COLOR PHOTOGRAPH SPECIFICATIONS

IDEAL PHOTOGRAPH ◄

IMAGE MUST FIT INSIDE THIS BOX ►

THE PICTURE AT LEFT IS IDEAL SIZE, COLOR, BACKGROUND, AND POSE. THE IMAGE SHOULD BE 30MM (1 3/16IN) FROM THE HAIR TO JUST BELOW THE CHIN, AND 26MM (1 IN) FROM LEFT CHEEK TO RIGHT EAR. THE IMAGE MUST FIT IN THE BOX AT RIGHT.

THE PHOTOGRAPH

* THE OVERALL SIZE OF THE PICTURE, INCLUDING THE BACKGROUND, MUST BE AT LEAST 40MM (1 9/16 INCHES) IN HEIGHT BY 35MM (1 3/8IN) IN WIDTH.

* PHOTOS MUST BE FREE OF SHADOWS AND CONTAIN NO MARKS, SPLOTCHES, OR DISCOLORATIONS.

* PHOTOS SHOULD BE HIGH QUALITY, WITH GOOD BACK LIGHTING OR WRAP AROUND LIGHTING, AND MUST HAVE A WHITE OR OFF-WHITE BACKGROUND.

* PHOTOS MUST BE A GLOSSY OR MATTE FINISH AND UN-RETOUCHED.

* POLAROID FILM HYBRID #5 IS ACCEPTABLE; HOWEVER SX-70 TYPE FILM OR ANY OTHER INSTANT PROCESSING TYPE FILM IS UNACCEPTABLE. NON-PEEL APART FILMS ARE EASILY RECOGNIZED BECAUSE THE BACK OF THE FILM IS BLACK. ACCEPTABLE INSTANT COLOR FILM HAS A GRAY-TONED BACKING.

THE IMAGE OF THE PERSON

* THE DIMENSIONS OF THE IMAGE SHOULD BE 30MM (1 3/16 INCHES) FROM THE HAIR TO THE NECK JUST BELOW THE CHIN, AND 26MM (1 INCH) FROM THE RIGHT EAR TO THE LEFT CHEEK. IMAGE CANNOT EXCEED 32MM BY 28MM (1 1/4IN X 1 1/16IN).

* IF THE IMAGE AREA ON THE PHOTOGRAPH IS TOO LARGE OR TOO SMALL, THE PHOTO CANNOT BE USED.

* PHOTOGRAPHS MUST SHOW THE ENTIRE FACE OF THE PERSON IN A 3/4 VIEW SHOWING THE RIGHT EAR AND LEFT EYE.

* FACIAL FEATURES **MUST BE IDENTIFIABLE.**

* CONTRAST BETWEEN THE IMAGE AND BACKGROUND IS ESSENTIAL. PHOTOS FOR VERY LIGHT SKINNED PEOPLE SHOULD BE SLIGHTLY UNDER-EXPOSED. PHOTOS FOR VERY DARK SKINNED PEOPLE SHOULD BE SLIGHTLY OVER-EXPOSED.

SAMPLES OF UNACCEPTABLE PHOTOGRAPHS

INCORRECT POSE	IMAGE TOO LARGE	IMAGE TOO SMALL	IMAGE TOO DARK UNDER-EXPOSED

IMAGE TOO LIGHT	DARK BACKGROUND	OVER-EXPOSED	SHADOWS ON PIC

Immigration & Naturalization Service
Form M-378 (6-92)

In addition they included a photocopy of their marriage certificate, a photocopy of David's birth certificate, and all the proofs required to be attached to David's Affidavit of Support (I-864).

U.S. Department of Justice
Immigration and Naturalization Service

OMB # 1115-0214

Affidavit of Support Under Section 213A of the Act

START HERE - Please Type or Print

Part 1. Information on Sponsor (You)

Last Name	First Name	Middle Name
Stone	David	B

Mailing Address (Street Number and Name)	Apt/Suite Number
46 Chester Street	3-L

City	State or Province
Madison	New Jersey

Country	ZIP/Postal Code	Telephone Number
USA	07941	(201) 123-4567

Place of Residence if different from above (Street Number and Name)	Apt/Suite Number
Same as above	

City	State or Province

Country	ZIP/Postal Code	Telephone Number ( )

Date of Birth (Month, Day, Year)	Place of Birth (City, State, Country)	Are you a U.S. Citizen?
3/2/75	Phila, PA USA	☒ Yes ☐ No

Social Security Number	A-Number (If any)
083-22-1111	N/A

FOR AGENCY USE ONLY

This Affidavit   Receipt

[ ] Meets

[ ] Does not meet

Requirements of Section 213A

Part 2. Basis for Filing Affidavit of Support

I am filing this affidavit of support because (check one):

a. ☒ I filed/am filing the alien relative petition.

b. ☐ I filed/am filing an alien worker petition on behalf of the intending immigrant, who is related to me as my _____. (relationship)

c. ☐ I have ownership interest of at least 5% of _____ (name of entity which filed visa petition) which filed an alien worker petition on behalf of the intending immigrant, who is related to me as my _____. (relationship)

d. ☐ I am a joint sponsor willing to accept the legal obligations with any other sponsor(s).

Officer's Signature _____

Location _____

Date _____

Part 3. Information on the Immigrant(s) You Are Sponsoring

Last Name	First Name	Middle Name
Stone	Carla	Rojas

Date of Birth (Month,Day,Year)	Sex:	Social Security Number (If any)
6/7/79	☐ Male ☒ Female	246-80-1234

Country of Citizenship	A-Number (If any)
Argentina	N/A

Current Address (Street Number and Name)	Apt/Suite Number	City
46 Chester Street	3-L	Madison

State/Province	Country	ZIP/Postal Code	Telephone Number
NJ	USA	07941	(201) 123-4567

List any spouse and/or children immigrating with the immigrant named above in this Part: *(Use additional sheet of paper if necessary.)*

Name	Relationship to Sponsored Immigrant			Date of Birth			A-Number (If any)	Social Security Number (If any)
	Spouse	Son	Daughter	Mo.	Day	Yr.		
None								

Form I-864 (10/6/97)

Part 4. Eligibility to Sponsor

To be a sponsor you must be a U.S. citizen or national or a lawful permanent resident. If you are not the petitioning relative, you must provide proof of status. To prove status, U.S. citizens or nationals must attach a copy of a document proving status, such as a U.S. passport, birth certificate, or certificate of naturalization, and lawful permanent residents must attach a copy of both sides of their Alien Registration Card (Form I-551).

The determination of your eligibility to sponsor an immigrant will be based on an evaluation of your demonstrated ability to maintain an annual income at or above 125 percent of the Federal poverty line (100 percent if you are a petitioner sponsoring your spouse or child and you are on active duty in the U.S. Armed Forces). The assessment of your ability to maintain an adequate income will include your current employment, household size, and household income as shown on the Federal income tax returns for the 3 most recent tax years. Assets that are readily converted to cash and that can be made available for the support of sponsored immigrants if necessary, including any such assets of the immigrant(s) you are sponsoring, may also be considered.

The greatest weight in determining eligibility will be placed on current employment and household income. If a petitioner is unable to demonstrate ability to meet the stated income and asset requirements, a joint sponsor who *can* meet the income and asset requirements is needed. Failure to provide adequate evidence of income and/or assets or an affidavit of support completed by a joint sponsor will result in denial of the immigrant's application for an immigrant visa or adjustment to permanent resident status.

A. Sponsor's Employment

I am: 1. ☒ Employed by __Barton Manufacturing Company__ *(Provide evidence of employment)*
Annual salary $ _60,000_ *or* hourly wage $ _____ *(for_____ hours per week)*

2. ☐ Self employed _____*(Name of business)*
Nature of employment or business _____

3. ☐ Unemployed or retired since _____

B. Use of Benefits

Have you or anyone related to you by birth, marriage, or adoption living in your household or listed as a dependent on your most recent income tax return received any type of means-tested public benefit in the past 3 years?
☐ Yes   ☒ No *(If yes, provide details, including programs and dates, on a separate sheet of paper)*

C. Sponsor's Household Size   Number

1. Number of persons (related to you by birth, marriage, or adoption) living in your residence, including yourself. *(Do NOT include persons being sponsored in this affidavit.)*   __1__
2. Number of immigrants being sponsored in this affidavit *(Include all persons in Part 3.)*   __1__
3. Number of immigrants **NOT** living in your household whom you are still obligated to support under a previously signed affidavit of support using Form I-864.   __0__
4. Number of persons who are otherwise dependent on you, as claimed in your tax return for the most recent tax year.   __0__
5. Total household size. *(Add lines 1 through 4.)*   **Total**   __2__

List persons below who are included in lines 1 or 3 for whom you previously have submitted INS Form I-864, *if your support obligation has not terminated.*
(If additional space is needed, use additional paper)

Name	A-Number	Date Affidavit of Support Signed	Relationship
None			

Part 4. Eligibility to Sponsor *(Continued)*

D. Sponsor's Annual Household Income

Enter total unadjusted income from your Federal income tax return for the most recent tax year below. If you last filed a joint income tax return but are using only your *own* income to qualify, list total earnings from your W-2 Forms, or, *if* necessary to reach the required income for your household size, include income from other sources listed on your tax return. If your *individual* income does not meet the income requirement for your household size, you may also list total income for anyone related to you by birth, marriage, or adoption currently living with you in your residence if they have lived in your residence for the previous 6 months, or any person shown as a dependent on your Federal income tax return for the most recent tax year, even if not living in the household. For their income to be considered, household members or dependents must be willing to make their income available for support of the sponsored immigrant(s) and to complete and sign Form I-864A, Contract Between Sponsor and Household Member. A sponsored immigrant/household member only need complete Form I-864A if his or her income will be used to determine your ability to support a spouse and/or children immigrating with him or her.

You must attach evidence of current employment and copies of income tax returns as filed with the IRS for the most recent 3 tax years for yourself and all persons whose income is listed below. See "Required Evidence" in Instructions. Income from all 3 years will be considered in determining your ability to support the immigrant(s) you are sponsoring.

- ☒ I filed a single/separate tax return for the most recent tax year.
- ☐ I filed a joint return for the most recent tax year which includes only my own income.
- ☐ I filed a joint return for the most recent tax year which includes income for my spouse and myself.
    - ☐ I am submitting documentation of my individual income (Forms W-2 and 1099).
    - ☐ I am qualifying using my spouse's income; my spouse is submitting a Form I-864A.

Indicate most recent tax year	2000
	(tax year)
Sponsor's individual income	$ 60,000
or	
Sponsor and spouse's combined income *(If joint tax return filed; spouse must submit Form I-864A.)*	$
Income of other qualifying persons. *(List names; include spouse if applicable. Each person must complete Form I-864A.)*	
_____	$
_____	$
_____	$
Total Household Income	$ 60,000

Explain on separate sheet of paper if you or any of the above listed individuals are submitting Federal income tax returns for fewer than 3 years, or if other explanation of income, employment, or evidence is necessary.

E. Determination of Eligibility Based on Income

1. ☒ I am subject to the 125 percent of poverty line requirement for sponsors.
   ☐ I am subject to the 100 percent of poverty line requirement for sponsors on active duty in the U.S. Armed Forces sponsoring their spouse or child.
2. Sponsor's total household size, from Part 4.C., line 5 ___2___ .
3. Minimum income requirement from the Poverty Guidelines chart for the year of __1999__ is $ _13,825_ for this household size. *(year)*

If you are currently employed and your household income for your household size is equal to or greater than the applicable poverty line requirement (from line E.3.), you do not need to list assets (Parts 4.F. and 5) or have a joint sponsor (Part 6) unless you are requested to do so by a Consular or Immigration Officer. You may skip to Part 7, Use of the Affidavit of Support to Overcome Public Charge Ground of Admissibility. Otherwise, you should continue with Part 4.F.

Form I-864 (10/6/97) **Page 3**

Part   4.   Eligibility to Sponsor   *(Continued)*

F. Sponsor's Assets and Liabilities

Your assets and those of your qualifying household members and dependents may be used to demonstrate ability to maintain an income at or above 125 percent (or 100 percent, if applicable) of the poverty line *if* they are available for the support of the sponsored immigrant(s) and can readily be converted into cash within 1 year. The household member, other than the immigrant(s) you are sponsoring, must complete and sign Form I-864A, Contract Between Sponsor and Household Member. List the cash value of each asset *after* any debts or liens are subtracted. Supporting evidence must be attached to establish location, ownership, date of acquisition, and value of each asset listed, including any liens and liabilities related to each asset listed. See "Evidence of Assets" in Instructions.

Type of Asset	Cash Value of Assets *(Subtract any debts)*
Savings deposits	$
Stocks, bonds, certificates of deposit	$
Life insurance cash value	$
Real estate	$
Other *(specify)*	$
Total Cash Value of Assets	$_____

Part 5.   Immigrant's Assets and Offsetting Liabilities

The sponsored immigrant's assets may also be used in support of your ability to maintain income at or above 125 percent of the poverty line *if* the assets are or will be available in the United States for the support of the sponsored immigrant(s) and can readily be converted into cash within 1 year.

The sponsored immigrant should provide information on his or her assets in a format similar to part 4.F. above. Supporting evidence must be attached to establish location, ownership, and value of each asset listed, including any liens and liabilities for each asset listed. See "Evidence of Assets" in Instructions.

Part 6.   Joint Sponsors

If household income and assets do not meet the appropriate poverty line for your household size, a joint sponsor is required. There may be more than one joint sponsor, but each joint sponsor must individually meet the 125 percent of poverty line requirement based on his or her household income and/or assets, including any assets of the sponsored immigrant. By submitting a separate Affidavit of Support under Section 213A of the Act (Form I-864), a joint sponsor accepts joint responsibility with the petitioner for the sponsored immigrant(s) until they become U.S. citizens, can be credited with 40 quarters of work, leave the United States permanently, or die.

Part 7.   Use of the Affidavit of Support to Overcome Public Charge Ground of Inadmissibility

Section 212(a)(4)(C) of the Immigration and Nationality Act provides that an alien seeking permanent residence as an immediate relative (including an orphan), as a family-sponsored immigrant, or as an alien who will accompany or follow to join another alien is considered to be likely to become a public charge and is inadmissible to the United States unless a sponsor submits a legally enforceable affidavit of support on behalf of the alien. Section 212(a)(4)(D) imposes the same requirement on an employment-based immigrant, and those aliens who accompany or follow to join the employment-based immigrant, if the employment-based immigrant will be employed by a relative, or by a firm in which a relative owns a significant interest. Separate affidavits of support are required for family members at the time they immigrate if they are not included on this affidavit of support or do not apply for an immigrant visa or adjustment of status within 6 months of the date this affidavit of support is originally signed. The sponsor must provide the sponsored immigrant(s) whatever support is necessary to maintain them at an income that is at least 125 percent of the Federal poverty guidelines.

I submit this affidavit of support in consideration of the sponsored immigrant(s) not being found inadmissible to the United States under section 212(a)(4)(C) (or 212(a)(4)(D) for an employment-based immigrant) and to enable the sponsored immigrant(s) to overcome this ground of inadmissibility. I agree to provide the sponsored immigrant(s) whatever support is necessary to maintain the sponsored immigrant(s) at an income that is at least 125 percent of the Federal poverty guidelines. I understand that my obligation will continue until my death or the sponsored immigrant(s) have become U.S. citizens, can be credited with 40 quarters of work, depart the United States permanently, or die.

Part 7.   Use of the Affidavit of Support to Overcome Public Charge Grounds   *(Continued)*

Notice of Change of Address.

Sponsors are required to provide written notice of any change of address within 30 days of the change in address until the sponsored immigrant(s) have become U.S. citizens, can be credited with 40 quarters of work, depart the United States permanently, or die. To comply with this requirement, the sponsor must complete INS Form I-865. Failure to give this notice may subject the sponsor to the civil penalty established under section 213A(d)(2) which ranges from $250 to $2,000, unless the failure to report occurred with the knowledge that the sponsored immigrant(s) had received means-tested public benefits, in which case the penalty ranges from $2,000 to $5,000.

> *If my address changes for any reason before my obligations under this affidavit of support terminate, I will complete and file INS Form I-865, Sponsor's Notice of Change of Address, within 30 days of the change of address. I understand that failure to give this notice may subject me to civil penalties.*

Means-tested Public Benefit Prohibitions and Exceptions.

Under section 403(a) of Public Law 104-193 (Welfare Reform Act), aliens lawfully admitted for permanent residence in the United States, with certain exceptions, are ineligible for most Federally-funded means-tested public benefits during their first 5 years in the United States. This provision does not apply to public benefits specified in section 403(c) of the Welfare Reform Act or to State public benefits, including emergency Medicaid; short-term, non-cash emergency relief; services provided under the National School Lunch and Child Nutrition Acts; immunizations and testing and treatment for communicable diseases; student assistance under the Higher Education Act and the Public Health Service Act; certain forms of foster-care or adoption assistance under the Social Security Act; Head Start programs; means-tested programs under the Elementary and Secondary Education Act; and Job Training Partnership Act programs.

Consideration of Sponsor's Income in Determining Eligibility for Benefits.

If a permanent resident alien is no longer statutorily barred from a Federally-funded means-tested public benefit program and applies for such a benefit, the income and resources of the sponsor and the sponsor's spouse will be considered (or deemed) to be the income and resources of the sponsored immigrant in determining the immigrant's eligibility for Federal means-tested public benefits. Any State or local government may also choose to consider (or deem) the income and resources of the sponsor and the sponsor's spouse to be the income and resources of the immigrant for the purposes of determining eligibility for their means-tested public benefits. The attribution of the income and resources of the sponsor and the sponsor's spouse to the immigrant will continue until the immigrant becomes a U.S. citizen or has worked or can be credited with 40 qualifying quarters of work, provided that the immigrant or the worker crediting the quarters to the immigrant has not received any Federal means-tested public benefit during any creditable quarter for any period after December 31, 1996.

> *I understand that, under section 213A of the Immigration and Nationality Act (the Act), as amended, this affidavit of support constitutes a contract between me and the U.S. Government. This contract is designed to protect the United States Government, and State and local government agencies or private entities that provide means-tested public benefits, from having to pay benefits to or on behalf of the sponsored immigrant(s), for as long as I am obligated to support them under this affidavit of support. I understand that the sponsored immigrants, or any Federal, State, local, or private entity that pays any means-tested benefit to or on behalf of the sponsored immigrant(s), are entitled to sue me if I fail to meet my obligations under this affidavit of support, as defined by section 213A and INS regulations.*

Civil Action to Enforce.

If the immigrant on whose behalf this affidavit of support is executed receives any Federal, State, or local means-tested public benefit before this obligation terminates, the Federal, State, or local agency or private entity may request reimbursement from the sponsor who signed this affidavit. If the sponsor fails to honor the request for reimbursement, the agency may sue the sponsor in any U.S. District Court or any State court with jurisdiction of civil actions for breach of contract. INS will provide names, addresses, and Social Security account numbers of sponsors to benefit-providing agencies for this purpose. Sponsors may also be liable for paying the costs of collection, including legal fees.

Part 7.   Use of the Affidavit of Support to Overcome Public Charge Grounds   *(Continued)*

I acknowledge that section 213A(a)(1)(B) of the Act grants the sponsored immigrant(s) and any Federal, State, local, or private agency that pays any means-tested public benefit to or on behalf of the sponsored immigrant(s) standing to sue me for failing to meet my obligations under this affidavit of support. I agree to submit to the personal jurisdiction of any court of the United States or of any State, territory, or possession of the United States if the court has subject matter jurisdiction of a civil lawsuit to enforce this affidavit of support. I agree that no lawsuit to enforce this affidavit of support shall be barred by any statute of limitations that might otherwise apply, so long as the plaintiff initiates the civil lawsuit no later than ten (10) years after the date on which a sponsored immigrant last received any means-tested public benefits.

Collection of Judgment.

I acknowledge that a plaintiff may seek specific performance of my support obligation. Furthermore, any money judgment against me based on this affidavit of support may be collected through the use of a judgment lien under 28 U.S.C. 3201, a writ of execution under 28 U.S.C. 3203, a judicial installment payment order under 28 U.S.C. 3204, garnishment under 28 U.S.C. 3205, or through the use of any corresponding remedy under State law. I may also be held liable for costs of collection, including attorney fees.

Concluding Provisions.

I, David B. Stone _____, *certify under penalty of perjury under the laws of the United States that:*

    (a) I know the contents of this affidavit of support signed by me;
    (b) All the statements in this affidavit of support are true and correct;
    (c) I make this affidavit of support for the consideration stated in Part 7, freely, and without any mental reservation or purpose of evasion;
    (d) Income tax returns submitted in support of this affidavit are true copies of the returns filed with the Internal Revenue Service; and
    (e) Any other evidence submitted is true and correct.

David B. Stone _____   9/1/2001 _____
          (Sponsor's Signature)   *(Date)*

Subscribed and sworn to *(or affirmed)* before me this

_____day of _____, _____
                         (Month)   *(Year)*

at _____.

My commission expires on _____.

_____
    (Signature of Notary Public or Officer Administering Oath)

_____
                           (Title)

Part 8.   If someone other than the sponsor prepared this affidavit of support, that person must complete the following:

I certify under penalty of perjury under the laws of the United States that I prepared this affidavit of support at the sponsor's request, and that this affidavit of support is based on all information of which I have knowledge.

Signature	Print Your Name	Date	Daytime Telephone Number
			( )

Firm Name and Address

David had a good job, but Carla was eager to go to work and did not know how long she would have to wait for her green card, so she completed Form I-765, Application for Employment Authorization.

This is how Carla completed Form I-765:

U. S. Department of Justice
Immigration and Naturalization Service

OMB # 1115-0163

Application for Employment Authorization

Do Not Write In This Block

Remarks	Action Stamp	Fee Stamp
A#		
Applicant is filing under 274a.12 _____		

☐ Application Approved. Employment Authorized / Extended (Circle One) _____ (Date).
    until _____ (Date).
    Subject to the following conditions: _____
☐ Application Denied.
    ☐ Failed to establish eligibility under 8 CFR 274a.12 (a) or (c).
    ☐ Failed to establish economic necessity as required in 8 CFR 274a.12(c) (14), (18) and 8 CFR 214.2(f)

I am applying for:
☑ Permission to accept employment
☐ Replacement (of lost employment authorization document).
☐ Renewal of my permission to accept employment (attach previous employment authorization document).

1. Name (Family Name in CAPS) (First) (Middle)
STONE   Carla   Rojas

2. Other Names Used (Include Maiden Name)
Carla A. Rojas (maiden)

3. Address in the United States (Number and Street) (Apt. Number)
46 Chester Street   3-L

(Town or City) (State/Country) (ZIP Code)
Madison   NJ   07941

4. Country of Citizenship/Nationality
Argentina

5. Place of Birth (Town or City) (State/Province) (Country)
Buenos Aires   Argentina

6. Date of Birth (Month/Day/Year)   7. Sex
6/7/79   ☐ Male ☑ Female

8. Marital Status   ☑ Married   ☐ Single
    ☐ Widowed   ☐ Divorced

9. Social Security Number (Include all Numbers you have ever used)
246-80-1234

10. Alien Registration Number (A-Number) or I-94 Number (if any)
I-94: 998567880 05

11. Have you ever before applied for employment authorization from INS?
☐ Yes (If yes, complete below)   ☑ No
Which INS Office?   Date(s)

Results (Granted or Denied - attach all documentation)

12. Date of Last Entry into the U.S. (Month/Day/Year)
8/20/95

13. Place of Last Entry into the U.S.
Newark, NJ

14. Manner of Last Entry (Visitor, Student, etc.)
J-2

15. Current Immigration Status (Visitor, Student, etc.)
F-1

16. Go to Part 2 of the instructions, Eligibility Categories. In the space below, place the letter and number of the category you selected from the instructions (For example, (a)(8), (c)(17)(iii), etc.).

Eligibility under 8 CFR 274a.12
(c) (9) (   )

Certification

Your Certification: I certify, under penalty of perjury under the laws of the United States of America, that the foregoing is true and correct. Furthermore, I authorize the release of any information which the Immigration and Naturalization Service needs to determine eligibility for the benefit I am seeking. I have read the Instructions in Part 2 and have identified the appropriate eligibility category in Block 16.

Signature	Telephone Number	Date
Carla R. Stone	(201) 123-4567	9/1/2001

Signature of Person Preparing Form If Other Than Above: I declare that this document was prepared by me at the request of the applicant and is based on all information of which I have any knowledge.

Print Name	Address	Signature	Date

Initial Receipt	Resubmitted	Relocated		Completed		
		Rec'd	Sent	Approved	Denied	Returned

Form I-765 (Rev. 10/13/98)N Page 7

Carla and David made photocopies of their entire submission so they would have a complete record of everything that they would file. Then Carla and David went down to the local office of the INS to file all of the documents in person (this can be done in family-immigration cases but not in most other cases). The INS Information Officer gave the couple a receipt that showed which documents they filed and when they filed them.

Some months after filing these documents, Carla and David were summoned to appear for an interview. They brought to the interview originals of all documents of which they had filed photo-copies. In addition, they brought along copies of all of the documents that they filed previously, their wedding folder, their wedding album and videotape, and snapshots taken of them together since their wedding day. At the interview, an examiner checked all of the forms and documentation that Carla and David had submitted.

Then the INS examiner questioned David and Carla separately. The questions concerned daily living habits, what they had eaten for dinner the previous Saturday, the brand of toothpaste each used, and the color of the sheets on the bed. David and Carla are married and are living together so they should have had no trouble answering the questions, but it is easy to get confused under this type of ques-tioning. Fortunately, they had been warned by friends that they would have to submit to this type of questioning, called a "*Stokes interview*," so they did their best to answer politely. The process may be unpleasant and even insulting, but the end result, the green card, is worth it. So smile, as they did.

At the conclusion of the interview, Carla and David were told that Carla would indeed be granted Conditional Resident Alien (CRA) status. (Remember that Carla and David had been married less than two years at the time they filed their papers.) To remove the conditions and obtain a permanent green card for Carla, the couple waited almost two years and then filed Form I-751, Petition to Remove the Conditions on Residence. This form should be filed 90 days before the second anniver-sary of the granting of CRA status. Along with this form, Carla and David submitted a photocopy of Carla's conditional green card and documents proving that Carla and David entered into the marriage in good faith and were in fact still married. Among other things, Carla and David submitted copies of the birth certificate of their son Adam, who was born within the two-year period, their joint tax returns, insurance policies naming each other as beneficiaries, joint loan agreements, and sworn affidavits from people who knew the couple.

Carla's and David's Form I-751 looked like this:

U.S. Department of Justice
Immigration and Naturalization Service

Petition to Remove the Conditions on Residence

OMB No. 1115-0145

START HERE - Please Type or Print

Part 1. Information about you.

Family Name Stone	Given Name Carla	Middle Initial R

FOR INS USE ONLY

Returned

Receipt

Resubmitted

Reloc Sent

Reloc Rec'd

☐ Applicant Interviewed

Remarks

Action

Address - C/O:

Street Number and Name 46 Chester Street	Apt #3-L
City Madison	State or Province NJ
Country USA	ZIP/Postal Code 07941
Date of Birth (month/day/year) 6/7/79	Country of Birth Argentina
Social Security # 246-80-1234	A # A066987002
Conditional residence expires on (month/day/year) 2/2/04	

Mailing address if different from residence in C/O:

Street Number and Name	Apt #
City	State or Province
Country	ZIP/Postal Code

Part 2. Basis for petition (check one).

a. ☑ My conditional residence is based on my marriage to a U.S. citizen or permanent resident, and we are filing this petition together.

b. ☐ I am a child who entered as a conditional permanent resident and I am unable to be included in a Joint Petition to Remove the Conditional Basis of Alien's Permanent Residence (Form I-751) filed by my parent(s).

My conditional residence is based on my marriage to a U.S. citizen or permanent resident, but I am unable to file a joint petition and I request a waiver because: (check one)

c. ☐ My spouse is deceased.

d. ☐ I entered into the marriage in good faith, but the marriage was terminated though divorce/annulment.

e. ☐ I am a conditional resident spouse who entered in to the marriage in good faith, or I am a conditional resident child, who has been battered or subjected to extreme mental cruelty by my citizen or permanent resident spouse or parent.

f. ☐ The termination of my status and deportation from the United States would result in an extreme hardship.

Part 3. Additional Information about you.

Other names used (including maiden name): Carla A. Rojas (maiden)	Telephone # (201) 123-4567
Date of Marriage 8/2/01	Place of Marriage Madison, NJ

If your spouse is deceased, give the date of death (month/day/year)

Are you in deportation or exclusion proceedings? ☐ Yes ☑ No

Was a fee paid to anyone other than an attorney in connection with this petition? ☐ Yes ☑ No

To Be Completed by Attorney or Representative, if any

☐ Fill in box if G-28 is attached to represent the applicant

VOLAG#

ATTY State License #

Continued on back.

Form I-751 (Rev. 10/13/98)N

Part 3. Additional Information about you. (con't)

Since becoming a conditional resident, have you ever been arrested, cited, charged, indicted, convicted, fined or imprisoned for breaking or violating any law or ordinance (excluding traffic regulations), or committed any crime for which you were not arrested?   ☐ Yes ☒ No

If you are married, is this a different marriage than the one through which conditional residence status was obtained?   ☐ Yes ☒ No

Have you resided at any other address since you became a permanent resident?   ☐ Yes ☒ No *(If yes, attach a list of all addresses and dates.)*

Is your spouse currently serving employed by the U. S. government and serving outside the U.S.?   ☐ Yes ☒ No

---

Part 4. Information about the spouse or parent through whom you gained your conditional residence .

Family Name	Given Name	Middle Initial	Phone Number
Stone	David	B	( ) 201-123-4567

Address 46 Chester Street, Apt. 3-L, Madison, NJ 07941

Date of Birth (month/day/year)	Social Security #	A#
3/2/75	083-22-1111	N/A

Part 5. Information about your children. *List all your children. Attach another sheet if necessary*

Name	Date of Birth (month/day/year)	If in U.S., give A#, current immigration status and U.S. Address	Living with you?
Adam Stone	6/17/03	U.S. Citizen	☒ Yes ☐ No
2			☐ Yes ☐ No
3			☐ Yes ☐ No
4			☐ Yes ☐ No

Part 6. Complete if you are requesting a waiver of the joint filing petition requirement based on extreme mental cruelty.

Evaluator's ID Number:	State: [ ]	Number: [ ][ ][ ][ ][ ][ ][ ][ ]	Expires on (month/day/year)	Occupation

Last Name	First Name	Address

Part 7. Signature. *Read the information on penalties in the instructions before completing this section. If you checked block "a" in Part 2 your spouse must also sign below.*

I certify, under penalty of perjury under the laws of the United States of America, that this petition, and the evidence submitted with it, is all true and correct. If conditional residence was based on a marriage, I further certify that the marriage was entered into in accordance with the laws of the place where the marriage took place, and was not for the purpose of procuring an immigration benefit. I also authorize the release of any information from my records which the Immigration and Naturalization Service needs to determine eligibility for the benefit being sought.

Signature *Carla R. Stone*	Print Name Carla R. Stone	Date 11/2/2003
Signature of Spouse *David B. Stone*	Print Name David B. Stone	Date 11/2/2003

Please note: If you do not completely fill out this form, or fail to submit any required documents listed in the instructions, then you cannot be found eligible for the requested benefit, and this petition may be denied.

Part 8. Signature of person preparing form if other than above.

I declare that I prepared this petition at the request of the above person and it is based on all information of which I have knowledge.

Signature	Print Name	Date

Firm Name and Address

Form I-751 (Rev. 10/13/98)N

They photocopied the Form I-751 and all the accompanying documentation and sent everything by certified mail, return receipt requested, to the INS Regional Service Center. Then they waited.

About three months later, they were summoned to appear for an interview. By now David and Carla had a suitcase full of documents to carry to the INS office. They brought all the materials they had brought to the original green card interview and copies of the materials sent with the petition requesting removal of the conditions. In addition they brought an album of photographs of them together taken during the past two years. They also brought little Adam.

David and Carla answered all of the INS examiner's questions politely, and the interview was soon over. Shortly thereafter, Carla received a permanent alien registration card, Form I-551.

Chapter 5

THE 1996 IMMIGRATION LAWS

INTRODUCTION TO THE 1996 IMMIGRATION LAWS

In 1996, two important new immigration laws took effect: the Illegal Immigration Reform and Immigrant Responsibility Act (IIRAIRA) and the Anti-Terrorism and Effective Death Penalty Act (AEDPA). Many congressmen and senators claimed that these laws would control illegal immigration. Although people have argued over the success of IIRAIRA and AEDPA in limiting illegal immigration, almost everyone agrees that these laws contain provisions that can have extremely harsh consequences on families, legal immigrants, and others who would like to enter the United States legally. As a person who is interested in eventually becoming a U.S. citizen, it is important for you to understand what these laws say and how you can avoid their (potentially) harsh consequences.

If you would like to read IIRAIRA and/or the AEDPA in their entirety, you can find them at the INS Web site, located at www.ins.usdoj.gov/. By the way, this Web site contains a wealth of information on a wide variety of immigration topics.

SUMMARY OF KEY PROVISIONS

Some of the most significant aspects of the new laws include the following:

- Expansion of the definition of *aggravated felony* and the limitation of relief from deportation for people convicted of aggravated felonies, regardless of the date of conviction.

- New public charge provisions.

- Bars to admissibility for unlawful presence in the United States.

Although IIRAIRA and AEDPA contain many other important new provisions (for example, the laws created a new expedited removal process for certain people and eliminated a judicial review for many kinds of cases), we will focus on these three issues.

AGGRAVATED FELONY PROVISIONS

Of course, aliens who have been convicted of or who admit to having committed certain crimes have always been treated harshly under the immigration laws, as well they should. Even under prior law, aliens who committed crimes of moral turpitude (usually defined as conduct that is inherently base, vile, or depraved, or contrary to accepted rules of morality), drug offenders, aliens convicted of multiple crimes, and aliens seeking to enter the United States to engage in espionage, sabotage, or any other unlawful activity were deemed *excludable*. (Today, we use the word *inadmissible*.) Those deemed excludable were subject to deportation. The old law also barred aliens convicted of aggravated felonies from obtaining green cards. Under the old law, an *aggravated felony* covered numerous crimes, including murder, illicit drug trafficking, money laundering, crimes of violence for which the term of imprisonment was at least five years, and many other serious offenses.

IIRAIRA greatly expanded the definition of aggravated felony for immigration purposes. Under the new law, many nonviolent crimes, including shoplifting, theft, and check kiting, are defined as aggravated felonies. Many other crimes, including crimes of violence for which the term of imprisonment is at least one year, are also deemed to be aggravated felonies. The Board of Immigration Appeals recently held that a felony DWI (a felony charge resulting from operating a motor vehicle under the influence of alcohol) constitutes a *crime of violence* under these new rules.

Perhaps more significantly, the new definitions are retroactive. That means that even lawful permanent residents (green card holders) can be placed in deportation proceedings today for minor offenses committed years ago. This is the case, even if the offense was not defined at the time as an aggravated felony, and even if the person has served his time in the criminal justice system. It is true even if the green card holder had no sentence imposed (for example, if the judge suspended the sentence).

If you are a green card holder who is thinking about applying for naturalization (citizenship), but you have a criminal record, you should think twice before filing that application. As we will discuss in more detail in Chapter 6, "Applying for Naturalization," you cannot meet the naturalization requirement of "good moral character" if, among other things, you have been convicted of an aggravated felony after November 29, 1990. You may even be placed in removal (deportation) proceedings when the INS checks your criminal history in connection with your application for naturalization.

NEW PUBLIC CHARGE PROVISIONS

In most cases, if you are applying for a green card, you must prove that you will not need public assistance—that you will not become a *public charge*—after you obtain your green card. This means that you must prove that you will not need Medicaid, food stamps, or other means-tested benefits for poor people. Refugees, asylees, and certain other individuals don't have to make this showing.

Under the old law, most people made the required showing by having a person in the United States, a sponsor, sign a Form I-134, Affidavit of Support, on their behalf. In the Affidavit of Support, the sponsor promised to provide financial support for the alien if necessary. To prove that he had the means to do so, the sponsor would attach evidence of his financial ability. Usually, this evidence would include a letter from the sponsor's employer, income tax returns, bank statements, and the like. Many aliens often prepared their own Affidavits of Support, attaching evidence of their own income and assets.

The public charge rules changed, effective December 19, 1997. For one thing, all immediate relatives and family-based immigrants must have a sponsor, and the sponsor must be the family member who filed the visa petition. Second, the sponsor must complete a new Affidavit of Support, Form I-864. Form I-864 is far more complicated than old Form I-134. (Form I-134 may still be used to meet the public charge requirements in most employment-based cases and all DV lottery cases.) Most sponsors must demonstrate that they earn an income of at least 125 percent of the federal poverty level, as determined by the Department of Health and Human Services (individuals on active duty in the armed forces must earn at least 100 percent of the federal poverty level). A sponsor must typically make this showing by attaching proof of current employment and his last three federal tax returns. A sponsor who cannot meet the income requirements can still satisfy the public charge rules by proving that he has sufficient assets to support the alien. The income of other household members, including the sponsored immigrant, *if* he has been living in the sponsor's residence for at least the previous six months, may be added to establish the appropriate income level. The value of the sponsored immigrant's assets may also be counted, if the sponsor does not meet the income requirement using his own income and/or assets.

If the sponsor cannot meet the required income or asset level, another person may serve as a joint sponsor. The joint sponsor must meet all sponsorship requirements, other than being the petitioning relative.

One of the biggest changes in this area is that the Affidavit of Support is now legally enforceable. This means that sponsors (or joint sponsors) who fail to support the immigrants they sponsor can be sued by any federal, state, local agency, or private entity that provides means-tested benefits, as well as by the immigrants they sponsored. As a result, a sponsor should make sure that he understands his obligations before undertaking this major responsibility.

The new income/asset requirements have had a tremendous effect on applicants for family-based green cards. Many people have been unable to meet the new requirements, and, as a result, they have been denied green cards. If *you* are thinking about applying for a green card based on a family relationship, make sure that your sponsor can satisfy the income/asset requirements before he files an application on your behalf.

UNLAWFUL PRESENCE AND BARS TO ADMISSIBILITY

The 1996 immigration laws also created new bars to entering the United States for people who have been *unlawfully present* in the country for six months or longer. These rules prevent anyone who has previously been in the United States unlawfully for more than 180 days, but less than one year, from re-entering the country for three years. Anyone who has been in the United States unlawfully for one year or longer may be barred from re-entering the United States for ten years. Remember, however, that the three- and ten-year bars do not take effect until after an alien leaves the United States and then tries to re-enter.

You are considered unlawfully present in the United States if you remain in the country after your authorized period of stay (as recorded on your Form I-94) or if you are present without being admitted or paroled (if, for example, you sneaked into the country).

The INS won't count against you any periods of unlawful presence when you were under 18 years of age, nor will it count days of unlawful presence prior to April 1, 1997, the effective date of the new law. In addition, the bars don't apply if you were present in the United States while a bona fide asylum application was pending (unless you were employed without authorization during that time) or if you fall into certain narrow categories of battered women and children.

In some cases, the INS may agree to waive the three- and ten-year bars. For example, if you are an alien spouse or parent of a U.S. citizen or lawful permanent resident, you may be able to get a waiver if you can prove that imposition of the bar will cause extreme hardship to your spouse or child.

Determining precisely what constitutes unlawful presence can be a tricky thing. If you think that you may have been unlawfully present for some period of time, you may want to consult with an immigration attorney before leaving the United States, if you plan to return in the future.

THE EFFECT OF THE 1996 IMMIGRATION LAWS

The 1996 immigration laws have had far-reaching effects on large numbers of intending immigrants. The new affidavit of support rules apply to all family-based applicants (and some employment-based applicants as well), and the three- and ten-year bars apply to anybody who has been unlawfully present in the United States since April 1, 1997. In addition, the new rules regarding criminal aliens, including the expanded definitions of aggravated felonies, have virtually eliminated the possibility of ever obtaining a green card, let alone citizenship, for many people.

If you are thinking about applying for a green card (or if you already have a green card and you are thinking about applying for naturalization), you need to understand how the new laws may affect your case. If you have a criminal background, do the research to see whether you can be deemed inadmissible or placed in removal proceedings. If a relative is sponsoring you for a green card, make sure that he has a high enough income or sufficient assets to meet the new Affidavit of Support requirements. And, if you have been unlawfully present in the United States since April 1, 1997, check with an immigration lawyer to see what your options are in terms of leaving the country and returning later.

It seems that the immigration laws are getting more complicated each day. As a person who ultimately wants to become a U.S. citizen, you need to remain informed about those laws.

Part III
NATURALIZATION

Chapter 6
APPLYING FOR NATURALIZATION

A lawful permanent resident (LPR) is authorized to remain in the United States indefinitely, to have a job and develop a career, and to sponsor certain family members for immigration under family preference categories. An LPR must pay taxes but cannot vote to affect the rate of taxation or to influence the use to which tax monies will be put. This right is reserved for citizens. You may become a citizen through the process of naturalization.

Because a green card does not expire (although green cards issued since 1989 must be replaced every 10 years), you are not under any time pressure to start the process. It is possible to remain in the United States as an LPR for an entire lifetime, but because you have purchased this book, you obviously are thinking about or planning on becoming a U.S. citizen. You may file Form N-400 when you reach a date 90 days or closer to the date by which you will have fulfilled your continuous residency requirement (see the following section). You may also wait until after you have fulfilled or surpassed the required term of residency. You do not have to meet a deadline, but the sooner after reaching eligibility that you apply, the sooner you can begin enjoying all the privileges of citizenship.

People who are 18 years of age or older use Form N-400, Application for Naturalization, to begin the naturalization process. Before completing Form N-400, however, you should make sure that you meet the requirements for naturalization.

REQUIREMENTS FOR NATURALIZATION

The first requirement for naturalization is that you must be an LPR. Certain exceptions are made to this rule for people who have served honorably in the U.S. Armed Forces during times of war or declared hostilities.

Second, you must be at least 18 years old, unless the INS waives the age requirement due to military involvement. Children under the age of 18 become naturalized automatically upon the naturalization of their parents. Different procedures must be followed for children who are applying for naturalization on their own.

Third, you must meet the continuous residence requirements. For most people, this means that you must prove that you have been a resident of the United States continuously for at least five years after you became an LPR. If (1) you are currently married to and living with a U.S. citizen; (2) you have been married to and living with your spouse for the past three years; and (3) your spouse has been a U.S. citizen for the past three years, then the continuous residence requirement is only three years, not five years.

What does the INS mean by "continuous residence?" It means that you have not left the United States for a long period of time. If you leave the country for too long, you could interrupt your continuous residence.

If you leave the United States for more than six months but less than one year, the law says that you have disrupted your continuous residence unless you can prove otherwise. (You can prove otherwise by filing certain tax information showing that you filed your income tax returns, among other things.) If you leave the United States for one year or longer, you will almost certainly be found to have disrupted your continuous residence. Still, if you return within two years, some of your time out of the country may count toward meeting your continuous residence requirement.

A few groups of people do not have to meet any continuous residence requirements. These include members of the U.S. Armed Forces. In addition, certain people may leave the country and not disrupt their continuous residence, if they file Form N-470, Application to Preserve Residence for Naturalization Purposes.

Fourth, you must meet the physical presence requirement of the law. You must be physically present in the United States for at least one-half of the five years (912.5 days) or one-half of three years (547.5 days), if you are the spouse of a U.S. citizen. It is hard to understand the difference between "continuous presence" and "physical presence," but we will try to explain it! Physical presence refers to the total number of days that you were outside the United States on all of your trips. Continuous presence refers to the number of days that you were outside the United States during a single trip. You may never have taken a trip that was long enough to break your continuous residence, but you may have taken so many short trips that you do not meet the physical presence requirement. For example, if you never took a trip outside the United States since becoming an LPR that lasted more than six months, but you took so many little trips to Canada, Mexico, and elsewhere that you were not present for at least one-half of the five- (or three-) year period, then you will not meet the physical presence requirement. Let's say that you must meet the physical presence requirement for spouses of U.S. citizens (one-half of three years). If you spent every weekend (three days) for three years in Canada visiting your family, you were not in the United States for 468 days (3 days × 52 weeks/year × 3 years = 468 days). Let's also say that during those three years, you took three trips to Europe; each trip was 30 days long. You would not meet the physical presence requirement, because you were not physically present in the United States for more than one-half of three years, or 547.5 days; you were absent from the United States for 558 days (468 + 90 days = 558 days).

A section on Form N-400 requires you to account for all of your absences from the United States. After filling out this section, you can evaluate whether you meet the continuous presence and physical presence requirements.

Fifth, you must have resided for at least three months within the INS district or state in which you plan to file your application for naturalization.

Sixth, you must be a person of "good moral character." Things that indicate a lack of good moral character include evidence that you have committed certain kinds of crimes, that you are a habitual drunkard or have driven while drunk, that you have lied to obtain immigration benefits or during your naturalization interview, or that you have failed to pay court-ordered child support or alimony. If you are a young man between the ages of 18 and 26, good moral character involves registering for the Selective Service System. In addition, if you have recently been ordered deported or removed, you are not eligible for naturalization.

Seventh, you must be willing to support and defend the United States and the U.S. Constitution. You must declare your *attachment* to the United States and the Constitution when you take the Oath of Allegiance. You must also renounce all foreign allegiances and be willing to serve the United States by fighting in the Armed Forces, performing noncombat service in the Armed Forces and performing civilian service. If you are against fighting or serving in the military due to your religious beliefs, you may be exempt from these requirements.

Finally, you must pass the English and civics tests at your naturalization interview. In the language of the law, you must demonstrate "an understanding of the English language, including an ability to read, write, and speak . . . simple words and phrases. . . ." You must also have "a knowledge and understanding of the fundamentals of the history, and of the principles and form of government, of the United States." We will discuss these tests in more detail later in this chapter.

If you are over the age of 50 and have lived in the United States as an LPR for at least 20 years, or if you are over the age of 55 and have lived in the United States as an LPR for at least 15 years, you may be excused from the English test. You are not excused from the civics test, but you may take it in the language of your choice. Finally, if you are over the age of 65 and have lived in the United States as an LPR for at least 20 years, you may take a simpler version of the civics test in the language of your choice (if you fit into this last category, you are called a *65/20 applicant*). In all of these special cases, you may sign your name in the alphabet of your own language if you do not know how to do it in English. Of course, special allowances are made for applicants who are unable to speak because of deafness or physical inability or who are unable to read or write because of blindness or paralysis.

Do not take the English and civics requirements lightly. People have been denied U.S. citizenship because they were unable to pass these tests. You can prepare yourself in a number of ways, as we will explain in the following section.

PREPARE YOURSELF BY GOING TO SCHOOL

If you are of school age and have an appropriate visa, enroll in public school and pursue secondary education to high school graduation. This course of action will serve two useful purposes. You will be well prepared for the civics test, and you will earn a high school diploma, which you need to get a job and advance in a career. If you want a college education, you must earn that high school diploma to qualify for college admission. A high school graduate should have no trouble proving English competency and knowledge of American history and government.

If you are over the age of 22 (the age may vary in different states), you are no longer eligible for daytime public education. However, many public school systems offer an opportunity to earn a high school diploma in a night school program. You may also earn a high school equivalency (a GED) diploma by enrolling in a GED preparation course and passing the GED examination.

If you can study on your own, you may take the GED examination without enrolling in a course. If Spanish is your native language, you may earn your GED diploma by taking and passing a GED exam in Spanish. (Your citizenship exam must still be taken in English unless you qualify for one of the waivers described.) Two ARCO publications provide valuable training and practice in the subjects and question styles of the GED exams. These books are *GED* and *GED en Español* and are available at local bookstores.

If you do not want to prepare for the tests by earning a U.S. high school diploma at this time, you can enroll in a citizenship class. Many public school systems offer an evening citizenship class. You may also find citizenship education offered at a community college, in a union- or company-sponsored program, or in classes offered by an organization of people who immigrated from your homeland and who are now eager to help others from their former country. These programs will give you excellent preparation for the tests.

PREPARE YOURSELF BY INDIVIDUAL STUDY

If you are able to read and understand printed English, you may choose to study on your own instead of attending scheduled classes.

Go to your local public library or bookstore and ask the librarian or clerk to assist you in choosing textbooks written at your level of English reading competency. If you complete a book on American history and another covering United States government, you should find yourself well prepared for any INS examination. Individual study from textbooks may take longer than individual study from government pamphlets, but it will give you a more complete education and understanding.

If your daily routine does not leave you a great deal of study time, some shorter study programs may prove adequate. The INS has prepared a series of booklets that it has published and made available through the Government Printing Office. The 100 sample citizenship questions from which examiners draw the questions they ask at the naturalization interview are entirely based on information in these booklets. (The 100 sample citizenship questions can be found in Chapter 8, "Practice Tests.")

In fact, the answer to every U.S. history or government question you will be asked is in these booklets. The booklets and their prices at the time of publication of this book are:

United States History: 1600–1987, Publication #M-289, $7.50 (free at some INS offices)

U.S. Government Structure, An English as a Second Language Text, Publication #M-303, $18.00

Citizenship Education and Naturalization Information, Publication #M-287 $4.00

Citizenship Education and Naturalization Information, An English as a Second Language Text, Publication #M-302, $8.00

The booklets are offered at more than one reading level. If you order by telephone, you should ask what reading levels are available for each booklet; the price may vary depending on level.

You can order by telephone and credit card by calling 1-202-512-1800, or you can fax your order to 1-202-512-2168. No sales tax and no shipping fee are charged for government publications.

You also can order these booklets by mail. Send a check or money order made out to Superintendent of Documents to

Government Printing Office
Washington, DC 20402

You should also get the list titled, "Sample Citizenship Questions" from your local INS office or from the INS's Web site (www.ins.usdoj.gov/). This document lists all of the questions that are typically asked at naturalization interviews, along with the answers. Occasionally, you will get an examiner who will ask you a question that is not on the list. Don't worry; if you study the topics covered in the publications listed here, you should have no trouble answering any of the questions.

If you are a 65/20 naturalization applicant, you can download the 25 sample naturalization questions that will form the basis of your modified civics test.

If you feel that you already have a reasonable knowledge of American history and government, you may find the chapter of this book titled "Preparing for Your Exam" sufficient as a compact and handy review. Or, you might start with this chapter and, if you find it puzzling, follow up with a textbook that can fill in the gaps in your knowledge.

The changes in immigration laws over the past years have permitted many previously unauthorized aliens to gain permanent status and to begin the naturalization process. The new welfare laws that treat permanent residents differently from U.S. citizens have encouraged many long-term permanent residents to apply for citizenship. Other provisions of the new laws have permitted greater numbers of immigrants to enter the country, to fulfill the requirements, and to petition for naturalization. At the same time, the government is trying to hold down operating costs and has reduced the number of immigration personnel. What this means to people who want to become citizens is that they may have to wait up to a year, or even a bit longer, from the time they file a Form N-400 to the time they are called for the interview.

PUT IT ALL TOGETHER

You are prepared for naturalization. You have a valid, permanent green card; you have fulfilled all of the residency requirements, or you will have fulfilled them within the next three months; and you are prepared to prove your literacy in English and your knowledge of U.S. government and history. Your next task is to assemble one more packet of forms. You will need the following:

N-400 Application for Naturalization.

Two more photos conforming to size and view regulations.

A check or money order for the proper fee; fees change so verify the current amount before filing.

Photocopies of your I-551 Alien Registration Receipt Card, front and back, and of your birth certificate.

Proof of termination of all previous marriages.

If you are applying for naturalization based on marriage to a U.S. citizen, send a copy of your current marriage certificate, proof of termination of all of your spouse's previous marriages, and proof that your spouse has been a U.S. citizen for at least the past three years (birth certificate, certificate of naturalization, certificate of citizenship, etc.)

Except for the N-400, you have been through all of this before. Maintain your sense of humor. Keep copies of everything that you are submitting to your local INS office. The N-400 must be filed with the appropriate Regional Service Center by mail. Be sure to send the packet by certified mail with return receipt requested, just as you have been doing throughout the process.

After you have filed your N-400 packet, the INS will send you a letter telling you where and when to have your fingerprints taken. In most cases, the letter will tell you to go to the nearest INS district office. Take your letter, your green card, and another form of photo identification (driver's license, passport, and so on) with you and get your fingerprints taken on the appointed day. After the INS takes your fingerprints, it will send them to the FBI. The FBI will use your fingerprints to do a criminal background check on you.

Now you have to wait. The INS may notify you that it requires additional documents, such as copies of your passport or tax information. Send whatever is requested. Keep records. Eventually, you will be called for your naturalization interview.

THE NATURALIZATION INTERVIEW

Arrive for the interview promptly and appropriately dressed. You want to show this examiner that you are exactly the kind of person he would like to see as a citizen of the United States. Your interview will take 40 minutes or more.

At this interview, the examiner will go over your application with you and will ask questions based on statements on your application. He will ask you about your background, place and length of residence, character, attachment to the U.S. Constitution, and your willingness to take the Oath of Allegiance to the United States.

Next, the examiner will test your English literacy and knowledge of U.S. government and history, unless you are exempt.

THE ENGLISH TEST

The examiner will test your ability to read, write, and speak English. He will test your reading ability by asking you to read aloud parts of the N-400, to read a group of civics questions and then answer them, or to read several simple sentences aloud. He will test your writing ability by asking you to write one or two simple sentences. Finally, the examiner will test your speaking ability by listening to you during the course of the interview. We will discuss the English test in more detail in Chapter 7, "Preparing for the English and Civics Tests."

THE CIVICS TEST

The examiner will test your knowledge of U.S. history and government by asking you to verbally answer a group of civics questions that are, in most cases, taken from the sample citizenship questions described earlier in this chapter. You may be asked to answer as many as 20 of these questions. In Chapter 7, we will start getting you prepared for the civics test, and in Chapter 8, "Practice Tests," you can find all of the sample questions.

If you pass the tests and satisfy the examiner with your answers, the examiner will sign your application and will recommend that your application for naturalization be approved.

THE OATH OF ALLEGIANCE

The final step in the process is the taking of the Oath of Allegiance to the United States. The INS will notify you by mail of the time and date of your oath ceremony. If you cannot attend the ceremony on the scheduled date, return the INS notice (Form N-445) to your local INS office, together with a note explaining your problem and asking the INS to reschedule your ceremony.

When you arrive at the ceremony, you must check in with the INS. One of the first things you will do is turn in your green card. Don't worry about this; you won't need your green card anymore, because you will be getting a Certificate of Naturalization at the ceremony!

You will also have to turn in the Form N-445 that you received in the mail. This is the notice regarding the oath ceremony, and it has questions on the back that you must complete and submit. These questions are simple and relate only to the time between your naturalization interview and the oath ceremony. One of the questions you must answer, for example, is, "Have you traveled outside the United States?"

Finally, you will take the Oath of Allegiance. When you take the oath, you will formally renounce (give up) all ties to the government of your former country and declare total allegiance to the United States.

Here is the Oath of Allegiance:

I hereby declare, on oath, that I absolutely and entirely renounce and abjure all allegiance and fidelity to any foreign prince, potentate, state, or sovereignty of whom or which I have heretofore been a subject or citizen; that I will support and defend the Constitution and laws of the United States of America against all enemies, foreign and domestic; that I will bear true faith and allegiance to the same; that I will bear arms on behalf of the United States when required by law; that I will perform noncombatant service in the Armed Forces of the United States when required by the law; that I will perform work of national importance under civilian direction when required by the law; and that I take this obligation freely without any mental reservation or purpose of evasion; so help me God.

If you prove to the INS's satisfaction that you are opposed to fighting on behalf of the United States because of your religious training and beliefs, you may take the oath without the following lines:

. . . that I will bear arms on behalf of the United States when required by law . . .

If you prove that you are opposed to any type of service in the Armed Forces because of your religious training and beliefs, you may also omit the following lines:

. . . that I will perform noncombatant service in the Armed Forces of the United States when required by law . . .

If you show the INS that you may not swear the oath using the words, "on oath," you may replace those words with the words, "and solemnly affirm." If you may not use the words, "so help me God," then you may omit those words.

Of course, as a new citizen, you may maintain ties of affection to your home country and its people. The oath refers to governments and governmental systems, not to family loyalties.

After you have taken the oath, you are officially a U.S. citizen. You will be given an official Certificate of Naturalization, which is proof of your citizenship. You may apply for a U.S. passport whenever you are ready.

Let us return one more time to our friend Carla and follow her as she attains citizenship. Life as a lawful permanent resident presented no difficulties for Carla, but her mother, who had now been back in Argentina for more than two years (required by her having been in the United States on a J-1 visa), was eager to immigrate to be closer to her daughter and grandson. Carla was aware that it would be easiest to bring in her mother as an immediate family member of a U.S. citizen, so she began steps to attain her own citizenship as soon as possible. After she had held her permanent, unconditional green card for a full nine months (which was after holding a conditional green card for two years), Carla filed the Form N-400, along with the supporting documents and the filing fee, with her Regional Service Center.

Shortly thereafter, Carla received a notice from the INS to have her fingerprints taken. She went on the appointed day and was fingerprinted.

U.S. Department of Justice
Immigration and Naturalization Service

OMB #1115-0009
Application for Naturalization

START HERE - Please Type or Print

FOR INS USE ONLY

Part 1.   Information about you.

Family Name Stone	Given Name Carla	Middle Initial R

U.S. Mailing Address - Care of

Street Number and Name 5 Allenby Drive   Apt. #

City Madison   County Madison

State New Jersey   ZIP Code 07941

Date of Birth (month/day/year) 6/7/79

Country of Birth Argentina

Social Security # 246-80-1234

A # A066987002

FOR INS USE ONLY
Returned   Receipt
Resubmitted
Reloc Sent
Reloc Rec'd
Applicant Interviewed
At Interview
request naturalization ceremony at court
Remarks
Action

Part 2.   Basis for Eligibility *(check one).*

a.   I have been a permanent resident for at least five (5) years .

b. ✔ I have been a permanent resident for at least three (3) years and have been married to a United States Citizen for those three years.

c.   I am a permanent resident child of United States citizen parent(s) .

d.   I am applying on the basis of qualifying military service in the Armed Forces of the U.S. and have attached completed Forms N-426 and G-325B

e.   Other. (Please specify section of law)_____

Part 3.   Additional information about you.

Date you became a permanent resident (month/day/year) 2/2/02

Port admitted with an immmigrant visa or INS Office where granted adjustment of status. Newark, NJ

Citizenship Argentina

Name on alien registration card (if different than in Part 1) same

Other names used since you became a permanent resident (including maiden name) None

| Sex Male ✔Female | Height 5'4" | Marital Status: Single ✔Married | Divorced Widowed |

Can you speak, read and write English ?   No ✔Yes.

Absences from the U.S.:

Have you been absent from the U.S. since becoming a permanent resident?   No ✔Yes.

If you answered "Yes" , complete the following, Begin with your most recent absence. If you need more room to explain the reason for an absence or to list more trips, continue on separate paper.

Date left U.S.	Date returned	Did absence last 6 months or more?	Destination	Reason for trip
10/4/02	11/1/02	☐Yes ☑No	Argentina	Visit
		☐Yes ☐No		
		☐Yes ☐No		
		☐Yes ☐No		
		☐Yes ☐No		
		☐Yes ☐No		

To Be Completed by *Attorney or Representative*, if any
☐ Fill in box if G-28 is attached to represent the applicant
VOLAG#
ATTY State License #

Continued on back.

Form N-400 (Rev. 01/15/99)N

Part 4. Information about your residences and employment.

List your addresses during the last five (5) years or since you became a permanent resident, whichever is less. Begin with your current address. If you need more space, continue on separate paper:

Street Number and Name, City, State, Country, and Zip Code	Dates (month/day/year)	
	From	To
5 Allenby Street, Madison, NJ 07941, USA	May, 2004	present
16 Chester Street, #3-L, Madison, NJ 07941, USA	Aug. 2001	May, 2004

3.   List your employers during the last five (5) years. List your present or most recent employer first. If none, write "None". If you need more space, continue on separate paper.

Employer's Name	Employer's Address	Dates Employed (month/day/year)		Occupation/position
	Street Name and Number - City, State and ZIP Code	From	To	
Madison County Schools	10 Hilltop Rd, Madison, NJ 07941	12/1/01	present	Teacher

Part 5. Information about your marital history.

A.   Total number of times you have been married __1__ . If you are now married, complete the following regarding your husband or wife.

Family name Stone	Given name David	Middle initial B

Address 5 Allenby Drive, Madison, NJ 07941

Date of birth (month/day/year) 3/2/75	Country of birth USA	Citizenship USA
Social Security# 083-22-1111	A# (if applicable) N/A	Immigration status (If not a U.S. citizen) U.S. Citizen

Naturalization (If applicable) N/A
(month/day/year)   Place   (City, State)

If you have ever previously been married or if your current spouse has been previously married, please provide the following on separate paper: Name of prior spouse, date of marriage, date marriage ended, how marriage ended and immigration status of prior spouse.

Part 6. Information about your children.

3.   Total Number of Children __1__ . Complete the following information for each of your children. If the child lives with you, state "with me" in the address column; otherwise give city/state/country of child's current residence. If deceased, write "deceased" in the address column.   If you need more space, continue on separate paper.

Full name of child	Date of birth	Country of birth	Citizenship	A - Number	Address
Adam Stone	6/17/03	USA	USA	N/A	with me

Continued on next page   Form N-400 (Rev. 01/15/99)N

Continued on back

Part 7. Additional eligibility factors.

Please answer each of the following questions. If your answer is **"Yes"**, explain on a separate paper.

1. Are you now, or have you ever been a member of, or in any way connected or associated with the Communist Party, or ever knowingly aided or supported the Communist Party directly, or indirectly through another organization, group or person, or ever advocated, taught, believed in, or knowingly supported or furthered the interests of communism?   ☐ Yes ☑ No

2. During the period March 23, 1933 to May 8, 1945, did you serve in, or were you in any way affiliated with, either directly or indirectly, any military unit, paramilitary unit, police unit, self-defense unit, vigilante unit, citizen unit of the Nazi party or SS, government agency or office, extermination camp, concentration camp, prisoner of war camp, prison, labor camp, detention camp or transit camp, under the control or affiliated with:

    a. The Nazi Government of Germany?   ☐ Yes ☑ No

    b. Any government in any area occupied by, allied with, or established with the assistance or cooperation of, the Nazi Government of Germany?   ☐ Yes ☑ No

3. Have you at any time, anywhere, ever ordered, incited, assisted, or otherwise participated in the persecution of any person because of race, religion, national origin, or political opinion?   ☐ Yes ☑ No

4. Have you ever left the United States to avoid being drafted into the U.S. Armed Forces?   ☐ Yes ☑ No

5. Have you ever failed to comply with Selective Service laws?   ☐ Yes ☑ No

    If you have registered under the Selective Service laws, complete the following information:

        Selective Service Number:_____   Date Registered:_____

    If you registered before 1978, also provide the following:

        Local Board Number:_____   Classification:_____

6. Did you ever apply for exemption from military service because of alienage, conscientious objections or other reasons?   ☐ Yes ☑ No

7. Have you ever deserted from the military, air or naval forces of the United States?   ☐ Yes ☑ No

8. Since becoming a permanent resident , have you ever failed to file a federal income tax return ?   ☐ Yes ☑ No

9. Since becoming a permanent resident , have you filed a federal income tax return as a nonresident or failed to file a federal return because you considered yourself to be a nonresident?   ☐ Yes ☑ No

10 Are deportation proceedings pending against you, or have you ever been deported, or ordered deported, or have you ever applied for suspension of deportation?   ☐ Yes ☑ No

11. Have you ever claimed in writing, or in any way, to be a United States citizen?   ☐ Yes ☑ No

12. Have you ever:

    a. been a habitual drunkard?   ☐ Yes ☑ No

    b. advocated or practiced polygamy?   ☐ Yes ☑ No

    c. been a prostitute or procured anyone for prostitution?   ☐ Yes ☑ No

    d. knowingly and for gain helped any alien to enter the U.S. illegally?   ☐ Yes ☑ No

    e. been an illicit trafficker in narcotic drugs or marijuana?   ☐ Yes ☑ No

    f. received income from illegal gambling?   ☐ Yes ☑ No

    g. given false testimony for the purpose of obtaining any immigration benefit?   ☐ Yes ☑ No

13. Have you ever been declared legally incompetent or have you ever been confined as a patient in a mental institution?   ☐ Yes ☑ No

14. Were you born with, or have you acquired in same way, any title or order of nobility in any foreign State?   ☐ Yes ☑ No

15. Have you ever:

    a. knowingly committed any crime for which you have not been arrested?   ☐ Yes ☑ No

    b. been arrested, cited, charged, indicted, convicted, fined or imprisoned for breaking or violating any law or ordinance excluding traffic regulations?   ☐ Yes ☑ No

(If you answer yes to 15 , in your explanation give the following information for each incident or occurrence the **city**, **state**, and **country**, where the offense took place, the **date** and **nature** of the offense, and the **outcome** or **disposition** of the case).

Part 8.   Allegiance to the U.S.

If your answer to any of the following questions is **"NO"**, attach a full explanation:

1. Do you believe in the Constitution and form of government of the U.S.?   ☑ Yes ☐ No

2. Are you willing to take the full Oath of Allegiance to the U.S.? (see instructions)   ☑ Yes ☐ No

3. If the law requires it, are you willing to bear arms on behalf of the U.S.?   ☑ Yes ☐ No

4. If the law requires it, are you willing to perform noncombatant services in the Armed Forces of the U.S.?   ☑ Yes ☐ No

5. If the law requires it, are you willing to perform work of national importance under civilian direction?   ☑ Yes ☐ No

---

Continued on back   Form N-400 (Rev. 01/15/99)N

Part 9. Memberships and organizations.

A. List your present and past membership in or affiliation with every organization, association, fund, foundation, party, club, society, or similar group in the United States or in any other place. Include any military service in this part. If none, write "none". Include the name of organization, location, dates of membership and the nature of the organization. If additional space is needed, use separate paper.

None

Part 10. Complete only if you checked block " C " in Part 2.

How many of your parents are U.S. citizens? ☐ One   ☐ Both   (Give the following about one U.S. citizen parent:)

Family Name	Given Name	Middle Name

Address

Basis for citizenship:
☐ Birth
☐ Naturalization Cert. No.

Relationship to you (check one):
☐ natural parent   ☐ adoptive parent
☐ parent of child legitimated after birth

If adopted or legitimated after birth, give date of adoption or, legitimation: *(month/day/year)*_____.

Does this parent have legal custody of you?   ☐ Yes   ☐ No

Attach a copy of relating evidence to establish that you are the child of this U.S. citizen and evidence of this parent's citizenship.)

Part 11. Signature.   *(Read the information on penalties in the instructions before completing this section).*

I certify or, if outside the United States, I swear or affirm, under penalty of perjury under the laws of the United States of America that this application, and the evidence submitted with it, is all true and correct. I authorize the release of any information from my records which the Immigration and Naturalization Service needs to determine eligibility for the benefit I am seeking.

Signature   *Carla R. Stone*   Date 3/20/2005

Please Note: *If you do not completely fill out this form, or fail to submit required documents listed in the instructions, you may not be found eligible for naturalization and this application may be denied.*

Part 12. Signature of person preparing form if other than above. *(Sign below)*

I declare that I prepared this application at the request of the above person and it is based on all information of which I have knowledge.

Signature   Print Your Name   Date

Firm Name
and Address

DO NOT COMPLETE THE FOLLOWING UNTIL INSTRUCTED TO DO SO AT THE INTERVIEW

I swear that I know the contents of this application, and supplemental pages 1 through____, that the corrections , numbered 1 through____, were made at my request, and that this amended application, is true to the best of my knowledge and belief.

_____
(Complete and true signature of applicant)

Subscribed and sworn to before me by the applicant.

_____
(Examiner's Signature)   Date

Form N-400 (Rev. 01/15/99)N

U.S. Department of Justice
Immigration and Naturalization Service

OMB No. 1115-0009

N-400, Application for Naturalization

Supplement A

PART A. INSTRUCTIONS

Please complete this supplement and file it with your application *(Form N-400)* to help us better process your request. If you have already filed your application, you may complete and submit this supplement to the Office where your application is pending.

If you are submitting this supplement with your application, sign your name in ink on the side of your photographs, but **DO NOT** write over your face. Sign your name as show on your green card unless you are seeking to change your name, in which case please sign your full name as you indicated it in question 7.

Public Report Burden for this supplement is estimated to average 6 minutes per response. *(See Form N-400 for more information on reporting burden hours.)*

This supplement is considered part of your application for naturalization. All the information provided must be true and correct.

PART B. ADDITIONAL INFORMATION ABOUT YOU. *(The applicant for naturalization.)*

Last Name Stone	First Name Carla	Middle Name

Daytime Phone# (201) 561-1234	Alien Registration # A066987002	Date of Birth *(Month/Day/Year)* 6/7/73	Date you became a permanent resident *(Month/Day/Year)* 2/2/02

1. A. Did you graduate from an accredited college in the U.S.? (Yes) No   B. Did you graduate from college outside the U.S.? Yes No

   *If Yes to either question, check the highest level of college degree you received: *(Attach a copy of your highest degree to this supplement.)*

   Associate's   ✓ Bachelor's   Master's   Doctorate

2. Did you graduate from High school in the U.S.?   Yes (No)   *If Yes, how many years of high school did you attend in the U.S.?
   Less than 1   One   Two   Three   Four or more

   (Attach a copy of your high school degree to this supplement or complete the following.)

   Name of School _____ Year Graduated _____

   Location *(City, State)* _____

3. Did you already passed an INS approved citizenship test?   Yes (No)
   (If Yes, attach a copy of the test results.)

4. Have you completed an INS approved Adult Education Course?   Yes (No)
   (If Yes, attach a copy of the certificate of completion.)

5. Within the past 5 years have you been required to pay child support through a separation agreement, divorce decree or other court order?   Yes (No)   *(If No, skip to question 6)*

   If YES:
   - At any time during the past 5 years were you more than 2 weeks behind in these payments?   Yes   No
   - Are you currently more than 2 weeks behind?   Yes   No

6. Naturalization involves a formal ceremony. This ceremony can be conducted by INS or by certain courts. In many parts of the country both conduct ceremonies. However, you may request that you only be naturalized in a court ceremony. This would mean you would not be scheduled for an INS ceremony even if one were available.
   - Would you like to only be scheduled for a court ceremony?   Yes   ✓ I have no preference

7. Your name as shown on your green card will normally be used when you naturalize. However, if you have changed your name through divorce or marriage since receiving your last green card we will update our records and issue your certificate in your current name. Any applicant also has the option of requesting a change of name when naturalizing; however, if you do we will schedule you for a court ceremony since only the court can grant a change of name.

   - Do you want to change your name as a result of your marriage or divorce?   Yes   ✓No
     (If Yes, attach a copy of the marriage or divorce decree.)
   - Do you otherwise want to change your name when you naturalize?   Yes   ✓No

   If you want to use a name other than the one on your current green card, Clearly Write it below:

Last Name	First Name	Middle Name

Form N-400 Supplement A (01-15-99)

Several months later, Carla received an appointment letter for her interview in the mail. As it happened, Carla was scheduled for her naturalization interview on the day of her birthday. She wore a new suit and a very pretty blouse for the important event and arrived at the INS offices 15 minutes before her scheduled appointment. The examiner was running behind schedule, however, and Carla had to wait two hours before she was finally called.

The examiner asked Carla what she especially liked about the United States, and Carla replied that she appreciated the opportunity to improve her social and economic status and to assume as much responsibility as she might wish. The examiner also questioned Carla about her absences from the United States, places of residence, and willingness to take the Oath of Allegiance. Obviously, Carla satisfied the interviewer with her answers. The examiner also administered the English and civics tests, which Carla passed with flying colors. At the end of the interview, the examiner signed the N-400 and shook Carla's hand with a welcoming smile.

Six weeks later, Carla received an invitation to appear at an oath ceremony to take the Oath of Allegiance. Carla, David, and the baby dressed up for the occasion and went to the ceremony. Carla took her oath. At the conclusion of the ceremony, Carla received her Certificate of Naturalization.

Later, Carla went to her local INS office and picked up a Form I-130, Petition for Alien Relative, so that she could begin the process of bringing her mother to join her family. That evening, Carla and David hired a baby-sitter and went out to dinner to celebrate.

Carla began the process of applying for a green card on behalf of her mother. She entered her naturalization certificate number on the otherwise completed I-130 and prepared to file the petition. The printed instructions accompanying this form say that original papers must be filed with the form. However, rules have changed since the instructions were printed. The INS will now accept photocopies, so Carla filed by mail following the usual precautions of keeping a full photocopied record of the filing and making use of certified mail and return receipts. Along with the I-130 and a photocopy of her Certificate of Naturalization, Carla included a copy of her own birth certificate to prove her relationship to her mother, one more G-325A for herself, a G-325A completed by her mother, sets of photos of herself and of her mother, and the required fee. A copy of the I-130 that Carla used can be found in the "Appendix of INS Forms."

If you have read carefully through the book to this page, you should understand the procedure for remaining in the United States legally, for adjusting your status from nonimmigrant to immigrant, and for applying for naturalization. The next chapter will help you to prepare for the English and civics tests. The "Appendix of INS Forms" at the back of the book includes printed instructions that accompany the forms. By seeing the forms and instructions in advance, you can gather documents that may be hard to find and get practice in filling in the spaces.

If you have some questions or find some requirements to be troublesome, seek advice from an attorney who specializes in immigration matters. Religious groups, ethnic clubs, fraternal organizations, unions, and bar associations can all refer you to reputable immigration attorneys. Some of these organizations offer limited services at low fees. If you decide to use an attorney, prepare your questions in advance. That way, you can take less of the attorney's time, and the consultation will cost you less money.

Chapter 7

PREPARING FOR THE ENGLISH AND CIVICS TESTS

As we have discussed, the INS will give you an English test and a civics test during your naturalization interview. This chapter is designed to help you pass both tests with flying colors.

THE ENGLISH TEST

The law requires you to prove that you can read, write, and speak basic English. If you are reading this book to learn how to become a U.S. citizen, you can probably read English very well. If you read well, you may also know how to write English well. If you are less certain of your ability to read and write English at a basic level, you should practice by having a friend read you short sentences that you can write. The information booklets published by the INS and other organizations include information about the subjects of examination, some sample questions, and samples of the kinds of sentences you must write.

UNDERSTANDING AND SPEAKING ENGLISH

You must show the INS examiner that you can understand and speak the English language. Generally, the examiner will determine whether you meet this requirement by watching and listening to you during the course of the interview. If you demonstrate an understanding of the language, then you should have no trouble with this part of the interview.

WRITING A SENTENCE IN ENGLISH

The examiner will then want to test your ability to write simple words and phrases in English. Generally, the examiner will dictate one or two sentences. You then write what you hear. You need only basic competency to pass this part. These are samples of the kinds of sentences you may be asked to write:

- The Fourth of July is the birthday of the United States.
- The colors of the American flag are red, white, and blue.
- The White House is the home of the President.
- When I am a citizen, I will be able to vote.

THE CIVICS TEST

The requirements in terms of knowledge of U.S. government and history are more demanding. You need to answer only a very few questions, but the body of knowledge covered is great, and you have no way of knowing in advance exactly which of the 100 sample citizenship questions you will be expected to answer. You may even be asked a question that is not listed on the sample citizenship questions (the examiner may ask such a question, if it is considered basic enough). You really do have to study for this portion of the examination. When you have finished studying, you will have much more information than you need to pass the exam.

A SHORT HISTORY OF THE UNITED STATES

In 1492, Christopher Columbus, believing the world to be round, sailed west from Spain hoping to reach the East Indies. Instead, he reached the West Indies, islands off the coast of North America. Columbus is therefore credited with discovering America. Following Columbus, Spanish explorers came to search for gold in Mexico, Central America, and parts of North America. Ponce de Leon landed on the east coast of Florida and spent many years searching for the Fountain of Youth. Many of the Spanish settlers settled in what is now the southwest.

Before the end of the century, England also began explorations of the New World. English expeditions were centered much farther north and along the east coast of North America. John Cabot, one of the earliest English explorers, landed on the coast of Canada.

A number of early English efforts to establish settlements failed, but in 1620 about 100 people set out from Plymouth, England, on a ship named the *Mayflower* in search of religious freedom. The ship headed for the area of Virginia, which has a mild climate, but navigation at that time was still inexact. Instead, the ship landed in Cape Cod Bay in Massachusetts. The settlers decided to remain despite the hardships presented by their lack of preparation for the harsh winters of the region. Because they recognized that they would be forced to live together and to rely upon one another and upon their own resources, this group, known as *pilgrims,* drew up a document they called the Mayflower Compact. A modern restatement of the meaning of the Mayflower Compact reads:

> We whose names are underwritten, having undertaken a voyage to plant the first colony in the northern parts of Virginia, do by these presents, solemnly and mutually in the presence of God and one of another, covenant and combine ourselves together into a civil body politic, for our better ordering and preservation; and by virtue hereof to enact, constitute, and frame such just and equal laws, ordinances, acts, constitutions and offices, from time to time, as shall be thought most meet and convenient for the general good of the colony; unto which we promise all due submission and obedience.

The signers of the Mayflower Compact had created a new government, in effect the first American government. The Mayflower Compact did not include any laws controlling religious beliefs. This feature of the Mayflower Compact found its way into the Bill of Rights of the United States Constitution in 1791.

In the early years, the English colonies in North America were not entirely self-sufficient. They relied upon England as their source of manufactured goods and for products from most nations other than England. As such, the colonies served as new markets for English merchants who encouraged emigration. Between 1660 and 1760, 13 English colonies were established in the New World. The English colonists were joined by settlers from other European nations—France, Ireland, Germany, and Holland. These non-English settlers increased the population and further expanded markets. They also brought their own cultures and lifestyles. Thus, began the wonderful mix of peoples who became North Americans.

As their areas and populations grew, the nature of the colonies and the colonial economy began to diversify. The northern colonies, those in New England, Pennsylvania, and New York (where the growing season is short, and the soil is rocky), became the commercial region, and the South remained agricultural. Even in the South, farming was hard and expensive in this era before time- and labor-saving farm machinery. Southern farmers came to rely on the use of slaves as a source of abundant, cheap labor. By 1740, about 150,000 slaves were in the South.

During the first century of the colonial period, the 13 colonies existed without much interference from the English king. Although the colonies did have English governors, they were self-governing insofar as their daily affairs were concerned. However, in 1752, the French, with the assistance of Indians hostile to the English, began to battle the English.

By the end of the French and Indian Wars, which coincided with the end of the Seven Years' War in Europe (1763), England was heavily in debt. In its frantic scramble for more money, England looked to the colonies. The colonies were expected to help the English economy by paying more taxes. Needless to say, the colonists, who were still busy establishing themselves on a far-away continent, were not eager to turn over their hard-earned money to pay for England's wars. But England persisted in trying to collect ever greater amounts of money.

As trouble developed between the colonists and the British army, some colonists began to suggest independence from England. The First Continental Congress met in Philadelphia in September, 1774. The Congress drew up a petition to the king, the "Declaration of Rights," in which it asked for specific changes in England's attitude toward the colonies.

Just the Facts

America was discovered by Christopher Columbus in 1492. American Indians, now called Native Americans, inhabited the United States before Columbus arrived. In the 1600s, settlers from England began to come to America, looking for religious freedom. The colonists settled in 13 colonies along the Atlantic seacoast and were called pilgrims. The English colonies were governed by England. Early settlers in the Southwest came from Spain.

THE REVOLUTIONARY WAR

England had been the *mother country* of most of the colonists. They did not all want to break away. The colonists' main objection was to taxation without representation. They felt that if they had representatives in the English government, they would be able to explain which taxes they found to be offensive and to propose ways in which the colonies could contribute to the well-being of the English economy.

England, however, would not permit colonial representation in Parliament. In fact, in January, 1775, England ordered its troops to fire upon colonists who were rebelling against taxes in the Massachusetts colony. That incident has been called "the shot heard round the world" because it effectively began the American Revolution. Most colonists who had wanted to remain loyal subjects of England reacted to the attack by the British and rallied to the cause of freedom. The Revolutionary War lasted for seven years before England finally lost and granted independence to the 13 colonies.

The Continental Congress named George Washington, a military leader during the French and Indian Wars, to serve as Commander-in-Chief of the Continental armed forces. Then, among its earliest acts, the Continental Congress asked Thomas Jefferson, who later became our third President, to draft a Declaration of Independence.

This Declaration was adopted on July 4, 1776. We now observe the Fourth of July every year as the birth date of our nation. The Declaration of Independence is a powerful document. It first makes clear the reluctance with which the colonies are declaring their independence. Then it sets forth a clear philosophy of human rights and catalogs all the misdeeds of the King of England. The language of the Declaration is the language of 1776, but when you understand the Declaration, you understand the causes of the Revolution and the basic roots of American government. Here is the full text of the Declaration of Independence:

> When in the course of human events, it becomes necessary for one people to dissolve the political bands which have connected them with another, and to assume among the powers of the earth, the separate and equal station to which the laws of Nature and of Nature's God entitle them, a decent respect to the opinions of mankind requires that they should declare the causes which impel them to separation.

> We hold these truths to be self-evident, that all men are created equal, that they are endowed by their Creator with certain unalienable rights, that among these are life, liberty and the pursuit of happiness. That to secure these rights, governments are instituted among men, deriving their just powers from the consent of the governed,—That whenever any form of government becomes destructive of these ends, it is the right of the people to alter or to abolish it, and to institute new government, laying its foundation on such principles and organizing its powers in such form, as to them shall seem most likely to effect their safety and happiness. Prudence, indeed, will dictate that governments long established should not be changed for light and transient causes; and accordingly all experience hath shown, that man-kind are more disposed to suffer, while evils are sufferable, than to right themselves by abolishing the forms to which they are accustomed. But when a long train of abuses and usurpations, pursuing invariably the same object evinces a design to reduce them under absolute despotism, it is their right, it is their duty, to throw off such government, and to provide new guards for their

future security.—Such has been the patient sufferance of these Colonies; and such is now the necessity which constrains them to alter their former systems of government. The history of the present King of Great Britain is a history of repeated injuries and usurpations, all having in direct object the establishment of an absolute tyranny over these States. To prove this, let facts be submitted to a candid world.

He has refused his assent to laws, the most wholesome and necessary for the public good.

He has forbidden his Governors to pass laws of immediate and pressing importance, unless suspended in their operation till his assent should be obtained; and when so suspended, he has utterly neglected to attend to them.

He has refused to pass other laws for the accommodation of large districts of people, unless those people would relinquish the right of representation in the legislature, a right inestimable to them and formidable to tyrants only.

He has called together legislative bodies at places unusual, uncomfortable, and distant from the depository of their public records, for the sole purpose of fatiguing them into compliance with his measures.

He has dissolved Representative Houses repeatedly, for opposing with manly firmness his invasions on the rights of the people.

He has refused for a long time, after such dissolutions, to cause others to be elected; whereby the legislative powers, incapable of annihilation, having returned to the people at large for their exercise; the State remaining in the mean time exposed to all the dangers of invasion from without, and convulsions within.

He has endeavoured to prevent the population of these States; for that purpose obstructing the laws for naturalization of foreigners; refusing to pass others to encourage their migrations hither, and raising the conditions of new appropriations of lands.

He has obstructed the administration of justice, by refusing his assent to laws for establishing judiciary powers.

He has made judges dependent on his will alone, for the tenure of their offices, and the amount and payment of their salaries.

He has erected a multitude of new offices, and sent hither swarms of officers to harass our people, and eat out their substance.

He has kept among us, in times of peace, standing armies without the consent of our legislatures.

He has affected to render the military independent of and superior to the civil power.

He has combined with others to subject us to a jurisdiction foreign to our constitution, and unacknowledged by our laws; giving his assent to their acts of pretended legislation:

For quartering large bodies of armed troops among us:

For protecting them, by a mock trial, from punishment for any murders which they should commit on the inhabitants of these States:

For cutting off our trade with all parts of the world:

For imposing taxes on us without our consent:

For depriving us in many cases, of the benefits of trial by jury:

For transporting us beyond seas to be tried for pretended offenses:

For abolishing the free system of English laws in a neighbouring province, establishing therein an arbitrary government and enlarging its boundaries so as to render it at once an example and fit instrument for introducing the same absolute rule into these colonies:

For taking away our charters, abolishing our most valuable laws, and altering fundamentally the forms of our governments:

For suspending our own legislatures, and declaring themselves invested with power to legislate for us in all cases whatsoever.

He has abdicated government here, by declaring us out of his protection and waging war against us.

He has plundered our seas, ravaged our coasts, burnt our towns, and destroyed the lives of our people.

He is at this time transporting large armies of foreign mercenaries to complete the works of death, desolation, and tyranny, already begun with circumstances of cruelty and perfidy scarcely paralleled in the most barbarous ages, and totally unworthy the head of a civilized nation.

He has constrained our fellow citizens taken captive on the high seas to bear arms against their country, to become the executioners of their friends and brethren, or to fall themselves by their hands.

He has excited domestic insurrections amongst us, and has endeavoured to bring on the inhabitants of our frontiers, the merciless Indian savages, whose known rule of warfare is an undistinguished destruction of all ages, sexes and conditions.

In every stage of these oppressions we have petitioned for redress in the most humble terms: Our repeated petitions have been answered only by repeated injury. A prince, whose character is thus marked by every act which may define a tyrant, is unfit to be the ruler of a free people.

Nor have we been wanting in attentions to our British brethren. We have warned them from time to time of attempts by their legislature to extend an unwarrantable jurisdiction over us. We have reminded them of the circumstances of our emigration and settlement here. We have appealed to their native justice and magnanimity, and we have conjured them by the ties of our common kindred to disavow these usurpations, which would inevitably interrupt our connections and correspondence. They too have been deaf to the voice of justice and of consanguinity. We must, therefore, acquiesce in the necessity which denounces our separation, and hold them, as we hold the rest of mankind, enemies in war, in peace friends.

WE, THEREFORE, the Representatives of the United States of America, in General Congress, Assembled, appealing to the Supreme Judge of the world for the rectitude of our intentions, do, in the name, and by authority of the good people of these Colonies, solemnly publish and declare, That these United Colonies are, and of right ought to be FREE AND INDEPENDENT STATES; that they are absolved from all allegiance to the British Crown, and that all political connection between them and the State of Great Britain, is and ought to be totally dissolved; and that as free and independent States, they have full power to levy war, conclude peace, contract alliances, establish commerce, and to do all other acts and things which independent States may of right do. And for the support of this Declaration, with a firm reliance on the protection of Divine Providence, we mutually pledge to each other our lives, our fortunes and our sacred honor.

Having declared itself a new nation, the United States found that it had to fight a war against England and learn to govern itself at the same time. Members of the Continental Congress drew up a document called the Articles of Confederation. When the war for independence was over, in 1783, they set about the task of governing the nation under the Articles of Confederation. The Articles had created a very loose federation of states with almost no national government. The country could not pay its debts. Without a strong national government to coordinate the country, a United States of America could not function. The whole country would soon fall apart.

Just the Facts

In the 1770s, colonists went to war with England to protest unfair laws and taxes. This war was called the Revolutionary War. General George Washington was chosen to lead the Americans. The Declaration of Independence, written by Thomas Jefferson, was the result of a meeting of colonists from all 13 English colonies at Independence Hall in Philadelphia. The Declaration of Independence was signed on July 4, 1776, which is now known as Independence Day. The Colonial Army fought and won the Revolutionary War, and our new nation was born.

THE CONSTITUTION

A Constitutional Convention met in Philadelphia's Independence Hall throughout the summer of 1787. James Madison, later to become our fourth President, wrote draft after draft, and the delegates argued and debated until they finally agreed on the Constitution under which the United States is still governed today. Many delegates at the convention were concerned that the Constitution as drafted set up an efficient means for governing the country but neglected the whole area of human fights. They felt that the new Constitution did not offer safeguards against the kinds of activities with which King George III of England had oppressed them.

The fears of these delegates were set aside with a firm promise that a Bill of Rights would be presented as a set of amendments to the Constitution as soon as possible. The Bill of Rights was indeed adopted in 1791. Much controversy and discussion centered on the subject of slavery. Most delegates from the northern states agreed that slavery was wrong, that one person should not be owned by another. Delegates from southern states argued that the southern economy, and indeed that of the United States, would falter without the contribution of slave labor. For some time it appeared that the delegates from the two sections of the country would never agree on a Constitution.

They finally arrived at a compromise by which slavery would be permitted to continue and slaves continue to be imported into the United States until at least 1808. The delegates assumed that by 1808 the economy would be in better shape and a fully functioning Congress could legislate according to the needs and conscience of the country at that time.

The delegates to the Constitutional Convention agreed that the new Constitution would go into effect when it had been *ratified*, that is approved, by the legislatures of nine of the states. The Constitution actually did go into effect in March, 1789, followed two years later by the Bill of Rights, which had by then been ratified by three-fourths of the states, as required by Article V of the Constitution.

The Constitution is a short document. It states its business in a few well-chosen words. Perhaps its clarity and simplicity is the secret of its endurance. The body of the Constitution consists of a Preamble stating its purpose and seven articles establishing the framework of the government, defining relationships among the states and between the states and the federal government, and prescribing the amendment process.

The entire Preamble is as follows:

WE THE PEOPLE of the United States, in order to form a more perfect Union, establish justice, insure domestic tranquillity, provide for the common defense, promote the general welfare, and secure the blessings of liberty to ourselves and our posterity, do ordain and establish this Constitution for the United States of America.

Your citizenship examination will probably include some questions about the Constitution, but it will not require you to know details nor know precisely where to find specific facts. The commentary that accompanies the full text of the Constitution on the following pages highlights the important information.

ARTICLE I

SECTION 1. All legislative powers herein granted shall be vested in a Congress of the United States, which shall consist of a Senate and House of Representatives.

SECTION 2. The House of Representatives shall be composed of members chosen every second year by the people of the several States, and the electors in each State shall have the qualifications requisite for electors of the most numerous branch of the State Legislature.

Members of the House of Representatives serve for two years and then must present themselves for re-election.

No person shall be a representative who shall not have attained to the age of twenty-five years, and been seven years a citizen of the United States, and who shall not, when elected, be an inhabitant of that State in which he shall be chosen.

Members of the House of Representatives must be at least 25 years old and must live in the state that they represent.

The following paragraph requires that state delegations to the House of Representatives be based on population. It provides for a population census to be made every ten years. The paragraph also states that Indians need pay no taxes but that if they are not taxed, they are not counted as persons and that slaves count as three-fifths of a person. This method of counting the population for representation in Congress was one of the major compromises reached in drafting a Constitution acceptable to delegates from all regions of the colonies.

Representatives and direct taxes shall be apportioned among the several States which may be included within this Union, according to their respective numbers, which shall be determined by adding to the whole number of free persons, including those bound to service for a term of years, and excluding Indians not taxed, three-fifths of all other persons. The actual enumeration shall be made within three years after the first meeting of the Congress of the United States, and within every subsequent term of ten years, in such manner as they shall by law direct. The number of representatives shall not exceed one for every thirty thousand, but each State shall have at least one representative; and until such enumeration shall be made, the State of New Hampshire shall be entitled to choose three, Massachusetts eight, Rhode Island and Providence Plantations one, Connecticut five, New York six, New Jersey four, Pennsylvania eight, Delaware one, Maryland six, Virginia ten, North Carolina five, South Carolina five, and Georgia three.

Impeachment is the means for removing the President, Vice President, and federal judges from office. All impeachment proceedings must begin in the House of Representatives.

When vacancies happen in the representation from any State, the Executive authority thereof shall issue writs of election to fill such vacancies.

The House of Representatives shall choose their Speaker and other officers; and shall have the sole power of impeachment.

SECTION 3. The Senate of the United States shall be composed of two senators from each State, chosen by the legislature thereof, for six years and each senator shall have one vote.

Senators serve a six-year term. The Constitution as originally written and passed provided that senators be elected by state legislatures rather than by the people. This method of electing senators was changed in 1913 by the 17th Amendment.

Immediately after they shall be assembled in consequence of the first election, they shall be divided as equally as may be into three classes. The seats of the senators of the first class shall be vacated at the expiration of the second year, of the second class at the expiration of the fourth year, and of the third class at the expiration of the sixth year, so that one-third

Terms of senators are staggered so that only one-third of the Senate is elected every two years. This paragraph sets that mechanism in motion.

A senator must be at least 30 years old and must live in the state from which elected.

The Vice President presides over the Senate and has the power to vote to break a tie.

If the House of Representatives votes to impeach the President, Vice President, or another impeachable official, the Senate conducts a trial. Two-thirds of the voting senators must agree for conviction.

One-fifth of the members present at a vote taken in either House of Congress may demand that a roll-call vote be taken. A roll-call vote allows for certainty as to whether or not the measure has passed and makes each member's vote a matter of public record. From this record, voters can follow the activities of their representatives in Congress.

may be chosen every second year; and if vacancies happen by resignation, or otherwise, during the recess of the legislature of any State, the executive thereof may make temporary appointments until the next meeting of the legislature, which shall then fill such vacancies.

No person shall be a senator who shall not have attained to the age of thirty years, and been nine years a citizen of the United States, and who shall not, when elected, be an inhabitant of that State for which he shall be chosen.

The Vice President of the United States shall be President of the Senate, but shall have no vote, unless they be equally divided.

The Senate shall choose their other officers, and also a President pro tempore, in the absence of the Vice President, or when he shall exercise the office of President of the United States.

The Senate shall have the sole power to try all impeachments. When sitting for that purpose, they shall be on oath or affirmation. When the President of the United States is tried, the Chief Justice shall preside: And no person shall be convicted without the concurrence of two thirds of the members present.

Judgment in cases of impeachment shall not extend further than to removal from office, and disqualification to hold and enjoy any office or honor, trust or profit under the United States; but the party convicted shall nevertheless be liable and subject to indictment, trial, judgment and punishment, according to law.

SECTION 4. The times, places and manner of holding elections for senators and representatives, shall be prescribed in each State by the legislature thereof; but the Congress may at any time by law make or alter such regulations, except as to the places of choosing senators.

The Congress shall assemble at least once in every year, and such meeting shall be on the first Monday in December, unless they shall by law appoint a different day.

SECTION 5. Each house shall be the judge of the elections, returns and qualifications of its own members, and a majority of each shall constitute a quorum to do business; but a smaller number may adjourn from day to day, and may be authorized to compel the attendance of absent members, in such manner, and under such penalties as each house may provide.

Each house may determine the rules of its proceedings, punish its members for disorderly behaviour, and, with the concurrence of two-thirds, expel a member.

Each house shall keep a journal of its proceedings, and from time to time publish the same, excepting such parts as may in their judgment require secrecy; and the yeas and the nays of the members of either house on any question shall, at the desire of one-fifth of those present, be entered on the journal.

Neither house, during the session of Congress, shall, without the consent of the other, adjourn for more than three days, nor to any other place than that in which the two houses shall be sitting.

SECTION 6. The senators and representatives shall receive a compensation for their services, to be ascertained by law, and paid out of the Treasury of the United States. They shall in all cases, except treason, felony and breach of the peace, be privileged from arrest during their attendance at the session of their respective houses, and in going to and returning from the same; and for any speech or debate in either house, they shall not be questioned in any other place.

In the interest of free and open debate, members of Congress may express any ideas or opinions without fear of being sued or punished.

No senator or representative shall, during the time for which he was elected, be appointed to any civil office under the authority of the United States, which shall have been created, or the emoluments whereof shall have been increased during such time; and no person holding any office under the United States, shall be a member of either house during his continuance in office.

In effect, a person cannot serve in Congress and hold an appointed office at the same time.

Every bill that has been passed by both Houses of Congress must be sent to the President. The President has 10 days (not including Sunday) to approve the bill and sign it into law or to reject the bill and return it to the body that proposed it. If, upon reconsideration, both Houses pass the bill by majorities of two-thirds or greater, the bill becomes law—even over the objections of the President. If the President neither signs nor returns the bill within 10 days, it becomes law automatically unless Congress adjourns within that time, in which case the bill does not become law. This last situation is called a *pocket veto*.

SECTION 7. All bills for raising revenue shall originate in the House of Representatives; but the Senate may propose or concur with amendments as on other bills.

The special power of the House of Representatives is initial control over the raising and spending of money. The House of Representatives is said to have the *power of the purse*. All other legislation may begin in the House of Representatives or the Senate.

Every bill which shall have passed the House of Representatives and the Senate, shall, before it become a law, be presented to the President of the United States; if he approves he shall sign it, but if not he shall return it, with his objections to that house in which it shall have originated, who shall enter for the objections at large on their journal, and proceed to reconsider it. If after such reconsideration two-thirds of the House shall agree to pass the bill, it shall be sent, together with the objections, to the other House, by which it shall likewise be reconsidered, and if approved by two-thirds of that House, it shall become a law. But in all cases the votes of both Houses shall be determined by yeas and nays, and the names of the persons voting for and against the bill shall be entered on the journal of each House respectively. If any bill shall not be returned by the President within ten days (Sundays excepted) after it shall have been presented to him, the same shall be a law, in like manner as if had signed it, unless the Congress by their adjournment prevent its return, in which case it shall not be a law.

Every order, resolution, or vote to which the concurrence of the Senate and House of Representatives may be necessary (except on a question of adjournment) shall be presented to the President of the United States; and before the same shall take effect, shall be approved by him, or being disapproved by him, shall be repassed by two-thirds of the Senate and House of Representatives, according to the rules and limitations prescribed in the case of a bill.

Congress can raise money to pay for all governmental business. The only restriction is that all states be treated equally with regard to revenue collection.

SECTION 8. The Congress shall have power to lay and collect taxes, duties, imposts and excises, to pay the debts and provide for the common defense and general welfare of the United States; but all duties, imposts and excises shall be uniform throughout the United States;

To borrow money on the credit of the United States;

To regulate commerce with foreign nations, and among the several States, and with the Indian tribes;

To establish a uniform rule of naturalization, and uniform laws on the subject of bankruptcies throughout the United States;

To coin money, regulate the value thereof, and of foreign coin, and fix the standard of weights and measures;

To provide for the punishment of counterfeiting the securities and current coin of the United States;

To establish post offices and post roads;

This clause provides for the patenting of inventions and the copyrighting of written works.

To promote the progress of science and useful arts, by securing for limited times to authors and inventors the exclusive right to their respective writings and discoveries;

Aside from the Supreme Court, which is established in Article III, the Congress is in charge of setting up a federal court system.

To constitute tribunals inferior to the Supreme Court;

To define and punish piracies and felonies committed on the high seas, and offenses against the law of nations;

To declare war, grant letters of marque and reprisal, and make rules concerning captures on land and water;

ONLY Congress has the power to declare war.

To raise and support armies, but no appropriation of money to that use shall be for a longer term than two years;

To provide and maintain a Navy;

To make rules for the government and regulation of the land and naval forces;

To provide for calling forth the militia to execute the laws of the Union, suppress insurrections and repel invasions;

To provide for organizing, arming, and disciplining the militia, and for governing such part of them as may be employed in the service of the United States, reserving to the States respectively, the appointment of officers, and the authority of training the militia according to the discipline prescribed by Congress;

To exercise exclusive legislation in all cases whatsoever, over such district (not exceeding ten miles square) as may, by cession of particular States, and the acceptance of Congress, become the seat of the Government of the United States, and to exercise like authority over all places purchased by the consent of the legislature of the State in which the same shall be, for the erection of forts, magazines, arsenals, dock-yards, and other needful buildings; —And

This is the authority by which the federal government governs Washington, D.C. (District of Columbia) and military bases throughout the country.

To make all laws which shall be necessary and proper for carrying into execution the foregoing powers and all other powers vested by this Constitution in the Government of the United States, or in any department or officer thereof.

SECTION 9. The migration or importation of such persons as any of the States now existing shall think proper to admit, shall not be prohibited by the Congress prior to the year one thousand eight hundred and eight, but a tax or duty may be imposed on such importation, not exceeding ten dollars for each person.

The privilege of the writ of habeas corpus shall not be suspended, unless when in cases of rebellion or invasion the public safety may require it.

No bill of attainder or ex post facto law shall be passed.

No capitation, or other direct, tax shall be laid unless in proportion to the census or enumeration herein before directed to be taken.

No tax or duty shall be laid on articles exported from any State.

No preference shall be given by any regulation of commerce revenue to the ports of one State over those of another: nor shall vessels bound to, or from, one State, be obliged to enter, clear, or pay duties in another.

Free trade is to exist among the states.

No money shall be drawn from the Treasury, but in consequence of appropriations made by law; and a regular statement and account of the receipts and expenditures of all public money shall be published from time to time.

No title of nobility shall be granted by the United States: And no person holding any office of profit or trust under them, shall, without consent of the Congress, accept of any present, emolument, office, or title, of any kind whatever, from any King, Prince, or foreign State.

SECTION 10. No State shall enter into any treaty, alliance, or confederation, grant letters of marque and reprisal; coin money; emit bills of credit; make any thing but gold and silver coin a tender in payment of debts, pass any bill of attainder, ex post facto law, or law impairing the obligation of contracts, or grant any rifle of nobility.

No State shall, without the consent of the Congress, lay any imposts or duties on imports or exports, except what may be absolutely necessary for executing its inspection laws; and the net produce of all duties and imposts, laid by any State on imports or exports, shall be for the use of the Treasury of the United States; and all such laws shall be subject to the revision and control of the Congress.

No State shall, without the consent of Congress, lay any duty of tonnage, keep troops, or ships of war in time of peace, enter into any agreement or compact with another State, or with a foreign power, or engage in war, unless actually invaded, or in such imminent danger as will not admit of delay.

ARTICLE II

SECTION 1. The executive power shall be vested in a President of the United States of America. He shall hold his office during the term of four years, and, together with the Vice President, chosen for the same term, be elected, as follows:

Each State, shall appoint in such manner as the legislature thereof may direct, a number of electors, equal to the whole number of senators and

This method of choosing the President and Vice President was changed in 1804 with the passage of the 12th Amendment. The President and Vice President must be able to cooperate and to work effectively together. Under the original provisions, the President and Vice President tended to be rivals. Under the current system, each Presidential nominee's choice is well known, and electors vote separately for President and for the President's choice as Vice President.

representatives to which the State may be entitled in the Congress; but no senator or representative, or person holding an office of trust or profit under the United States, shall be appointed an elector.

The electors shall meet in their respective States, and vote by ballot for two persons, of whom one at least shall not be an inhabitant of the same State with themselves. And they shall make a list of all the persons voted for, and of the number of votes for each; which list they shall sign and certify, and transmit sealed to the seat of the Government of the United States, directed to the President of the Senate. The President of the Senate shall, in the presence of the Senate and House of Representatives, open all the certificates, and the votes shall then be counted. The person having the greatest number of votes shall be the President, if such number be a majority of the whole number of electors appointed; and if there be more than one who have such majority, and have an equal number of votes, then the House of Representatives shall immediately choose by ballot one of them for President; and if no person have a majority, then from the five highest on the list the said House shall in like manner choose the President. But in choosing the President, the votes shall be taken by States, the representation from each State having one vote; a quorum for this purpose shall consist of a member or members from two thirds of the States, and a majority of all the States shall be necessary to a choice. In every case, after the choice of the President, the person having the greatest number of votes of the electors shall be the Vice President. But if there should remain two or more who have equal votes, the Senate shall choose from them by ballot the Vice President.

The Congress may determine the time of choosing the electors, and the day on which they shall give their votes; which day shall be the same throughout the United States.

The President must be at least 35 years old and may not be a naturalized citizen.

No person except a natural born citizen, or a citizen of the United States, at the time of the adoption of this Constitution, shall be eligible to the office of President; neither shall any person be eligible to that office who shall not have attained to the age of thirty-five years, and been fourteen years a resident within the United States.

In case of the removal of the President from office, or of his death, resignation, or inability to discharge the powers and duties of the said office, the same shall devolve on the Vice President, and the Congress may by law provide for the case of removal, death, resignation or inability, both of the President and Vice President, declaring what officer shall then act as President, and such officer shall act accordingly, until the disability be removed, or a President shall be elected.

The President shall, at stated times, receive for his services, a compensation, which shall neither be increased nor diminished during the period for which he shall have been elected, and he shall not receive within that period any other emolument from the United States, or any of them.

Before he enter on the execution of this office, he shall take the following oath or affirmation:—"I do solemnly swear (or affirm) that I will faithfully execute the office of President of the United States, and will to the best of my ability, preserve, protect, and defend the Constitution of the United States."

Just as the President must approve all acts of Congress before they may become law, so the Senate must approve treaties into which the President hopes to enter and must approve all of the President's appointments to positions of power and authority. This system, by which those in one branch of the government must ratify actions by persons in another branch, is called the system of *checks and balances*. By instituting these checks and balances, the framers of the Constitution hoped to avoid the abuse of power by members of any one branch—Executive (the President), Legislative (the Congress), or Judiciary (the Supreme Court).

SECTION 2. The President shall be Commander-in-Chief of the Army and Navy of the United States, and of the militia of the several States, when called into the actual service of the United States; he may require the opinion, in writing, of the principal officer in each of the Executive Departments, upon any subject relating to the duties of their respective offices, and he shall have power to grant reprieves and pardons for offenses against the United States, except in cases of impeachment.

He shall have power, by and with the advice and consent of the Senate, to make treaties, provided two-thirds of the Senators present concur; and he shall nominate, and by and with the advice and consent of the Senate, shall appoint ambassadors, other public ministers and consuls, Judges of the Supreme Court, and all other officers of the United States, whose appointments are not herein otherwise provided for, and which shall be established by law: but the Congress may by law vest the appointment of such inferior officers, as they think proper, in the President alone, in the courts of law, or in the heads of departments.

The President shall have power to fill up all vacancies that may happen during the recess of the Senate, by granting commissions which shall expire at the end of their next session.

SECTION 3. He shall from time to time give to the Congress information of the state of the Union, and recommend to their consideration such measures as he shall judge necessary and expedient; he may, on extraordinary occasions, convene both houses, or either of them, and in case of disagreement between them, with respect to the time of adjournment, he may adjourn them to such time as he shall think proper; he shall receive ambassadors and other public ministers; he shall take care that the laws be faithfully executed, and shall commission all the officers of the United States.

SECTION 4. The President, Vice President, and all civil officers of the United States, shall be removed from office on impeachment for, and conviction of, treason, bribery, or other high crimes or misdemeanors.

ARTICLE III

SECTION 1. The judicial power of the United States, shall be vested in one Supreme Court, and in such inferior courts as the Congress may from time to time ordain and establish. The judges, both of the supreme and inferior courts, shall hold their offices during good behaviour, and shall, at stated times, receive for their services, a compensation, which shall not be diminished during their continuance of office.

Federal judges are appointed for life. The reason for the lifetime appointments is the desire to have a judiciary department totally without political influence or any outside interference. Federal judges do not need to satisfy any appointing authority nor the public at large. They are free to exercise their judgment in deliberations and decisions. This is the concept of an *independent judiciary.*

SECTION 2. The judicial power shall extend to all cases, in law and equity, arising under this Constitution, the laws of the United States, and treaties made, or which shall be made, under their authority; to all cases affecting ambassadors, other public ministers and consuls; to all cases of admiralty and maritime jurisdiction; to controversies to which the United States shall be a party; to controversies between two or more States; between a State and citizens of another State; between citizens of different States; between citizens of the same State claiming lands under grants of different States, and between a State, or the citizens thereof, and foreign States, citizens or subjects.

In all cases affecting ambassadors, other public ministers and consuls, and those in which a State shall be a party, the Supreme Court shall have original jurisdiction. In all the other cases before mentioned, the Supreme Court shall have appellate jurisdiction, both as to law and fact, with such exceptions, and under such regulations as the Congress shall make.

The trial of all crimes, except in cases of impeachment, shall be by jury; and such trial shall be held in the State where the said crimes shall have been committed; but when not committed within any State, the trial shall be at such place or places as the Congress may by law have directed.

Only the individual actually convicted of treason (or, for that matter, any other crime) is guilty, and only the guilty may be punished. The family of the guilty party bears no guilt unless also tried and convicted.

SECTION 3. Treason against the United States, shall consist only in levying war against them, or in adhering to their enemies, giving them aid and comfort. No person shall be convicted of treason unless on the testimony of two witnesses to the same overt act, or on confession in open court.

The Congress shall have power to declare the punishment of treason, but no attainder of treason shall work corruption of blood, or forfeiture except during the life of the person attained.

ARTICLE IV

This section constitutes what is known as the *full faith and credit clause.* Each state is entitled to make and interpret its own laws; all other states must respect those laws and rulings.

SECTION 1. Full faith and credit shall be given in each State to the public acts, records, and judicial proceedings of every other State. And the Congress may by general laws prescribe the manner in which such acts, records, and proceedings shall be proved, and the effect thereof.

Article III, Section 2 provides that trials take place in the states in which the crimes were committed. This section provides for *extradition* of an accused who may have fled the state of commission in hope of avoiding trial.

Slaves presented a special problem that the Constitution addressed as a specific issue. In some states, slavery was entirely legal. Under the laws of those states, a slave was property. If a slave managed to escape from his home state to a state in which slavery was not legally protected, was the slave to be afforded the privileges and immunities of a citizen of that state or were the laws of the state from which the slave had fled to be afforded full faith and credit? In this special case, full faith and credit of the home state's laws was to be upheld, and the slave was to be returned to the slave state from which he had fled.

SECTION 2. The citizens of each State shall be entitled to all privileges and immunities of citizens in the several States.

A person charged in any State with treason, felony, or other crime, who shall flee from justice, and be found in another State, shall on demand of the executive authority of the State from which he fled, be delivered up, to be removed to the State having jurisdiction of the crime.

No person held to service or labour in one State, under the laws thereof, escaping into another, shall, in consequence of any law or regulation therein, be discharged from such service or labour, but shall he delivered up on claim of the party to whom such service or labour may be due.

SECTION 3. New States may be admitted by the Congress into this Union; but no new State shall be formed or erected within the jurisdiction of any other State; nor any State be formed by the junction of two or more States, or parts of States, without the consent of the legislatures of the States concerned as well as of the Congress.

The Congress shall have power to dispose of and make all needful rules and regulations respecting the Territory or other property belonging to the United States; and nothing in this Constitution shall be so construed as to prejudice any claims of the United States, or of any particular State.

SECTION 4. The United States shall guarantee to every State in this Union a republican form of Government, and shall protect each of them against invasion; and on application of the legislature, or of the executive (when the legislature cannot be convened) against domestic violence.

A citizen of any state is a citizen of the United States and when within any state other than his own is to be treated in the same way as is a citizen of that state.

ARTICLE V

The Congress, whenever two-thirds of both Houses shall deem it necessary, shall propose amendments to this Constitution, or on the application of the legislatures of two-thirds of the several States, shall call a convention for proposing amendments, which, in either case, shall be valid to all intents and purposes, as part of the Constitution, when ratified by the legislatures of three-fourths of the several States, or by conventions in three-fourths thereof, as the one or the other mode of ratification may be proposed by the Congress; provided that no amendment which may be made prior to the year one thousand eight hundred and eight shall in any manner affect the first and fourth clauses in the Ninth Section of the First Article; and that no State, without its consent, shall be deprived of its equal suffrage in the Senate.

The Constitution (along with U.S. treaties) is the SUPREME LAW OF THE LAND. All Congressional acts and all state laws must comply with the provisions of the Constitution. If a citizen feels that Congress has enacted a law that is contrary to the intent of the Constitution, the citizen may disobey that law, be convicted, and challenge the law through appeals. The appeals process goes from the court in which the citizen was convicted to an appelate court. If the appelate court maintains the conviction, the appeal may be brought to the Supreme Court for final determination as to the constitutionality of the law. This process is known as *Judicial Review* and is another aspect of the system of checks and balances.

ARTICLE VI

Adherence to any particular religion or to no religion at all is neither a qualification nor disqualification for any office.

All debts contracted and engagements entered into, before the adoption of this Constitution, shall be as valid against the United States under this Constitution, as under the Confederation. This Constitution, and the laws of the United States which shall be made in pursuance thereof; and all treaties made, or which shall be made, under the authority of the United States, shall be the supreme law of the land; and the judges in every State shall be bound thereby, anything in the Constitution or laws of any State to the contrary notwithstanding.

The senators and representatives before mentioned, and the members of the several State legislatures, and all executive and judicial officers, both of the United States and of the several States, shall be bound by oath or affirmation, to support this Constitution; but no religious test shall ever be required as a qualification to any office or public trust under the United States.

ARTICLE VII

The ratification of the conventions of nine States shall be sufficient for the establishment of this Constitution between the States so ratifying the same.

Done in convention by the unanimous consent of the States present the seventeenth day of September in the year of our Lord one thousand seven hundred and eighty seven and of the Independence of the United States of America the twelfth. In witness whereof we have hereunto subscribed our names,

(*here follow the signatures*)

ARTICLES IN ADDITION TO, AND AMENDMENTS OF, THE CONSTITUTION

ARTICLE I

Most people associate the 1st Amendment with free speech and freedom of religion.

Congress shall make no law respecting an establishment of religion, or prohibiting the free exercise thereof; or abridging the freedom of speech, or of the press; or the right of the people peaceably to assemble, and to petition the Government for a redress of grievances.

ARTICLE II

A well regulated militia, being necessary to the security of a free State, the right of the people to keep and bear arms, shall not be infringed.

ARTICLE III

No soldier shall, in time of peace be quartered in any house, without the consent of the owner, nor in time of war, but in a manner to be prescribed by law.

ARTICLE IV

The right of the people to be secure in their persons, houses, papers, and effects, against unreasonable searches and seizures, shall not be violated, and no warrants shall issue, but upon probable cause, supported by oath or affirmation, and particularly describing the place to be searched, and the persons or things to be seized.

This article guarantees personal privacy and protection from search unless the reason for the search can be justified.

You should be aware of two protections provided for in this article. The protection against double jeopardy means that when acquitted, a person cannot be tried again on the same charge, even if new evidence may point toward guilt. The protection against self-incrimination permits an accused to refuse to serve as a witness against him- or herself.

ARTICLE V

No person shall be held to answer for a capital, or otherwise infamous crime, unless on a presentment or indictment of a Grand Jury, except in cases arising in the land or naval forces, or in the militia, when in actual service in time of war or public danger; nor shall any person be subject for the same offense to be twice put in jeopardy of life or limb; nor shall be compelled in any criminal case to be a witness against himself, nor be deprived of life, liberty, or property, without due process of law; nor shall private property be taken for public use, without just compensation.

ARTICLE VI

This amendment is important for guaranteeing rights and protections to the accused, particularly the rights to trial by jury, to confront and interrogate witnesses against the accused, and to have counsel (an attorney).

In all criminal prosecutions, the accused shall enjoy the right to a speedy and public trial, by an impartial jury of the State and district wherein the crime shall have been committed, which district shall have been previously ascertained by law, and to be informed of the nature and cause of the accusation; to be confronted with the witnesses against him; to have compulsory process for obtaining witnesses in his favor, and to have the assistance of counsel for his defense.

ARTICLE VII

In suits at common law, where the value in controversy shall exceed twenty dollars, the right of trial by jury shall be preserved, and no fact tried by a jury, shall be otherwise reexamined in any court of the United States, than according to the rules of the common law.

ARTICLE VIII

Excessive bail shall not be required, nor excessive fines imposed, nor cruel and unusual punishments inflicted.

ARTICLE IX

The enumeration in the Constitution, of certain rights, shall not be construed to deny or disparage others retained by the people.

ARTICLE X

The powers not delegated to the United States by the Constitution, nor prohibited by it to the States, are reserved to the States respectively, or to the people.

ARTICLE XI

The judicial power of the United States shall not be construed to extend to any suit in law or equity, commenced or prosecuted against one of the United States by citizens of another State, or by citizens or subjects of any foreign State.

The following amendment changes the methods of voting for President and Vice President originally described in Article II, Section 1. The March 4 date by which a President must be chosen was later changed by the 22nd Amendment to January 20.

ARTICLE XII

The electors shall meet in their respective States, and vote by ballot for President and Vice President, one of whom, at least, shall not be an inhabitant of the same State with themselves; they shall name in their ballots the person voted for as President, and in distinct ballots the person voted for as Vice President, and they shall make distinct lists of all persons voted for as President, and of all persons voted for as Vice President, and of the number of votes for each, which lists they shall sign and certify, and transmit sealed to the seat of the government of the United States, directed to the President of the Senate;—The President of the Senate shall, in the presence of the Senate and House of Representatives, open all the certificates and the votes shall then be counted;—The person having the greatest number of votes for President, shall be the President, if such number be a majority of the whole number of electors appointed; and if no person have such majority, then from the persons having the highest numbers not exceeding three on the list of those voted for as President, the House of Representatives shall choose immediately, by ballot, the President. But in choosing the President, the votes shall be taken by States, the representation from each State having one vote; a quorum for this purpose shall consist of a member or members from two-thirds of the States, and a majority of all the States shall be necessary to a choice. And if the House of Representatives shall not choose a President whenever the fight of choice shall devolve upon them, before the fourth day of March next following, then the Vice President shall act as President, as in the case of the death or other constitutional disability of the President.—The person having the greatest number of votes as Vice President, shall be the Vice President, if such number be a majority of the whole number of electors appointed, and if no person have a majority, then from the two highest numbers on the list, the Senate shall choose the Vice President; a quorum for the purpose shall consist of two-thirds of the whole number of Senators, and a majority of the whole number shall be necessary to a choice.

But no person constitutionally ineligible to the office of President shall be eligible to that of Vice President of the United States.

The following amendment proposed in February and ratified in December, 1865, following the Civil War, abolished slavery in the United States.

ARTICLE XIII

SECTION 1. Neither slavery nor involuntary servitude, except as a punishment for crime whereof the party shall have been duly convicted, shall exist within the United States, or any place subject to their jurisdiction.

SECTION 2. Congress shall have power to enforce this article by appropriate legislation.

ARTICLE XIV

This section defines citizenship and extends protection of the Constitution to all citizens. States are not permitted to discriminate among citizens in the application of state laws.

SECTION 1. All persons born or naturalized in the United States, and subject to the jurisdiction thereof, are citizens of the United States and of the State wherein they reside. No State shall make or enforce any law which shall abridge the privileges or immunities of citizens of the United States; nor shall any State deprive any person of life, liberty, or property, without due process of law; nor deny to any person within its jurisdiction the equal protection of the laws.

SECTION 2. Representatives shall be apportioned among the several States according to their respective numbers, counting the whole number of persons in each State, excluding Indians not taxed. But when the right to vote at any election for the choice of electors for President and Vice President of the United States, Representatives in Congress, the executive and judicial officers of a State, or the members of the legislature thereof, is denied to any of the male inhabitants of such State, being twenty-one years of age, and citizens of the United States, or in any way abridged, except for participation in rebellion, or other crime, the basis of representation therein shall be reduced in the proportion which the number of such male citizens shall bear to the whole number of male citizens twenty-one years of age in such State.

Each state may define the qualifications of its voters, but if a state disqualifies any group of male citizens over the age of 21 for other than a cause such as criminal conviction, that state's number of seats in the House of Representatives may be reduced accordingly.

The following section was meant to penalize participation in the Civil War by persons who had formerly been in power in federal or state government. In effect, the section accused of treason those who had taken an oath to support the Constitution of the United States and who had then engaged in insurrection or rebellion. While condemning these people as *traitors*, the section also gives Congress the power to forgive.

SECTION 3. No person shall be a Senator or Representative in Congress, or elector of President and Vice President, or hold any office, civil or military, under the United States, or under any State, who, having previously taken an oath, as a member of Congress, or as an officer of the United States, or as member of any State legislature, or as an executive or judicial officer of any State, to support the Constitution of the United States, shall have engaged in insurrection or rebellion against the same, or given aid or comfort to the enemies thereof. But Congress may by a vote of two-thirds of each house, remove such disability.

SECTION 4. The validity of the public debt of the United States, authorized by law, including debts incurred for payment of pensions and bounties for services in suppressing insurrection or rebellion, shall not be questioned. But neither the United States nor any State shall assume or pay any debt or obligation incurred in aid of insurrection or rebellion against the United States, or any claim for the loss or emancipation of any slave; but all such debts, obligations and claims shall be held illegal and void.

SECTION 5. The Congress shall have power to enforce, by appropriate legislation, the provisions of this article.

ARTICLE XV

The 15th Amendment gave former slaves, and all other U.S. male citizens regardless of race or skin color, the right to vote.

SECTION 1. The right of citizens of the United States to vote shall not be denied or abridged by the United States or by any State on account of race, color, or previous condition of servitude.

SECTION 2. The Congress shall have power to enforce this article by appropriate legislation.

ARTICLE XVI

This amendment introduced the personal income tax by which the federal government gathers revenues directly from the people to pay for the business and services of the government.

The Congress shall have power to lay and collect taxes on incomes, from whatever source derived, without apportionment among the several States, and without regard to any census or enumeration.

This amendment provides for the direct election of senators by the people. Originally, the Constitution provided for election of senators by the state legislatures. The amendment also says that a person who is qualified by state law to vote for members of the most numerous house of the state legislature is qualified to vote for that state's senators.

ARTICLE XVII

SECTION 1. The Senate of the United States shall be composed of two senators from each State, elected by the people thereof, for six years; and each senator shall have one vote. The electors in each State shall have the qualifications requisite for electors of the most numerous branch of the State legislatures.

SECTION 2. When vacancies happen in the representation of any State in the Senate, the executive authority of such State shall issue writs of election to fill such vacancies: Provided that the legislature of any State may empower the executive thereof to make temporary appointments until the people fill the vacancies by election as the legislature may direct.

SECTION 3. This amendment shall not be so construed as to affect the election or term of any senator chosen before it becomes valid as part of the Constitution.

ARTICLE XVIII

SECTION 1. After one year from the ratification of this article the manufacture, sale, or transportation of intoxicating liquors within, the importation thereof into, or the exportation thereof from the United States and all territory subject to the jurisdiction thereof for beverage purposes is hereby prohibited.

Ratification of this amendment began the period known as Prohibition, in which the sale and possession of liquor was prohibited by law.

SECTION 2. The Congress and the several States shall have concurrent power to enforce this article by appropriate legislation.

SECTION 3. This article shall be inoperative unless it shall have been ratified as an amendment to the Constitution by the legislatures of the several States, as provided in the Constitution, within seven years from the date of the submission hereof to the States by the Congress.

ARTICLE XIX

The right of citizens of the United States to vote shall not be denied or abridged by the United States or by any State on account of sex.

The 19th Amendment gave women the right to vote.

You may recall that under the 12th Amendment, the terms of President and Vice President began on March 4. Experience over the years showed that a President who had not been re-elected in November had very little power over the new Congress at the beginning of the year. For this reason, the date that the new Presidential term took effect was moved closer to the beginning of the Congressional year.

ARTICLE XX

SECTION 1. The terms of the President and Vice President shall end at noon on the 20th day of January, and the terms of Senators and Representatives at noon on the 3rd day of January, of the years in which such terms would have ended if this article had not been ratified; and the terms of their successors shall then begin.

The required annual meeting of Congress was moved from the first Monday in December (Article I, Section 4) to the third day of January to allow just enough time for internal organization within the new Congress before the President takes office.

SECTION 2. The Congress shall assemble at least once in every year, and such meeting shall begin at noon on the 3rd day of January, unless they shall by law appoint a different day.

SECTION 3. If, at the time fixed for the beginning of the term of the President, the President elect shall have died, the Vice President elect shall become President. If a President shall not have been chosen before the time fixed for the beginning of his term, or if the President elect shall have failed to qualify, then the Vice President elect shall act as President until a President shall have qualified; and the Congress may by law provide for the case wherein neither a President elect nor a Vice President elect shall have qualified, declaring who shall then act as President, or the manner in which one who is to act shall be selected, and such person shall act accordingly until a President or Vice President shall have qualified.

SECTION 4. The Congress may by law provide for the case of the death of any of the persons from whom the House of Representatives may choose a President whenever the right of choice shall have devolved upon them, and for the case of the death of any of the persons from whom the Senate may choose a Vice President whenever the right of choice shall have devolved upon them.

SECTION 5. Sections 1 and 2 shall take effect on the 15th day of October following the ratification of this article.

SECTION 6. This article shall be inoperative unless it shall have been ratified as an amendment to the Constitution by the legislatures of three-fourths of the several States within seven years from date of its submission.

ARTICLE XXI

Prohibition as national policy was a failure, and this amendment repeals the 18th Amendment.

SECTION 1. The eighteenth article of amendment to the Constitution of the United States is hereby repealed.

Even though the 10th Amendment specifically grants to the states or to the people all rights not expressly given to the federal government, this section of the amendment repealing Prohibition makes a point of granting to the states the right to institute Prohibition within their own borders under Constitutional protection.

SECTION 2. The transportation or importation into any State, Territory, or possession of the United States for delivery or use therein of intoxicating liquors, in violation of the laws thereof, is hereby prohibited.

SECTION 3. This article shall be inoperative unless it shall have been ratified as an amendment to the Constitution by conventions in the several States, as provided in the Constitution, within seven years from the date of the submission hereof to the States by the Congress.

This amendment served to limit future presidents to two terms in office. The only president to be elected to more than two terms was Franklin D. Roosevelt, who served three full terms and was elected to a fourth. He died in office during his fourth term.

ARTICLE XXII

SECTION 1. No person shall be elected to the office of the President more than twice, and no person who has held the office of President, or acted as President, for more than two years of a term to which some other person was elected President shall be elected to the office of the President more than once. But this Article shall not apply to any person holding the office of President when this Article was proposed by the Congress, and shall not prevent any person who may be holding the office of President, or acting as President, during the term within which this Article becomes operative from holding the office of President or acting as President during the remainder of such term.

SECTION 2. This Article shall be inoperative unless it shall have been ratified as an amendment to the Constitution by the legislatures of three-fourths of the several States within seven years from the date of its submission to the States by the Congress.

By the terms of this amendment, citizens of the District of Columbia became able to vote for President of the United States. They had never had this right before because they are not citizens of any state, and the Constitution, as originally adopted, provided only for electors appointed by states.

ARTICLE XXIII

SECTION 1. The District constituting the seat of Government of the United States shall appoint in such manner as the Congress may direct:

A number of electors of President and Vice President equal to the whole number of Senators and Representatives in Congress to which the District would be entitled if it were a State, but in no event more than the least populous State; they shall be in addition to those appointed by the States, but they shall be considered, for the purposes of the election of President and Vice President, to be electors appointed by a State; and they shall meet in the District and perform such duties as provided by the twelfth article of amendment.

SECTION 2. The Congress shall have power to enforce this article by appropriate legislation.

Some states had chosen to discriminate against the poor or the poorly informed by requiring the payment of a poll tax at some time before the election. The poorly informed did not hear of the requirement or of the time and place for payment; the poor were unable to pay. Thus, the poor were effectively denied the right to vote. At the same time, politicians were able to get the information to those expected to vote the "right way" and to pay the tax for poor people who agreed to vote for their candidates or their issues, thereby affecting the outcome of the vote. This source of discrimination and corruption was eliminated by the 24th Amendment.

ARTICLE XXIV

SECTION 1. The right of citizens of the United States to vote in any primary or other election for President or Vice President, for electors for President or Vice President, or for Senator or Representative in Congress, shall not be denied or abridged by the United States or any State by reason of failure to pay any poll tax or other tax.

SECTION 2. The Congress shall have power to enforce this article by appropriate legislation.*

ARTICLE XXV

SECTION 1. In case of the removal of the President from office or of his death or resignation, the Vice President shall become President.

SECTION 2. Whenever there is a vacancy in the office of the Vice President, the President shall nominate a Vice President who shall take office upon confirmation by a majority vote of both Houses of Congress.

SECTION 3. Whenever the President transmits to the President pro tempore of the Senate and the Speaker of the House of Representatives his written declaration that he is unable to discharge the powers and duties of his office, and until he transmits to them a written declaration to the contrary, such powers and duties shall be discharged by the Vice President as Acting President.

SECTION 4. Whenever the Vice President and a majority of either the principal officers of the executive departments or of such other body as Congress may by law provide, transmit to the President pro tempore of the Senate and the Speaker of the House of Representatives their written declaration that the President is unable to discharge the powers and duties of his office, the Vice President shall immediately assume the powers and duties of the office of Acting President.

Thereafter, when the President transmits to the President pro tempore of the Senate and the Speaker of the House of Representatives his written declaration that no inability exists, he shall resume the powers and duties of his office unless the Vice President and a majority of either the principal officers of the executive departments or of such other body as Congress may by law provide, transmit within four days to the President pro tempore of the Senate and Speaker of the House of Representatives their written declaration that the President is unable to discharge the powers and duties of his office. Thereupon Congress shall decide the issue, assembling within forty-eight hours for that purpose if not in session. If the Congress, within twenty-one days after receipt of the latter written declaration, or if Congress is not in session, within twenty-one days after Congress is required to assemble, determines by two-thirds vote of both Houses that the President is unable to discharge the powers and duties of his office, the Vice President shall continue to discharge the same as Acting President; otherwise the President shall resume the powers and duties of his office.

This amendment lowers the voting age from 21 to 18.

ARTICLE XXVI

SECTION 1. The right of citizens of the United States, who are eighteen years of age or older, to vote shall not be denied or abridged by the United States or by any state on account of age.

SECTION 2. The Congress shall have power to enforce this article by appropriate legislation.

The ninth state to ratify the new Constitution, New Hampshire, did so in June, 1788. The unanimous election of George Washington to the office of President followed. (This was the only time that a President was elected unanimously.) Because of his role as leader of the victorious Revolutionary army and as first President, George Washington has been called *the father of our country*.

Just the Facts

After the war was over, delegates from the 13 states met at Independence Hall in Philadelphia to write a new Constitution. This Constitution was accepted by all the states in 1789. The new Constitution set up a strong national government that has three branches:

The Legislative Branch, Congress, is made up of the Senate and the House of Representatives. Congress meets in the Capitol Building in Washington, D.C., and makes laws. Each state elects two members to represent them in the Senate. The number of members elected to the House of Representatives for each state is based on the state's population, which is determined by the U.S. Census Bureau.

The Judicial Branch includes the Supreme Court and other federal courts. These courts have the right and the responsibility for interpreting and applying the Constitution and the laws that are passed by Congress.

The Executive Branch, headed by the President, sees that the laws are carried out. The President is the Chief Executive of the United States and also Commander-in-Chief of the Armed Forces. Presidential elections are held every four years.

Each branch of the government is meant to keep the other branches in balance. For instance, the President may veto (not approve) an act passed by Congress, but Congress can still pass the act if two-thirds of its members vote for it. The Supreme Court may, however, declare that act unconstitutional; then it cannot become a law.

The Constitution can be changed, and these changes are called amendments. The first 10 amendments passed in 1791 are called the Bill of Rights. The Bill of Rights guarantees rights and liberties such as the freedom of speech, freedom of the press, and freedom of religion. A later amendment to the Constitution gave women the right to vote. Now, all citizens who are at least 18 years of age now have the right to vote. Another amendment states that after a required period of lawful permanent residence, an immigrant may apply for citizenship.

YEARS OF EXPANSION

While the 13 original colonies were forming themselves into the United States, adventurous Americans were exploring lands to the south and west, establishing farms and towns. The areas they settled petitioned to join the Union and were admitted as new states. The vast midsection of the country, from the Mississippi River to the Rocky Mountains and from the Gulf of Mexico to the Canadian border had been explored and claimed by France. The United States acquired this large land mass by buying it from France. This acquisition was known as the Louisiana Purchase, and the territory was called the Louisiana Territory, even though the current state of Louisiana is only a tiny part of it. Westward exploration and expansion continued through the nineteenth century (the 1800s) and included the entire Pacific coast by 1853 and added the Alaska purchase in 1867 and Hawaii in 1898.

Groups of communities formed themselves into states and, one by one, joined the Union. In 1912, Arizona joined the Union as the 48th state. Much later, Alaska became the 49th state in January, 1959, and Hawaii became the 50th state in August, 1959. The United States now consists of 50 states represented on the flag by 13 alternating red and white stripes (seven red and six white) for the 13 original colonies and 50 white stars on a blue field for the total number of states. Each state has its own constitution, a legislature, a governor, and a judiciary system.

The locations, climates, and geographic features of the various states led to great diversity among lifestyles. Its long winters, rocky soil, and deep sea ports for trade with Europe led the North to industrialize and to depend on manufacturing and trade for its livelihood rather than depending on agriculture. The fast-moving rivers created water power for the mills. Small towns clustered around these mills, and larger cities grew along the coast. Many immigrants came from Europe to work in these mills and to establish new lives in America.

The climate and soil of the southern states allowed for large-scale planting of a few profitable crops. Tobacco and cotton were grown on large plantations. Cultivating and harvesting these crops was backbreaking work. Slave labor was available and, from the standpoint of the plantation owners, very economical. Thus, the development of the southern economy was very different from that of the northern states.

With expansion to the west, more economic styles developed. The center of the country proved to be well suited for growing food crops. In fact, the Midwest is commonly called *America's breadbasket*. The southwestern regions proved to be the perfect areas for raising sheep and cattle. Each area had its own labor needs. As the territories spread out and as new states joined the Union, slavery became an important issue. From 1808 onward, the right to import and own slaves was a constant point of debate in Congress. Compromises were made with regard to the admission of each new state, but tempers often rose. The slavery question was eventually settled by the Civil War.

Even while the United States was growing, all was not peaceful. Westward expansion involved displacement of the native American Indians who had lived here before settlers arrived. In some cases, relations were friendly, but many times they were hostile.

Wars with the Indians were not the only problem. In 1812, the United States declared war against England. The main reason for this war was freedom of the high seas. England had been stopping American ships and taking American seamen from them to serve in the British navy. The United States won the war, but not before the British had burned down the entire new city of Washington, D.C. The War of 1812 was the last war to be fought with a European power on American soil. This was not, unfortunately, the last foreign war on American soil. The Mexican War, which began in 1846, was the last. When the United States defeated Mexico, it gained parts of Texas, California, and New Mexico.

Just the Facts

For almost 100 years, the United States continued to expand and acquire new territory, eventually becoming the country that you see on the map now. The Northwest Territories were annexed in 1785. For a feeling of where northwest was at that time, this area later became Ohio, Indiana, Illinois, Michigan, Minnesota, and North Dakota. The 1803 Louisiana Purchase from France added land from the Gulf of Mexico to the Canadian border and from the Mississippi River west to the Rockies. Florida was purchased from Spain in 1819. In the mid-1840s, the United States acquired much of the West and Southwest after war with Mexico—some by annexation, some by purchase. In 1867, Alaska was purchased from Russia. Hawaii, an independent republic, chose to become a territory of the United States in 1900. As the country grew, economies of different regions had different needs.

THE CIVIL WAR

The problems of the United States did not disappear with the defeat of its foreign enemies. The struggle between the North and South was highlighted by differences over slavery, but many other differences existed as well. The argument can be summed up as a dispute over states' rights. The southern states felt that the federal government was wielding too much power. They felt that they should have more rights as individual states. The southern states threatened to secede (to separate themselves) from the Union and backed up their threat by attacking Fort Sumter in South Carolina.

The federal government refused to accept the idea that states could resign from the Union and treated the attackers as rebellious states rather than as another nation. Eleven states declared that they had seceded and formed the Confederate States of America. The member states of the Confederacy were South Carolina, Mississippi, Florida, Alabama, Georgia, Louisiana, Texas, Virginia, Arkansas, North Carolina, and Tennessee. Their President was Jefferson Davis.

Four other slave states—Delaware, Kentucky, Maryland, and Missouri—chose to remain in the Union. The Civil War, also known as the War Between the States, lasted from 1861 to 1865. This was a very unhappy period in the history of the United States. Because no border restrictions existed among the states, members of families were often scattered in different parts of the nation. This meant that fathers might be fighting against sons and brothers against brothers. Medical science was inadequate for the wounds inflicted, and sanitation was almost nonexistent. Casualties were high, and the land itself was devastated.

By the Emancipation Proclamation on January 1, 1863, President Abraham Lincoln declared that all slaves in any parts of the country that were in rebellion against the United States were now free. Slaves in states that had remained loyal to the United States were not affected by the Emancipation Proclamation. These slaves were freed by the 13th Amendment, which was passed shortly after the end of the Civil War.

The Civil War ended in 1865, and the reunited country began a process of reconstruction. Agriculture was revived; industrialization proceeded at a very rapid pace; and the population grew quickly. Immigrants contributed significantly to the progress of the nation.

Just the Facts

The difference in needs between the different regions of the United States led to many disagreements. One of these disagreements resulted in the Civil War. The South tried to leave the Union (secede) over the issues of slavery and states' rights.

Abraham Lincoln was the President of the North during the war to preserve the Union; Jefferson Davis was the President of the South. Generals Robert E. Lee and Thomas J. "Stonewall" Jackson were leaders of the Confederate army (the South). The Civil War between the Union and the Confederacy was eventually won by the Union.

MODERN HISTORY

Aside from involvement in the Spanish-American War in 1898, provoked when the Spanish destroyed the U.S. battleship *Maine* in Havana harbor, times were relatively peaceful. But it was a busy time for industry, for labor, for Congress, and for the American people. Between the end of the Civil War in 1865 and our entry into World War I in 1917, the country as a whole grew and prospered, and the United States became a powerful nation in the world. Immigrants flowed into the country and rapidly found their way into American society and the American economy. The United States absorbed so many immigrants that it was called a *melting pot* of cultures and races.

In this period, labor began to organize, and legislation was passed in attempts to control child labor and to encourage safe working conditions for coal miners. Amendments to the Constitution clarified ways in which Constitutional protections governed the actions of the states and how they extended directly to the people. Other amendments defined citizenship and extended the rights of citizens, including granting the right to vote to former slaves. This was also the era of Prohibition, the time in which the production and sale of liquor was constitutionally prohibited throughout the United States, but it was nevertheless a time of fun, happiness, and lively music and dance.

Americans were pleased with their own lives. Their attitude toward Europe and its problems was that Europe was far away. Americans wanted to remain isolated even as Europe was at war.

In 1915, a German submarine sank the passenger liner *Lusitania* with many American civilians aboard. This action led many Americans to change their minds, and in 1917 the United States entered the war. (You will notice that the sinking of ships brought the United States into a number of wars. Sinking of the battleship *Maine* led to the Spanish American War; sinking of the liner *Lusitania* drew us into the First World War; and the bombing of Pearl Harbor and total destruction of the aircraft carrier *Arizona* along with many other ships caused our entry into the Second World War.)

The First World War was over in 1918. It had been a very expensive war for all the countries involved. Recovery was also expensive, and money was mishandled and invested unwisely. On October 24, 1929, the American stock market fell in a *great crash*, and many banks failed. There was no money with which to pay workers, so millions of Americans lost their jobs. Unemployment was high, and poverty spread rapidly. This was the period of the Great Depression, which continued from 1929 to 1939. The Great Depression was not limited to the United Sates. Europe was undergoing a similar depression.

In the United States, people elected President Franklin D. Roosevelt. President Roosevelt was a strong leader with many creative ideas for social programs and federally funded work projects to help people to recover and to improve the economy. President Roosevelt is credited with bringing the United States and its people out of the Great Depression. In Europe, the depression and misery led the people to turn to dictators who promised a better life.

The rise of dictatorship in Europe did indeed lead to improvements in the lives of the people for a short period. However, in some cases, dictatorship and the power that accompanies it can lead to a desire for still more power. The German dictator, Adolf Hitler, was a very ruthless dictator. He led his armies to occupy one European country after another, imposing his own immorality on citizens of occupied countries. American isolationists did their best to keep the United States from becoming involved. The United States was just emerging from the depression and many citizens wanted a chance to recover in peace.

At the same time, the Japanese government was attempting to dominate the Far East just as the German government was attempting to absorb all of Europe. The United States joined the war after the Japanese carried out a surprise attack on the U.S. naval base at Pearl Harbor, Hawaii, on December 7, 1941. The surprise attack early on a Sunday morning caused more than 3,300 American deaths. President Roosevelt called December 7, "a date that will live in infamy." Congress promptly declared war against both Japan and Germany. The United States entered World War II as a major participant.

The war in Europe was won by the allied forces of the United States, England, Canada, Russia, and soldiers of European nations. The war in the Far East ended abruptly when the United States dropped an atomic bomb on the Japanese city of Hiroshima and then three days later dropped an atomic bomb on Nagasaki. President Harry Truman, who had succeeded President Roosevelt, made the difficult decision to use atomic weapons on civilian populations in order to save thousands of American servicemen's lives.

When the war ended, the victorious nations met and discussed forming some sort of world government that could help prevent such a devastating war from occurring again. They hoped to develop a United Nations that could solve problems through discussion, debate, and compromise. They hoped that a multinational peace-keeping force could stop tiny conflicts and prevent them from growing into full-scale wars. The United Nations was established with its headquarters in New York City. It has had some successes and some failures and still exists today.

With the end of World War II in 1945 came new governments and new alliances. Russian communism emerged as a new form of dictatorship and was expanding throughout Europe. The Russian communist government never directly attacked the United States or our citizens , so we never entered into a full-fledged war. The hostility and strained relations between the United States and Russia were called the Cold War. At the same time, another style of communism, Chinese communism, was taking hold in Asia and was spreading into North Korea and the northern part of the Indochinese peninsula.

In 1950, North Korea, with the assistance of Chinese communist troops, attacked its neighbor, South Korea. The United States went to battle to help defend South Korea, but this time as a member of the international United Nations forces rather than as an individual nation. The Korean Conflict ended in 1953.

The American government was very fearful of communism. It felt that once communist governments gained control, they tended to spread their influence rapidly and threatened the peace of the entire world. Because of this fear, the United States attempted to stop the spread of communism in Southeast Asia by assisting the South Vietnamese in their war against the North Vietnamese.

The Vietnamese War extended from 1964 to 1973. It was an unpopular cause. Many Americans felt that we were fighting an undefined enemy for an undefined reason. They felt that we were interfering in a Vietnamese civil war and had no business there. They did not want the United States to become a nation that was always at war. When the conflict was finally over, the American people wanted to show the world how kind-hearted and peaceful we really are. The United States opened its doors to war refugees and to victims of tyranny and oppression. We became much more hospitable and friendly to immigrants. Now you can benefit from this friendly attitude.

This brief history dwells heavily on the wars in which the United States has been involved. Wars and their dates and circumstances are good anchor dates for discussions of what was happening in the United States and abroad at a given time. War has not, however, been the chief motivating force of the American government or the American people. Americans are devoted to the goals of justice and equality and to an ever-improving quality of life. The middle of the twentieth century was marked by many social struggles. Dr. Martin Luther King, Jr. was a leader in a national civil rights movement to get rid of laws and practices that are unfair to minority group members. Between and even during wars, amendments and legislation granted greater equality, civil rights, and human rights to members of minority groups, to women, to the elderly, to the handicapped, and even to those accused of crimes.

Just the Facts

In the late 1800s and through the first half of 1900, millions of people immigrated to the United States. Immigration led to huge population growth and the expansion of population throughout the land area of the United States. The increase in population led to an increase in industrial production and, therefore, to an increase in the industrial workforce. Labor unions were created to improve working conditions and to raise workers' wages in industry, mining, and the railroads. During the Great Depression, which began with the stock market crash of 1929, many people were out of work.

In the twentieth century, the United States has been involved in a number of wars. In WWI, America fought alongside Britain and Russia against German expansion. American involvement in World War II began in the Pacific with the bombing of Pearl Harbor, Hawaii, by the Japanese and ended with the atomic bombing of Japan by the United States.

STATE AND LOCAL GOVERNMENTS

Each state has its own constitution and its own government divided into three branches. The state Legislative Branch usually has two elected groups, which in many states are called the Senate and the Assembly. The Executive Branch is headed by the state's Governor, who is elected by the people. The Judicial Branch is made up of the state courts, which interpret state laws.

All states have equal rights, and each state sets up counties, towns, and cities to provide for local government. The elected head of a city is most often called a mayor.

OTHER IMPORTANT FACTS

Knowing the general history of the United States will help you to answer many of the questions the examiner is likely to ask you. The following facts, even though they are not part of our history, are also important.

- The American flag is red, white, and blue.

- There are currently 50 states, each with its own star on the flag.

- The Statue of Liberty, a symbol of freedom, is in New York Harbor.

- Independence Hall and the Liberty Bell in Philadelphia are symbols of freedom.

- Most people earning income in the United States must file income tax forms, even if they are not U.S. citizens.

Chapter 8
PRACTICE TESTS

The following multiple-choice questions will give you plenty of practice with the subject matter of the civics test. These questions are not actually taken from the test, but they are very similar. Some may be asked by the INS examiner who gives you the test.

We will give you 20 questions on each multiple-choice exam. You have 30 minutes in which to answer the 20 questions on each exam. Limit yourself to the 30 minutes to answer questions on each of these practice tests. Answer every question. If you are not certain of an answer, eliminate answers that you are sure are wrong and choose from those remaining. When you finish, compare your answers with those provided. You must correctly answer 12 questions on one exam in order to pass. If you cannot answer 12 questions correctly, or if you feel that many of your correct answers were lucky guesses, then you should return to the Federal Textbooks on Citizenship listed in Chapter 6, "Applying for Naturalization." You may also find it very helpful to reread Chapter 7, "Preparing for the English and Civics Tests."

Use a piece of scratch paper to record your answers.

PRACTICE TEST ONE

1. In order to vote, a person must be 18 years of age or older and be a

    A. property owner
    B. woman
    C. citizen
    D. taxpayer

2. A person cannot become Vice President unless he or she was born

    A. in one of the original 13 states
    B. in the United States
    C. later than the President
    D. in the same state as the President

3. The system of checks and balances gives the

    A. President power to overrule state governors
    B. Supreme Court the power to amend the Constitution
    C. House of Representatives power to pass bills that the Senate refuses to approve
    D. Senate power to approve treaties

4. In which war was the city of Washington, D.C., burned down?

    A. War of 1812
    B. Civil War
    C. Revolutionary War
    D. Spanish-American War

5. A member of the Senate may not at the same time

    A. serve as an Ambassador
    B. own a home outside of the state from which he or she was elected
    C. travel abroad
    D. campaign for office

6. The state most recently admitted to the Union is

    A. Alaska
    B. Hawaii
    C. Delaware
    D. Washington

7. The number of members in the House of Representatives is

    A. 100
    B. 109
    C. 435
    D. 535

8. The amendment to the Constitution that protects citizens from unwarranted search of their homes or seizure of their property is the

   A. First
   B. Second
   C. Fourth
   D. Sixth

9. The President of the United States must be a native-born citizen and must be at least how many years old?

   A. 25
   B. 30
   C. 35
   D. 39

10. The National Anthem of the United States is called

    A. "America the Beautiful"
    B. "The Star-Spangled Banner"
    C. "Battle Hymn of the Republic"
    D. "God Bless America"

11. If a federal official is impeached and is found guilty, he or she will

    A. go to prison
    B. be deported
    C. pay a fine
    D. lose his or her job

12. Which of these states did *not* secede from the Union?

    A. Florida
    B. Tennessee
    C. Maryland
    D. Texas

13. Which document begins with the words, "We the People of the United States . . ."?

    A. Declaration of Independence
    B. Constitution
    C. Mayflower Compact
    D. Bill of Rights

14. The term "President's cabinet" refers to

    A. the piece of furniture in which unsigned bills are filed
    B. Congressional committee heads
    C. the President's secretarial staff
    D. a group of advisors

15. Of the following structures, the one that is *not* in Washington, D.C., is

    A. Independence Hall
    B. White House
    C. Thomas Jefferson Memorial
    D. Washington Monument

16. If the President vetoes a bill, that bill can still become law by a vote of

    A. a majority of both houses meeting in joint session
    B. $2/3$ of the members of each house of Congress
    C. $3/4$ of the members of each house of Congress
    D. $3/4$ of all the states

17. The Civil War was fought in

    A. New England
    B. Central America
    C. the southern United States
    D. Cuba

18. A ruling of the Supreme Court

    A. may be resubmitted to the Supreme Court on appeal
    B. may be appealed directly to the President
    C. may be overturned by a $3/4$ vote of both Houses of Congress
    D. must be accepted

19. A divorce granted in one state is recognized as valid in all states by virtue of

    A. the "full faith and credit clause" of the Constitution
    B. a law passed by Congress
    C. the Bill of Rights
    D. the principle of states' rights

20. What was the effect of the dropping of the first atomic bombs?

    A. The Korean War was begun.
    B. World War II was ended in the Far East.
    C. World War II was ended in Europe.
    D. Members of disadvantaged minority groups rioted in Los Angeles.

ANSWER KEY—PRACTICE TEST ONE

Check your answers to the questions in Practice Test One against these correct answers. If you passed comfortably, take the next two tests for more practice. If you failed or just barely passed, or if you simply feel uncomfortable, do some more study and review before you try another practice test.

1.	C	6.	B	11.	D	16.	B
2.	B	7.	C	12.	C	17.	C
3.	D	8.	C	13.	B	18.	D
4.	A	9.	C	14.	D	19.	A
5.	A	10.	B	15.	A	20.	B

PRACTICE TEST TWO

1. The first English settlers in the Massachusetts colony came to this country

   A. instead of serving time in debtor's prison
   B. to escape famine
   C. in search of religious freedom
   D. to avoid paying taxes to the king

2. Why did George Washington serve only two terms as President?

   A. The Constitution limits a President to two terms.
   B. He retired.
   C. He was not re-elected.
   D. He died.

3. The call "Remember the *Maine*" rallied American forces to battle in which war?

   A. French and Indian War
   B. Spanish-American War
   C. Civil War
   D. World War II

4. The Statue of Liberty may be seen and visited in

   A. Plymouth, Massachusetts
   B. Washington, D.C.
   C. Philadelphia's Independence Hall
   D. New York Harbor

5. What is the term of office served by a federal judge?

   A. six years
   B. thirteen years
   C. his or her lifetime
   D. until the next President is elected

6. In World War II, the group of countries including Germany, Italy, and Japan was called the

   A. Axis
   B. Allies
   C. Central Powers
   D. United Front

7. The heads of executive departments serve as members of the President's cabinet. One of these, the head of the Department of Justice, is the Attorney General. Every other cabinet member bears the title

   A. Department Head
   B. Secretary
   C. Executive
   D. General Attorney

8. From the standpoint of the states that seceded from the Union at the start of the Civil War, the chief issue was states' rights and their desire to live under laws that favored the southern economy. From the standpoint of the federal government, and most especially that of President Lincoln, the issue over which the war was fought was

   A. the South's allegiance with France
   B. the price of cotton
   C. the indivisibility of the Union
   D. freedom of the seas

9. In the history of the United States, only one President prior to President Clinton has been impeached, and that President also was not convicted by the Senate and, therefore, served out the remainder of his term. Who was that President?

    A. Richard Nixon
    B. Andrew Jackson
    C. Lyndon Johnson
    D. Andrew Johnson

10. The group of men who debated independence was called the

    A. Continental Congress
    B. Mayflower Compact
    C. Senate
    D. Conference of Governors

11. Who has the power to declare war?

    A. House of Representatives
    B. Commander-in-Chief of the Armed Forces
    C. Senate
    D. Congress

12. The Supreme Law of the Land is

    A. the final ruling of the Supreme Court
    B. the most recent amendment to the Constitution
    C. the Constitution
    D. a joint resolution of Congress

13. Which group received the right to vote most recently?

    A. women
    B. former slaves
    C. poor people
    D. 18-year-olds

14. Who is called "the Father of Our Country?"

    A. King George III of England
    B. George Washington
    C. Abraham Lincoln
    D. Martin Luther King

15. Political parties are not mentioned in the Constitution, but the right for the people to peaceably assemble, as granted by the First Amendment, clearly allows for political parties. The two political parties most active in the United States today are the

    A. Liberal Party and the Conservative Party
    B. Labor Party and Conservative Party
    C. Democrat Party and Republican Party
    D. Republican Party and People's Party

16. The right to trial by jury means that

    A. the trial will be fair
    B. a panel of three judges must agree on a verdict
    C. trial judges are elected by a vote of the people
    D. guilt or innocence is determined by ordinary citizens who listen to the evidence

17. What happens if the President dies in office?

    A. The Vice President automatically becomes President.
    B. The Electoral College meets and elects a new President.
    C. The House of Representatives chooses a new President.
    D. The Chief Justice appoints a new President.

18. Since the passage of the Thirteenth Amendment,

    A. a general census has been taken every 10 years
    B. slavery has been illegal
    C. naturalized citizens have been permitted to vote
    D. all wage earners have been required to pay an income tax

19. All but one of the following statements are

true. Which statement is *not* true?

A. Every state has its own constitution by which that state is governed.
B. A state cannot pass and enforce a law that is in conflict with the United States Constitution.
C. Each state can restrict trade with other states.
D. Every state has its own judicial system, that is, its own set of courts.

20. If a person who has committed a crime in one state leaves that state and is caught in another state, the state in which the person was caught will

A. try him or her for the crime
B. return him or her to the state in which the crime was committed
C. send him or her to the state of which he or she is a citizen
D. send him or her to a state in which he or she is unknown so as to ensure an impartial jury

ANSWER KEY—PRACTICE TEST TWO

1.	C	6.	A	11.	D	16.	D
2.	B	7.	B	12.	C	17.	A
3.	B	8.	C	13.	D	18.	B
4.	D	9.	D	14.	B	19.	C
5.	C	10.	A	15.	C	20.	B

PRACTICE TEST THREE

1. Where were the original 13 American colonies located?

A. on the East Coast
B. on the West Coast
C. in the Midwest
D. in the Southwest

2. When is Independence Day?

A. May 30
B. July 4
C. September 7
D. November 24

3. A naturalized U.S. citizen may be required to

A. vote
B. serve on a jury
C. make campaign contributions
D. bring family members to the United States

4. The first ten amendments to the United States Constitution are called

A. the Bill of Rights
B. the Rights of States
C. the Articles of Confederation
D. the Declaration of Independence

5. Freedom of speech and religion are protected by

A. the Declaration of Independence
B. the Bill of Rights
C. early laws of Congress
D. state laws

6. The first President of the United States was

A. Abraham Lincoln
B. James Madison
C. Thomas Jefferson
D. George Washington

7. The term "Reconstruction" refers to

    A. the time after the War of 1812 during which Washington, D.C., was rebuilt
    B. creation of the memorial to victims on the battleship Arizona at Pearl Harbor
    C. the post-Civil War era in the South
    D. mine safety improvements won by the United Mine Workers

8. During the Civil War, the U.S. President was

    A. Ulysses S. Grant
    B. Andrew Jackson
    C. Abraham Lincoln
    D. Jefferson Davis

9. An amendment to the Constitution gave women the right to

    A. vote
    B. speak freely
    C. own property
    D. serve in the army

10. When the Japanese attacked Pearl Harbor, the United States entered

    A. World War I
    B. World War II
    C. the Korean War
    D. the Vietnam War

11. Dr. Martin Luther King, Jr. was a

    A. senator
    B. governor
    C. medical scientist
    D. civil rights leader

12. Which city is the United States capital?

    A. Washington, D.C.
    B. New York City
    C. Philadelphia, Pennsylvania
    D. Boston, Massachusetts

13. The head of the Executive branch of the United States government is the

    A. Governor
    B. President
    C. Chief Justice
    D. Speaker of the House

14. A presidential election is held every

    A. year
    B. two years
    C. four years
    D. six years

15. The Cold War was

    A. fought in Alaska
    B. a period of hostility but no fighting
    C. another name for the Civil War
    D. begun with the dropping of the first atomic bomb

16. The United States Congress is made up of the Senate and the

    A. Assembly
    B. Lower House
    C. House of Commons
    D. House of Representatives

17. A state government is headed by a

    A. governor
    B. secretary of state
    C. president
    D. senator

18. A mayor governs a

    A. city
    B. county
    C. province
    D. region

19. The United Nations is an international organization

    A. of which the United States is a member
    B. with power to override the Constitution of the United States
    C. to which the United States does not belong
    D. dominated by the United States

20. A U.S. citizen has the right to do all of the following *except*

    A. march in front of the White House to protest immigration policies
    B. plot to overthrow the government by force
    C. burn the American flag
    D. choose to work in a hospital instead of serving in the armed forces

ANSWER KEY—PRACTICE TEST THREE

1.	A	6.	D	11.	D	16.	D
2.	B	7.	C	12.	A	17.	A
3.	B	8.	C	13.	B	18.	A
4.	A	9.	A	14.	C	19.	A
5.	B	10.	B	15.	B	20.	B

THE OFFICIAL INS INTERVIEW QUESTIONS

Now that you are an expert on U.S. history and government, you should review the 100 sample questions that INS examiners generally use as the basis for the real civics test. Under current INS policy, examiners will ask between ten and 20 of the questions on this list. You must answer at least 60 percent of the questions correctly to pass the test. If you do not pass the test during your initial naturalization interview, you will have another chance to pass it (or, for that matter, the English test) within 90 days after you take it for the first time.

1. What are the colors of our flag?

2. How many stars are there on our flag?

3. What color are the stars on our flag?

4. What do the stars on the flag mean?

5. How many stripes are on the flag?

6. What color are the stripes?

7. What do the stripes on the flag mean?

8. How many states are there in the union?

9. What is the Fourth of July?

10. What is the date of Independence Day?

11. Independence from whom?

12. What country did we fight during the Revolutionary War?

13. Who was the first President of the United States?

14. Who is the President of the United States today?

15. Who is the Vice President of the United States today?

16. Who elects the President of the United States?

17. Who becomes President of the United States if the President should die?

18. For how long do we the elect the President?

19. What is the Constitution?

20. Can the Constitution be changed?

21. What do we call a change to the Constitution?

22. How many changes or amendments are there to the Constitution?

23. How many branches are there in our government?

24. What are the three branches of our government?

25. What is the Legislative Branch of our government?

26. Who makes the laws in the United States?

27. What is Congress?

28. What are the duties of Congress?

29. Who elects Congress?

30. How many senators are there in Congress?

31. Can you name the two senators from your state?

32. For how long do we elect each senator?

33. How many representatives are there in Congress?

34. For how long do we elect the representatives?

35. What is the Executive Branch of our government?

36. What is the Judiciary Branch of our government?

37. What are the duties of the Supreme Court?

38. What is the supreme law of the United States?

39. What is the Bill of Rights?

40. What is the capital of your state?

41. Who is the current governor of your state?

42. Who becomes President of the United States if the President and Vice President should die?

43. Who is the Chief Justice of the Supreme Court?

44. Can you name the 13 original states?

45. Who said "Give me liberty or give me death"?

46. Which countries were our enemies during World War II?

47. What are the 49th and 50th states of the Union?

48. How many terms can a President serve?

49. Who was Martin Luther King, Jr.?

50. Who is the head of your local government?

51. According to the Constitution, a person must meet certain requirements in order to be eligible to become President. Name one of these requirements.

52. Why are there 100 senators in the Senate?

53. Who selects the Supreme Court Justices?

54. How many Supreme Court Justices are there?

55. Why did the pilgrims come to America?

56. What is the head executive of a state government called?

57. What is the head executive of a city government called?

58. What holiday was celebrated for the first time by the American colonists?

59. Who was the main writer of the Declaration of Independence?

60. When was the Declaration of Independence adopted?

61. What is the basic belief of the Declaration of Independence?

62. What is the National Anthem of the United States?

63. Who wrote "The Star-Spangled Banner"?

64. Where does freedom of speech come from?

65. What is the minimum voting age in the United States?

66. Who signs bills into law?

67. What is the highest court in the United States?

68. Who was President during the Civil War?

69. What did the Emancipation Proclamation do?

70. What special group advises the President?

71. Which President is called "the Father of Our Country"?

72. What Immigration and Naturalization Service form is used to apply for naturalized citizenship?

73. Who helped the pilgrims in America?

74. What is the name of the ship that brought the pilgrims to America?

75. What were the 13 original states of the United States called?

76. Name three rights or freedoms guaranteed by the Bill of Rights.

77. Who has the power to declare war?

78. What kind of government does the United States have?

79. Which President freed the slaves?

80. In what year was the Constitution written?

81. What are the first ten Amendments to the Constitution called?

82. Name one purpose of the United Nations.

83. Where does Congress meet?

84. Whose rights are guaranteed by the Constitution and the Bill of Rights?

85. What is the introduction to the Constitution called?

86. Name one benefit of being a citizen of the United States.

87. What is the most important right granted to U.S. citizens?

88. What is the United States capitol?

89. What is the White House?

90. Where is the White House located?

91. What is the name of the President's official home?

92. Name one right guaranteed by the First Amendment.

93. Who is the Commander-in-Chief of the U.S. military?

94. Which President was the first Commander-in-Chief of the U.S. military?

95. In what month do we vote for the President?

96. In what month is the new President inaugurated?

97. How many times may a senator be re-elected?

98. How many times may a congressman be re-elected?

99. What are the two major political parties in the United States today?

100. How many states are there in the United States?

ANSWERS

1. Red, white, and blue

2. 50

3. White

4. One for each state in the Union

5. 13

6. Red and white

7. They represent the original 13 states.

8. 50

9. Independence Day

10. July 4th

11. England

12. England

13. George Washington

14. [insert correct answer]

15. [insert correct answer]

16. The Electoral College

17. Vice President

18. Four years

19. The supreme law of the land

20. Yes

21. An amendment

22. 27

23. Three

24. Legislative, Executive, and Judiciary

25. Congress

26. Congress

27. The Senate and the House of Representatives

28. To make laws

29. The people

30. 100

31. [determine by locality]

32. Six years

33. 435

34. Two years

35. The President, Cabinet, and departments under the cabinet members

36. The Supreme Court

37. To interpret laws

38. The Constitution

39. The first ten Amendments of the Constitution

40. [determine by locality]

41. [determine by locality]

42. Speaker of the House of Representatives

43. William Rehnquist

44. Connecticut, New Hampshire, New York, New Jersey, Massachusetts, Pennsylvania, Delaware, Virginia, North Carolina, South Carolina, Georgia, Rhode Island, and Maryland

45. Patrick Henry

46. Germany, Italy, and Japan

47. Hawaii and Alaska

48. Two

49. A civil rights leader

50. [determine by locality]

51. Must be a natural born citizen of the United States, must be at least 35 years old by the time he/she will serve, must have lived in the United States for at least 14 years

52. Two from each state

53. Appointed by the President

54. Nine

55. For religious freedom

56. Governor

57. Mayor

58. Thanksgiving

59. Thomas Jefferson

60. July 4, 1776

61. That all men are created equal

62. "The Star-Spangled Banner"

63. Francis Scott Key

64. The Bill of Rights

65. 18

66. The President

67. The Supreme Court

68. Abraham Lincoln

69. Freed many slaves

70. The Cabinet

71. George Washington

72. Form N-400 (Application for Naturalization)

73. The American Indians (native Americans)

74. The Mayflower

75. Colonies

76. (a)Freedom of speech, press, religion, peaceable assembly, and requesting change of government

(b)The right to bear arms (the right to have weapons or own a gun, though subject to certain regulations)

(c)The government may not quarter, or house, soldiers in citizens' homes during peacetime without their consent

(d)The government may not search or take a person's property without a warrant

(e)A person may not be tried twice for the same crime and does not have to testify against him/herself

(f)A person charged with a crime still has some rights, such as the right to a fair trial and to have a lawyer

(g)The right to trial by jury, in most cases

(h)Protection of people against excessive or unreasonable fines or cruel and unusual punishment

(i)The people have rights other than those mentioned in the Constitution

(j)Any power not given to the federal government by the Constitution is a power of either the states or the people

77. The Congress

78. A Republic

79. Abraham Lincoln

80. 1787

81. The Bill of Rights

82. For countries to discuss and try to resolve world problems, to provide economic aid to many countries

83. In the Capitol in Washington, D.C.

84. Everyone (citizens and noncitizens living in the United States)

85. The Preamble

86. Obtain federal government jobs, travel with a U.S. passport, petition for close relatives to come to the United States to live

87. The right to vote

88. The place where Congress meets

89. The President's official home

90. 1600 Pennsylvania Ave. Northwest, Washington, D.C.

91. The White House

92. Freedom of Speech, Press, Religion, Peaceable Assembly and Requesting Change of the Government

93. The President

94. George Washington

95. November

96. January

97. There is no limit.

98. There is no limit.

99. Democrat and Republican

100. 50

QUESTIONS FOR APPLICANTS MEETING THE 65/20 EXCEPTION

Applicants for naturalization who have been living in the United States subsequent to lawful admission for permanent residence for at least 20 years and who are 65 years of age or older on the date of filing are given special consideration in satisfying the civics requirement.

This means that these applicants can take a simpler version of the civics test. Applicants entitled to special consideration will be asked ten questions from the following list. Applicants must answer at least six questions correctly to pass.

Because these applicants are also exempt from the English literacy requirement, they may be tested in the language of their choice.

1. Why do we celebrate the Fourth of July?

2. Who was the first President of the United States?

3. Who is President of the United States today?

4. What is the Constitution?

5. What are the first ten amendments of the Constitution called?

6. Who elects Congress?

7. How many senators are there in Congress?

8. For how long do we elect each senator?

9. For how long do we elect the representative in Congress?

10. Who nominates judges to the Supreme Court?

11. What are the three branches of our government?

12. What is the highest court in the United States?

13. What major river running north to south divides the United States?

14. The Civil War was fought over what important issue?

15. Name the two major political parties in the United States today.

16. How many states are there in the United States?

17. What is the capital of the United States?

18. What is the minimum voting age in the United States?

19. Who was Martin Luther King, Jr.?

20. What nation was first to land a man on the moon?

21. What is the capital of your state?

22. What is it called if the President refuses to sign a bill into law and returns it to Congress with his objections?

23. What two oceans bound the United States?

24. What famous American invented the electric light bulb?

25. What is the National Anthem of the United States?

ANSWERS

1. The Fourth of July is Independence Day.
2. George Washington
3. [insert correct answer]
4. The supreme law of the land
5. The Bill of Rights
6. The people
7. 100
8. Six years
9. Two years
10. The President
11. Legislative, Executive, and Judicial
12. The Supreme Court
13. The Mississippi River
14. Slavery or states rights
15. Democratic and Republican
16. 50
17. Washington, D.C.
18. 18
19. A civil rights leader
20. The United States of America
21. [insert local information]
22. Veto
23. The Atlantic and Pacific oceans
24. Edison
25. "The Star-Spangled Banner"

After reading this chapter and taking our three practice tests, you should be well-prepared for the civics test. Good luck; we will see you at the oath ceremony!

Part IV
APPENDIX OF INS FORMS

APPENDIX OF INS FORMS

The following forms, along with their accompanying instructions, appear in the order that they are first mentioned in the text. You should find these copies and instructions very useful as you gather information and documents. You might also practice filling out these copies, adjusting your words and handwriting to fit the spaces. You can't use these copies for actual filing. You must get original forms and fill them out according to their attached instructions. You may obtain INS forms, instructions, and fee schedules from your local INS office or by calling the INS Forms Request Line at 1-800-870-3676. You may also download INS forms, instructions, and fee schedules from the INS's Web site, which may be found at http://www.ins.usdoj.gov. Please note that in most cases, the INS has increased the filing fees that are printed on the forms. As a result, you should obtain a current fee schedule before you file anything with the INS.

Form I-539: Application to Extend/Change Nonimmigrant Status

Form I-134: Affidavit of Support

Form I-20: Certificate of Eligibility for Nonimmigrant (F-1) Student Status

Form I-130: Petition for Alien Relative

Form I-485: Application to Register Permanent Residence or Adjust Status

Form G-325A: Biographic Information

Form 9003: Department of the Treasury—Internal Revenue Service Additional Questions

Form M378: Color Photograph Specifications

Form I-864: Affidavit of Support Under Section 213A of the Act

Form I-864A: Contract Between Sponsor and Household Member

Form I-765: Application for Employment Authorization

Form I-751: Petition to Remove Conditions on Residence

Form N-400: Application for Naturalization

U.S. Department of Justice
Immigration and Naturalization Service

OMB No. 1115-0093

Application to Extend/Change Nonimmigrant Status

Purpose Of This Form.
This form is for a nonimmigrant to apply for an extension of stay or change to another nonimmigrant status. However, an employer should file Form I-129 to request an extension/change to E, H, L, O, P, Q or R status for an employee or prospective employee. Dependents of such employees should file for an extension/change of status on this form, not on Form I-129. This form is also for a nonimmigrant F-1 or M-1 student to apply for reinstatement.

This form consists of a basic application and a supplement to list co-applicants.

Who May File.
For extension of stay or change of status.
If you are a nonimmigrant in the U.S., you may apply for an extension of stay or a change of status on this form except as noted above. However, you may not be granted an extension or change of status if you were admitted under the Visa Waiver Program or if your current or proposed status is as:

- an alien in transit (C) or in transit without a visa (TWOV);
- a crewman (D); or
- a fiance(e) or dependent of a fiance(e) (K).

There are additional limits on change of status.

- A J-1 exchange visitor whose status was for the purpose of receiving graduate medical training is ineligible for change of status.
- A J-1 exchange visitor subject to the foreign residence requirement who has not received a waiver of that requirement, is only eligible for a change of status to A or G.
- An M-1 student is not eligible for a change to F-1 status, and is not eligible for a change to any H status if training received as an M-1 student helped him/her qualify for the H status.
- You may not be granted a change to M-1 status for training to qualify for H status.

For F-1 or M-1 student reinstatement. You will only be considered for reinstatement if you establish when filing this application:

- that the violation of status was solely due to circumstances beyond your control or that failure to reinstate you would result in extreme hardship;
- you are pursuing, or will pursue, a full course of study;
- you have not been employed off campus without authorization or, if an F-1 student, that your only unauthorized off-campus employment was pursuant to a scholarship, fellowship, or assistantship, or did not displace a U.S. resident; and
- you are not in deportation proceedings.

Multiple Applicants.
You may include your spouse and your unmarried children under age 21 as co-applicants in your application for the same extension or change of status if you are all in the same status now or they are all in derivative status.

General Filing Instructions.
Please answer all questions by typing or clearly printing in black ink. Indicate that an item is not applicable with "N/A". If the answer is "none," please so state. If you need extra space to answer any item, attach a sheet of paper with your name and your alien registration number (A#), if any, and indicate the number of the item to which the answer refers. Your application must be filed with the required Initial Evidence. Your application must be properly signed and filed with the correct fee. If you are under 14 years of age, your parent or guardian may sign your application.

Copies. If these instructions state that a copy of a document may be filed with this application and you choose to send us the original, we may keep that original for our records.

Translations. Any foreign language document must be accompanied by a full English translation which the translator has certified as complete and correct, and by the translator's certification that he or she is competent to translate from the foreign language into English.

Initial Evidence.
Form I-94, Nonimmigrant Arrival-Departure Record. You must file your application with the original Form I-94, Nonimmigrant Arrival/Departure Record, of each person included in the application, if you are filing for:

- an extension as a B-1 or B-2, or change to such status;
- reinstatement as an F-1 or M-1 or filing for change to F or M status; or
- an extension as a J, or change to such status.

In all other instances, file this application with a copy of the Form I-94 of each person included in the application.

If the required Form I-94 or required copy cannot be submitted, you must file Form I-102, Application for Replacement/Initial Nonimmigrant Arrival/Departure Document, with this application.

Valid Passport. A nonimmigrant who is required to have a passport to be admitted must keep that passport valid during his/her entire nonimmigrant stay. If a required passport is not valid when you file this application, submit an explanation with your application.

Additional Initial Evidence. An application must also be filed with the following evidence.

- If you are filing for an extension/change of status as the dependent of an employee who is an E, H, L, O, P, Q or R nonimmigrant, this application must be filed with:
  - the petition filed for that employee or evidence it is pending with the Service; or
  - a copy of the employee's Form I-94 or approval notice showing that he/she has already been granted status to the period requested in your application.
- If you are requesting an extension/change to A-3 or G-5 status, this application must be filed with:
  - a copy of your employer's Form I-94 or approval notice demonstrating A or G status;
  - an original letter from your employer describing your duties and stating that he/she intends to personally employ you; and
  - an original Form I-566, certified by the Department of State, indicating your employer's continuing accredited diplomatic status.
- If you are filing for an extension/change to other A or G status, you must submit Form I-566, certified by the Department of State to indicate your accredited diplomatic status.
- If you are filing for an extension/change to B-1 or B-2 status, this application must be filed with a statement explaining, in detail,:
  - the reasons for your request;
  - why your extended stay would be temporary including what arrangement you have made to depart the U.S.; and
  - any effect of the extended stay on your foreign employment and residency.
- If you are requesting an extension/change to F-1 or M-1 student status, this application must be filed with an original Form I-20 issued by the school which has accepted you. If you are requesting reinstatement to F-1 or M-1 status, you must also submit evidence establishing that you are eligible for reinstatement.
- If you are filing for an extension/change to I status, this application must be filed with a letter describing the employment and establishing that it is as the representative of qualifying foreign media.
- If you are filing for an extension/change to J-1 exchange visitor status, this application must be filed with an original Form IAP-66 issued by your program sponsor.
- If you are filing for an extension/change to N-1 or N-2 status as the parent or child of an alien admitted as a special immigrant under section 101(a)(27)(I), this application must be filed with a copy of that person's alien registration card.

When To File.
You must submit an application for extension of stay or change of status before your current authorized stay expires. We suggest you file at least 45 days before your stay expires, or as soon as you determine you need to change status. Failure to file before the expiration date may be excused if you demonstrate when you file the application:

- the delay was due to extraordinary circumstances beyond your control;
- the length of the delay was reasonable;
- that you have not otherwise violated your status;
- that you are still a bona fide nonimmigrant; and
- that you are not in deportation proceedings

Form I-539 (Rev. 10/30/98)N

Where To File.
File this application at your local INS office if you are filing:

- for an extension as a B-1 or B-2, or change to such status;
- for reinstatement as an F-1 or M-1 or filing for change to F or M status; or
- for an extension as a J, or change to such status.

In all other instances, file your application at an INS Service Center, as follows:

If you live in Connecticut, Delaware, District of Columbia, Maine, Maryland, Massachusetts, New Hampshire, New Jersey, New York, Pennsylvania, Puerto Rico, Rhode Island, Vermont, Virgin Islands, Virginia, or West Virginia, mail your application to: USINS Eastern Service Center, 75 Lower Welden Street, St. Albans, VT 05479-0001.

If you live in Alabama, Arkansas, Florida, Georgia, Kentucky, Louisiana, Mississippi, New Mexico, North Carolina, Oklahoma, South Carolina, Tennessee, or Texas, mail your application to: USINS Southern Service Center, P.O. Box 152122, Dept. A, Irving, TX 75015-2122.

If you live in Arizona, California, Guam, Hawaii, or Nevada, mail your application to: USINS Western Service Center, P.O. Box 30040, Laguna Niguel, CA 92607-0040.

If you live elsewhere in the United States, mail your application to: USINS Northern Service Center, 100 Centennial Mall North, Room, B-26, Lincoln, NE 68508.

Fee.
The fee for this application is $120.00. The fee must be submitted in the exact amount. It cannot be refunded. DO NOT MAIL CASH.

All checks and money orders must be drawn on a bank or other institution located in the United States and must be payable in United States currency. The check or money order should be made payable to the Immigration and Naturalization Service, except that:

- If you live in Guam, and are filing this application in Guam, make your check or money order payable to the "Treasurer, Guam."
- If you live in the Virgin Islands, and are filing this application in the Virgin Islands, make your check or money order payable to the "Commissioner of Finance of the Virgin Islands."

Checks are accepted subject to collection. An uncollected check will render the application and any document issued invalid. A charge of $30.00 will be imposed if a check in payment of a fee is not honored by the bank on which it is drawn.

Processing Information.
Acceptance. Any application that is not signed or is not accompanied by the correct fee will be rejected with a notice that the application is deficient. You may correct the deficiency and resubmit the application. An application is not considered properly filed until accepted by the Service.

Initial processing. Once the application has been accepted, it will be checked for completeness. If you do not completely fill out the form, or file it without required initial evidence, you will not establish a basis for eligibility, and we may deny your application.

Requests for more information or interview. We may request more information or evidence or we may request that you appear at an INS office for an interview. We may also request that you submit the originals of any copy. We will return these originals when they are no longer required.

Decision. An application for extension of stay, change of status, or reinstatement may be approved in the discretion of the Service. You will be notified in writing of the decision on your application.

Penalties.
If you knowingly and willfully falsify or conceal a material fact or submit a false document with this request, we will deny the benefit you are filing for, and may deny any other immigration benefit. In addition, you will face severe penalties provided by law, and may be subject to criminal prosecution.

Privacy Act Notice.
We ask for the information on this form, and associated evidence, to determine if you have established eligibility for the immigration benefit you are filing for. Our legal right to ask for this information is in 8 USC 1184, and 1258. We may provide this information to other government agencies. Failure to provide this information, and any requested evidence, may delay a final decision or result in denial of your request.

Paperwork Reduction Act Notice.
A person is not required to respond to a collection of information unless it displays a currently valid OMB control number. We try to create forms and instructions that are accurate, can be easily understood, and which impose the least possible burden on you to provide us with information. Often this is difficult because some immigration laws are very complex. The estimated average time to complete and file this application is as follows: (1) 10 minutes to learn about the law and form; (2) 10 minutes to complete the form; and (3) 25 minutes to assemble and file the application; for a total estimated average of 45 per application. If you have comments regarding the accuracy of this estimate, or suggestions for making this form simpler, you can write to both the Immigration and Naturalization Service, 425 I Street, N.W., Room 5307, Washington, D.C. 20536; OMB No. 1115-0093. DO NOT MAIL YOUR COMPLETED APPLICATION TO THIS ADDRESS.

Mailing Label--Complete the following mailing label and submit this page with your application if you are required to submit your original Form I-94.

Name and address of applicant

Name

Street

City, State, & Zip Code

Your I-94 Arrival-Departure Record is attached. It has been amended to show the extension of stay/change of status granted.

U.S. Department of Justice
Immigration and Naturalization Service

OMB No. 1115-0093

Additional Instructions for Form I-539

The North American Free Trade Agreement (NAFTA), which entered into force on January 1, 1994, created a new nonimmigrant classification, TN. TN nonimmigrants are Canadian citizen or Mexican citizen business persons who are coming to the United States to engage in business activities at a professional level.

Dependents of TN Nonimmigrants:
The dependents (spouse or unmarried minor children) of a TN nonimmigrant professional are designated as TD nonimmigrants. A TD nonimmigrant may accompany or follow to join the TN professional. TD nonimmigrants may not work in the United States.

Form I-539 shall be used by a TD nonimmigrant to request an extension of stay or by an alien to request a change of nonimmigrant status to TD classification.

Requirements:
(1) If applying for an extension of stay at the same time as the TN professional, the TD dependent shall file Form I-539 along with the Form I-129 for the TN professional. The same is true if the alien is applying for a change of nonimmigrant status to TD at the same time that the professional is applying for a change of nonimmigrant status to TN.

(2) If the alien is not applying for an extension of stay as a TD at the same time that the TN professional is applying for an extension, or is applying for a change of nonimmigrant status to TD after the TN nonimmigrant obtains status, the alien must present a copy of the TN's Form I-94, Nonimmigrant Arrival/Departure Record, to establish that the TN is maintaining valid nonimmigrant status.

(3) Dependents of TN nonimmigrants must be physically present in the United States at the time the application to extend or change nonimmigrant status is filed.

Where to File:
When filing for an extension of TD status or for a change of nonimmigrant status to TD, Form I-539 should be filed with the Director of the Northern Service Center.

Fee:
An application for extension of TD status or for a change of nonimmigrant status to TD must be submitted with the fee required by Form I-539.

Form I-539 (Rev. 10/01/93)N

U.S. Department of Justice
Immigration and Naturalization Service

OMB No.1115-0093
Application to Extend/ChangeNonimmigrant Status

START HERE - Please Type or Print

Part 1. Information about you.

Family Name	Given Name	Middle Initial

Address - In Care of:

Street # and Name		Apt. #

City	State

Zip Code	

Date of Birth (month/day/year)	Country of Birth

Social Security # (if any)	A# (if any)

Date of Last Arrival Into the U.S.	I-94#

Current Nonimmigrant Status	Expires on (month/day/year)

Part 2. Application Type. (See Instructions for fee.)

1. I am applying for: (check one)
   a. ☐ an extension of stay in my current status
   b. ☐ a change of status. The new status I am requesting is: _____
2. Number of people included in this application: (check one)
   a. ☐ I am the only applicant
   b. ☐ Members of my family are filing this application with me.
      The Total number of people included in this application is _____
      (complete the supplement for each co-applicant)

Part 3. Processing Information.

1. I/We request that my/our current or requested status be extended until (month/day/year) _____

2. Is this application based on an extension or change of status already granted to your spouse, child or parent?
   ☐ No   ☐ Yes (receipt #_____)

3. Is this application being filed based on a separate petition or application to give your spouse, child or parent an extension or change of status?
   ☐ No   ☐ Yes, filed with this application   ☐ Yes, filed previously and pending with INS

4. If you answered yes to question 3, give the petitioner or applicant name:

If the application is pending with INS, also give the following information.

   Office filed at_____ Filed on_____ (date)

Part 4. Additional Information.

1. For applicant #1, provide passport information:
Country of issuance	Valid to: (month/day/year)
2. Foreign address:
Street # and Name		Apt#

City or Town	State or Province

Country	Zip or Postal Code

FOR INS USE ONLY

Returned	Receipt
Date	
Resubmitted	
Date	
Reloc Sent	
Date	
Reloc Rec'd	
Date	
Date	
☐ Applicant Interviewed	

☐ *Extension Granted*
   to (date):_____

☐ *Change of Status/Extension Granted*
New Class:_____ To (date):_____

If denied:
☐ Still within period of stay

☐ V/D to: _____

☐ S/D to:_____

☐ Place under docket control

Remarks

Action Block

To Be Completed by
Attorney or Representative, if any

☐ Fill in box if G-28 is attached to represent the applicant

VOLAG#

ATTY State License #

Continued on back.

Form I-539 (Rev. 10/03/91)N

Part 4.   Additional Information. *(continued)*

3. Answer the following questions. If you answer yes to any question, explain on separate paper.	Yes	No
a. Are you, or any other person included in this application, an applicant for an immigrant visa or adjustment of status to permanent residence?		
b. Has an immigrant petition ever been filed for you, or for any other person included in this application?		
c. Have you, or any other person included in this application ever been arrested or convicted of any criminal offense since last entering the U.S.?		
d. Have you, or any other person included in this application done anything which violated the terms of the nonimmigrant status you now hold?		
e. Are you, or any other person included in this application, now in exclusion or deportation proceedings?		
f. Have you, or any other person included in this application, been employed in the U.S. since last admitted or granted an extension or change of status?		

If you answered YES to question 3f, give the following information on a separate paper: Name of person, name of employer, address of employer, weekly income, and whether specifically authorized by INS.

If you answered NO to question 3f, fully describe how you are supporting yourself on a separate paper. Include the source and the amount and basis for any income.

Part 5.   Signature.   *Read the information on penalties in the instructions before completing this section. You must file this application while in the United States.*

I certify under penalty of perjury under the laws of the United States of America that this application, and the evidence submitted with it, is all true and correct. I authorize the release of any information from my records which the Immigration and Naturalization Service needs to determine eligibility for the benefit I am seeking.

Signature	Print your name	Date

Please Note: *If you do not completely fill out this form, or fail to submit required documents listed in the instructions, you cannot be found eligible for the requested document and this application will have to be denied.*

Part 6.   Signature of person preparing form if other than above. *(Sign below)*

I declare that I prepared this application at the request of the above person and it is based on all information of which I have knowledge.

Signature	Print Your Name	Date

Firm Name
and Address

(Please remember to enclose the mailing label with your application)

Form I-539 (Rev. 10/91) N

OMB No. 1115-0062

U. S. Department of Justice
Immigration and Naturalization Service

Affidavit of Support

(ANSWER ALL ITEMS: FILL IN WITH TYPEWRITER OR PRINT IN BLOCK LETTERS IN INK.)

I, _____, *residing at* _____
　　　　　　　(Name)　　　　　　　　　　　　　　　　　　　　　　　　(Street and Number)

_____
　　　　(City)　　　　　　　　　　(State)　　　　　　　(ZIP Code if in U.S.)　　　　　(Country)

BEING DULY SWORN DEPOSE AND SAY:

1. I was born on_____ at _____
　　　　　　　　　(Date)　　　　　　　　　　　　(City)　　　　　　　　　(Country)

　　If you are *not* a native born United States citizen, answer the following as appropriate:

　　a. If a United States citizen through naturalization, give certificate of naturalization number _____

　　b. If a United States citizen through parent(s) or marriage, give citizenship certificate number _____

　　c. If United States citizenship was derived by some other method, attach a statement of explanation.

　　d. If a lawfully admitted permanent resident of the United States, give "A" number _____

2. That I am_____years of age and have resided in the United States since (date) _____

3. That this affidavit is executed in behalf of the following person:

Name		Sex	Age
Citizen of–(Country)	Marital Status	Relationship to Deponent	
Presently resides at–(Street and Number)	(City)	(State)	(Country)

Name of spouse and children accompanying or following to join person:

Spouse	Sex	Age	Child	Sex	Age
Child	Sex	Age	Child	Sex	Age
Child	Sex	Age	Child	Sex	Age

4. That this affidavit is made by me for the purpose of assuring the United States Government that the person(s) named in item 3 will not become a public charge in the United States.

5. That I am willing and able to receive, maintain and support the person(s) named in item 3. That I am ready and willing to deposit a bond, if necessary, to guarantee that such person(s) will not become a public charge during his or her stay in the United States, or to guarantee that the above named will maintain his or her nonimmigrant status if admitted temporarily and will depart prior to the expiration of his or her authorized stay in the United States.

6. That I understand this affidavit will be binding upon me for a period of three (3) years after entry of the person(s) named in item 3 and that the information and documentation provided by me may be made available to the Secretary of Health and Human Services and the Secretary of Agriculture, who may make it available to a public assistance agency.

7. That I am employed as, or engaged in the business of _____ with _____
　　　　　　　　　　　　　　　　　　　　　　　　　(Type of Business)　　　　　　　　　　(Name of concern)

at _____
　　　(Street and Number)　　　　　　　　(City)　　　　　　　　(State)　　　　　(Zip Code)

I derive an annual income of *(if self-employed, I have attached a copy of my last income tax return or report of commercial rating concern which I certify to be true and correct to the best of my knowledge and belief. See instruction for nature of evidence of net worth to be submitted.)*　　　　　　　　　　　　　　　　　　　　　　　　　$_____

I have on deposit in savings banks in the United States　　　　　　　$_____

I have other personal property, the reasonable value of which is　　　$_____

OVER

I have stocks and bonds with the following market value, as indicated on the attached list
which I certify to be true and correct to the best of my knowledge and belief. $ _____

I have life insurance in the sum of $ _____

With a cash surrender value of $ _____

I own real estate valued at $ _____

With mortgages or other encumbrances thereon amounting to $ _____

Which is located at _____
(Street and Number)   (City)   (State)   (Zip Code)

8. That the following persons are dependent upon me for support: (*Place an "X" in the appropriate column to indicate whether the person named is wholly or partially dependent upon you for support.*)

Name of Person	Wholly Dependent	Partially Dependent	Age	Relationship to Me

9. That I have previously submitted affidavit(s) of support for the following person(s). If none, state *"None"*

Name   Date submitted
_____

_____

_____

10. That I have submitted visa petition(s) to the Immigration and Naturalization Service on behalf of the following person(s). If none, state none.

Name   Relationship   Date submitted
_____

_____

_____

11.(*Complete this block only if the person named in item 3 will be in the United States temporarily.*)
   That I ☐ do intend   ☐ do not intend, to make specific contributions to the support of the person named in item 3. (*If you check "do intend", indicate the exact nature and duration of the contributions. For example, if you intend to furnish room and board, state for how long and, if money, state the amount in United States dollars and state whether it is to be given in a lump sum, weekly, or monthly, or for how long.*)

_____

_____

_____

OATH OR AFFIRMATION OF DEPONENT

I acknowledge at that I have read Part III of the Instructions, Sponsor and Alien Liability, and am aware of my responsibilities as an immigrant sponsor under the Social Security Act, as amended, and the Food Stamp Act, as amended.

I swear (affirm) that I know the contents of this affidavit signed by me and the statements are true and correct.

Signature of deponent _____

Subscribed and sworn to (affirmed) before me this _____ *day of* _____ , 19_____

at _____ . *My commission expires on* _____

Signature of Officer Administering Oath _____ *Title* _____

If affidavit prepared by other than deponent, please complete the following: I declare that this document was prepared by me at the request of the deponent and is based on all information of which I have knowledge.

_____
(*Signature*)   (*Address*)   (*Date*)

U.S. Department of Justice
Immigration and Naturalization Service
Please Read Instructions on Page 2

Certificate of Eligibility for Nonimmigrant (F-1) Student Status - For Academic and Language Students

OMB No. 1115-0051

Page 1

This page must be completed and signed in the U.S. by a designated school official.

1. Family Name (surname)

   First (given) name (do not enter middle name)

Country of birth	Date of birth (mo./day/year)

Country of citizenship	Admission number (Complete if known)

   For Immigration Official Use

Visa issuing post	Date Visa issued

   Reinstated, extension granted to:

2. School (school district) name

   School official to be notified of student's arrival in U.S. (Name and Title)

   School address (include zip code)

   School code (including 3-digit suffix, if any) and approval date

   _____ 214F_____ approved on _____

3. This certificate is issued to the student named above for:
   (Check and fill out as appropriate)

   a. ☐ Initial attendance at this school

   b. ☐ Continued attendance at this school

   c. ☐ School transfer.
   Transferred from _____

   d. ☐ Use by dependents for entering the United States.

   e. ☐ Other _____

4. Level of education the student is pursuing or will pursue in the United States:
   (check only one)

   a. ☐ Primary   e. ☐ Master's

   b. ☐ Secondary   f. ☐ Doctorate

   c. ☐ Associate   g. ☐ Language training

   d. ☐ Bachelor's   h. ☐ Other

5. The student named above has been accepted for a full course of study at this school, majoring in_____

   The student is expected to report to the school no later than (date) _____ and complete studies not later than (date)_____

   The normal length of study is _____

6. ☐ English proficiency is required:

   ☐ The student has the required English proficiency

   ☐ The student is not yet proficient, English instructions will be given at the school.

   ☐ English proficiency is not required because_____

7. This school estimates the student's average costs for an academic term of _____ (up to 12) months to be:

   a. Tuition and fees $_____

   b. Living expenses $_____

   c. Expenses of dependents $_____

   d. Other(specify):books $_____

   Total $_____ 0.00

8. This school has information showing the following as the students means of support, estimated for an academic term of _____ months (Use the same number of months given in item 7).

   a. Student's personal funds $_____

   b. Funds from this school
   (specify type) $_____

   c. Funds from another source
   (specify type and source) $_____

   d. On-campus employment (if any) $_____

   Total $_____ 0.00

9. Remarks: _____
   _____
   _____
   _____
   _____
   _____

10. School Certification: I certify under penalty of perjury that all information provided above in items 1 through 8 was completed before I signed this form and is true and correct; I executed this form in the United States after review and evaluation in the United States by me or other officials of the school of the student's application, transcripts or other records of courses taken and proof of financial responsibility, which were received at the school prior to the execution of this form; the school has determined that the above named student's qualifications meet all standards for admission to the school; the student will be required to pursue a full course of study as defined by 8 CFR 214.2(f)(6); I am a designated official of the above named school and I am authorized to issue this form.

Signature of designated school official	Name of school official (print or type)	Title	Date issued	Place issued (city and state)

11. Student Certification: I have read and agreed to comply with the terms and conditions of my admission and those of any extension of stay as specified on page 2. I certify that all information provided on this form refers specifically to me and is true and correct to the best of my knowledge. I certify that I seek to enter or remain in the United States temporarily, and solely for the purpose of pursuing a full course of study at the school named on page 1 of this form. I also authorize the named school to release any information from my records which is needed by the INS pursuant to 8 CFR 214.3(g) to determine my nonimmigrant status.

Signature of student	Name of student		Date

Signature of parent or guardian if student is under 18	Name of parent/guardian (Print or type)	Address(city)	(State or province)	(Country)	(Date)

Form I20 A-B/I20ID(Rev 04-27-88)N

For official use only
Microfilm Index Number

Authority for collecting the information on this and related student forms is contained in 8 U.S.C. 1101 and 1184. The information solicited will be used by the Department of State and the Immigration and Naturalization Service to determine eligibility for the benefits requested.

INSTRUCTIONS TO DESIGNATED SCHOOL OFFICIALS

1. The law provides severe penalties for knowingly and willfully falsifying or concealing a material fact or using any false document in the submission of this form. Designated school officials should consult regulations pertaining to the issuance of Form I-20 A-B at 8 CFR 214.3 (K) before completing this form. Failure to comply with these regulations may result in the withdrawal of the school approval for attendance by foreign students by the Immigration and Naturalization Service (8 CFR 214.4).

2. ISSUANCE OF FORM I-20 A-B. Designated school officials may issue a Form I-20 A-B to a student who fits into one of the following categories, if the student has been accepted for full-time attendance at the institution: a) a prospective F-1 nonimmigrant student; b) an F-1 transfer student; c) an F-1 student advancing to a higher educational level at the same institution; d) an out of status student seeking reinstatement. The form may also be issued to the dependent spouse or child of an F-1 student for securing entry into the United States.

When issuing a Form I-20 A-B, designated school officials should complete the student's admission number whenever possible to ensure proper data entry and record keeping.

3. ENDORSEMENT OF PAGE 4 FOR REENTRY. Designated school officials may endorse page 4 of the Form I-20 A-B for reentry if the student and/or the F-2 dependents is to leave the United States temporarily. This should be done only when the information on the Form I-20 remains unchanged. If there have been substantial changes in item 4, 5, 7, or 8, a new Form I-20 A-B should be issued.

4. REPORTING REQUIREMENT. Designated school official should always forward the top page of the form I-20 A-B to the INS data processing center at P.O. Box 140, London, Kentucky 40741 for data entry except when the form is issued to an F-1 student for initial entry or reentry into the United States, or for reinstatement to student status. (Requests for reinstatement should be sent to the Immigration and Naturalization Service district office having jurisdiction over the student's temporary residence in this country.)

The INS data processing center will return this top page to the issuing school for disposal after data entry and microfilming.

5. CERTIFICATION. Designated school officials should certify on the bottom part of page 1 of this form that the Form I-20 A-B is completed and issued in accordance with the pertinent regulations. The designated school official should remove the carbon sheet from the completed and signed Form I-20 A-B before forwarding it to the student.

6. ADMISSION RECORDS. Since the Immigration and Naturalization Service may request information concerning the student's immigration status for various reasons, designated school officials should retain all evidence which shows the scholastic ability and financial status on which admission was based, until the school has reported the student's termination of studies to the Immigration and Naturalization Service.

INSTRUCTIONS TO STUDENTS

1. Student Certification. You should read everything on this page carefully and be sure that you understand the terms and conditions concerning your admission and stay in the United States as a nonimmigrant student before you sign the student certification on the bottom part of page 1. **The law provides severe penalties for knowingly and willfully falsifying or concealing a material fact, or using any false document in the submission of this form.**

2. ADMISSION. A nonimmigrant student may be admitted for duration of status. This means that you are authorized to stay in the United States for the entire length of time during which you are enrolled as a full-time stu-

dent in an educational program and any period of authorized practical training plus sixty days. While in the United States, you must maintain a valid foreign passport unless you are exempt from passport requirements.

You may continue from one educational level to another, such as progressing from high school to a bachelor's program or a bachelor's program to a master's program, etc., simply by invoking the procedures for school transfers.

3. SCHOOL. For initial admission, you must attend the school specified on your visa. If you have a Form I-20 A-B from more than one school, it is important to have the name of the school you intend to attend specified on your visa by presenting a Form I-20 A-B from that school to the visa issuing consular officer. Failure to attend the specified school will result in the loss of your student status and subject you to deportation.

4. REENTRY. A nonimmigrant student may be readmitted after a temporary absence of five months or less from the United States, if the student is otherwise admissible. You may be readmitted by presenting a valid foreign passport, a valid visa, and either a new Form I-20 A-B or a page 4 of the Form I-20 A-B (the I-20 ID Copy) properly endorsed for reentry if the information on the I-20 form is current.

5. TRANSFER. A nonimmigrant student is permitted to transfer to a different school provided the transfer procedure is followed. To transfer school, you should first notify the school you are attending of the intent to transfer, then obtain a Form I-20 A-B from the school you intend to attend. Transfer will be effected only if you return the Form I-20 A-B to the designated school official within 15 days of beginning attendance at the new school. The designated school official will then report the transfer to the Immigration and Naturalization Service.

6. EXTENSION OF STAY. If you cannot complete the educational program after having been in student status for longer than the anticipated length of the program plus a grace period in a single educational level, or for more than eight consecutive years, you must apply for extension of stay. An application for extension of stay on a Form I-538 should be filed with the Immigration and Naturalization Service district office having jurisdiction over your school at least 15 days but no more than 60 days before the expiration of your authorized stay.

7. EMPLOYMENT. As an F-1 student, you are not permitted to work off campus or to engage in business without specific employment authorization. After your first year in F-1 student status, you may apply for employment authorization on Form I-538 based on financial needs arising after receiving student status, or the need to obtain practical training.

8. Notice of Address. If you move, you must submit a notice within 10 days of the change of address to the Immigration and Naturalization Service. (Form AR-11 is available at any INS office.)

9. Arrival/Departure. When you leave the United States, you must surrender your Form I-94 Departure Record. Please see back side of Form I-94 for detailed instructions. You do not have to turn in the I-94 if you are visiting Canada, Mexico, or adjacent islands other than Cuba for less than 30 days.

10. Financial Support. You must demonstrate that you are financially able to support yourself for the entire period of stay in the United States while pursuing a full course of study. You are required to attach documentary evidence of means of support.

11. Authorization to Release Information by School. To comply with requests from the United States Immigration & Naturalization Service for information concerning your immigration status, you are required to give authorization to the named school to release such information from your records. The school will provide the Service your name, country of birth, current address, and any other information on a regular basis or upon request.

12. Penalty. To maintain your nonimmigrant student status, you must be enrolled as a full-time student at the school you are authorized to attend. You may engage in employment only when you have received permission to work. Failure to comply with these regulations will result in the loss of your student status and subject you to deportation.

Public Reporting Burden. Reporting burden for this collection of information is estimated to average 30 minutes per response. If you have comments regarding the accuracy of this estimate, or suggestions for simplifying this form, you can write to both the U.S. Department of Justice, Immigration and Naturalization Service (Room 5304), Washington, D.C., 20536; and to the Office of Management and Budget, Paperwork Reduction Project: OMB No. 1115-0051; Washington, D.C. 20503.

U.S. Department of Justice
Immigration and Naturalization Service
Please Read Instructions on Page 2

**Certificate of Eligibility for Nonimmigrant (F-1) Student
Status - For Academic and Language Students**

OMB No. 1115-0051

Page 3

This page must be completed and signed in the U.S. by a designated school official.

1. Family Name (surname)

   First (given) name (do not enter middle name)

Country of birth	Date of birth (mo./day/year)

Country of citizenship	Admission number (Complete if known)

   For Immigration Official Use

Visa issuing post	Date Visa issued

2. School (school district) name

   School official to be notified of student's arrival in U.S. (Name and Title)

   School address (include zip code)

   School code (including 3-digit suffix, if any) and approval date

   _____ 214F_____ approved on _____

   Reinstated, extension granted to:

3. This certificate is issued to the student named above for:
   (Check and fill out as appropriate)
   a. ☐ Initial attendance at this school
   b. ☐ Continued attendance at this school
   c. ☐ School transfer.
      Transferred from _____
   d. ☐ Use by dependents for entering the United States.
   e. ☐ Other _____

4. Level of education the student is pursuing or will pursue in the United States:
   (check only one)
   a. ☐ Primary   e. ☐ Master's
   b. ☐ Secondary   f. ☐ Doctorate
   c. ☐ Associate   g. ☐ Language training
   d. ☐ Bachelor's   h. ☐ Other

5. The student named above has been accepted for a full course of study at
   this school, majoring in_____
   The student is expected to report to the school no later than (date)
   _____ and complete studies not later than (date)_____
   The normal length of study is _____

6. ☐ English proficiency is required:
   ☐ The student has the required English proficiency
   ☐ The student is not yet proficient, English instructions will be given at
      the school.
   ☐ English proficiency is not required because_____

7. This school estimates the student's average costs for an academic term of
   _____ (up to 12) months to be:
   a. Tuition and fees $ _____
   b. Living expenses $ _____
   c. Expenses of dependents $ _____
   d. Other(specify):books $ _____
   Total $ _____ 0.00

8. This school has information showing the following as the students means of
   support, estimated for an academic term of _____ months (Use the same
   number of months given in item 7).
   a. Student's personal funds $ _____
   b. Funds from this school $ _____
      (specify type)   _____
   c. Funds from another source $ _____
      (specify type and source)   _____
   d. On-campus employment (if any) $ _____
   Total $ _____ 0.00

9. Remarks: _____
   _____
   _____
   _____
   _____

10. School Certification: I certify under penalty of perjury that all information provided above in items 1 through 8 was completed before I signed this form and is true and correct; I executed this form in the United States after review and evaluation in the United States by me or other officials of the school of the student's application, transcripts or other records of courses taken and proof of financial responsibility, which were received at the school prior to the execution of this form; the school has determined that the above named student's qualifications meet all standards for admission to the school; the student will be required to pursue a full course of study as defined by 8 CFR 214.2(f)(6); I am a designated official of the above named school and I am authorized to issue this form.

Signature of designated school official	Name of school official (print or type)	Title	Date issued	Place issued (city and state)

11. Student Certification: I have read and agreed to comply with the terms and conditions of my admission and those of any extension of stay as specified on page 2. I certify that all information provided on this form refers specifically to me and is true and correct to the best of my knowledge. I certify that I seek to enter or remain in the United States temporarily, and solely for the purpose of pursuing a full course of study at the school named on page 1 of this form. I also authorize the named school to release any information from my records which is needed by the INS pursuant to 8 CFR 214.3(g) to determine my nonimmigrant status.

Signature of student	Name of student		Date

Signature of parent or guardian if student is under 18	Name of parent/guardian (Print or type)	Address(city)	(State or province)	(Country)	(Date)

    For official use only
    Microfilm Index Number

Form I20 A-B/I20ID(Rev 04-27-88)N

Page 4

IF YOU NEED MORE INFORMATION CONCERNING YOUR F-1 NONIMMIGRANT STUDENT STATUS AND THE RELATING IMMIGRATION PROCEDURES, PLEASE CONTACT EITHER YOUR FOREIGN STUDENT ADVISOR ON CAMPUS OR A NEARBY IMMIGRATION AND NATURALIZATION SERVICE OFFICE.

THIS PAGE, WHEN PROPERLY ENDORSED, MAY BE USED FOR ENTRY OF THE SPOUSE AND CHILDREN OF AN F-1 STUDENT FOLLOWING TO JOIN THE STUDENT IN THE UNITED STATES OR FOR REENTRY OF THE STUDENT TO ATTEND THE SAME SCHOOL AFTER A TEMPORARY ABSENCE FROM THE UNITED STATES.

For reentry of the student and/or the F-2 dependents (EACH CERTIFICATION SIGNATURE IS VALID FOR ONLY ONE YEAR.)

Signature of Designated School Official	Name of School Official(print or type)	Title	Date
Signature of Designated School Official	Name of School Official(print or type)	Title	Date
Signature of Designated School Official	Name of School Official(print or type)	Title	Date
Signature of Designated School Official	Name of School Official(print or type)	Title	Date
Signature of Designated School Official	Name of School Official(print or type)	Title	Date
Signature of Designated School Official	Name of School Official(print or type)	Title	Date

Dependent spouse and children of the F-1 student who are seeking entry/reentry to the U.S.

Name family (caps) first	Date of birth	Country of birth	Relationship to the F-1 student

Student Employment Authorization and other Records

U.S. Department of Justice
Immigration and Naturalization Service (INS)

Petition for Alien Relative

Instructions

Read the instructions carefully. If you do not follow the instructions, we may have to return your petition, which may delay final action. If more space is needed to complete an answer continue on separate sheet of paper.

1. Who can file?
A citizen or lawful permanent resident of the United States can file this form to establish the relationship of certain alien relatives who may wish to immigrate to the United States. You must file a separate form for each eligible relative.

2. For whom can you file?
A. If you are a citizen, you may file this form for:
   1) your husband, wife, or unmarried child under 21 years old
   2) your unmarried child over 21, or married child of any age
   3) your brother or sister if you are at least 21 years old
   4) your parent if you are at least 21 years

B. If you are a lawful permanent resident you may file this form for:
   1) your husband or wife
   2) your unmarried child

Note: If your relative qualifies under instruction A(2) or A(3) above, separate petitions are not required for his or her husband or wife or unmarried children under 21 years old. If your relative qualifies under instruction B(2) above, separate petitions are not required for his or her unmarried children under 21 years old. These persons will be able to apply for the same type of immigrant visa as your relative.

3. For whom can you not file?
You cannot file for people in the following categories:
A. An adoptive parent or adopted child, if the adoption took place after the child became 16 years old, or if the child has not been in the legal custody and living with the parent(s) for at least two years.
B. A natural parent if the United States citizen son or daughter gained permanent residence through adoption.
C. A stepparent or stepchild, if the marriage that created this relationship took place after the child became 18 years old.
D. A husband or wife, if your were not both physically present at the marriage ceremony, and the marriage was not consummated.
E. A husband or wife if you gained lawful permanent resident status by virtue of a prior marriage to a United States citizen or lawful permanent resident unless:
   1) a period of five years has elapsed since you became a lawful permanent resident; OR
   2) you can establish by clear and convincing evidence that the prior marriage (through which you gained your immigrant status) was not entered into for the purpose of evading any provision of the immigration laws; OR
   3) your prior marriage (through which you gained your immigrant status) was terminated by the death of your former spouse.
F. A husband or wife if he or she was in exclusion, deportation, rescission, or judicial proceedings regarding his or her right to remain in the United States when the marriage took place, unless such spouse has resided outside the United States for a two-year period after the date of the marriage.
G. A husband or wife if the Attorney General has determined that such an alien has attempted or conspired to enter into a marriage for the purpose of evading the immigration laws.
H. A grandparent, grandchild, nephew, niece, uncle, aunt, cousin, or in-law.

4. What documents do you need?
You must give INS certain documents with this form to prove you are eligible to file. You must also give the INS certain documents to prove the family relations between you and your relative.
A. For each document needed, give INS the original and one copy. However, because it is against the law to copy a Certificate of Naturalization, a Certificate of Citizenship or an Alien Registration Receipt Card (Form I-151 or I-551) give INS the original only. Originals will be returned to you.
B. If you do not wish to give INS the original document, you may give INS a copy. The copy must be certified by:
   1) an INS or U.S. consular officer, or
   2) an attorney admitted to practice law in the United States, or
   3) an INS accredited representative (INS may still require originals).
C. Documents in a foreign language must be accompanied by a complete English translation. The translator must certify that the translation is accurate and that he or she is competent to translate.

5. What documents do you need to show you are a United States citizen?
A. If you were born in the United States, give INS your birth certificate.
B. If you were naturalized, give INS your original Certificate of Naturalization.
C. If you were born outside the United States, and you are a U.S. citizen through your parents, give INS:
   1) your original Certificate of Citizenship, or
   2) your Form FS-240 (Report of Birth Abroad of a United States Citizen).
D. In place of any of the above, you may give INS your valid unexpired U.S. passport that was initially issued for at least 5 years.
E. If you do not have any of the above and were born in the United States, see instruction under 8 below. *"What if a document is not available?"*

6. What documents do you need to show you are a permanent resident?
You must give INS your alien registration receipt card (Form I-151 or Form I-551). Do not give INS a photocopy of the card.

7. What documents do you need to prove family relationship?
You have to prove that there is a family relationship between your relative and yourself.

In any case where a marriage certificate is required, if either the husband or wife was married before, you must give INS documents to show that all previous marriages were legally ended. In cases where the names shown on the supporting documents have changed, give INS legal documents to show how the name change occurred (for example a marriage certificate, adoption decree, court order, etc.)

Find the paragraph in the following list that applies to the relative for whom you are filing.

Form I-130 (Rev. 10/13/98)N

If you are filing for your:

A. **husband or wife,** give INS
   1) your marriage certificate
   2) a color photo of you and one of your husband or wife, taken within 30 days of the date of this petition. These photos must have a white background. They must be glossy, unretouched, and not mounted. The dimension of the facial image should be about 1 inch from chin to top of hair in 3/4 frontal view, showing the right side of the face with the right ear visible. Using pencil or felt pen, lightly print name (and Alien Registration Number, if known) on the back of each photograph.
   3) a completed and signed G-325A (Biographic Information) for you and one for your husband or wife. Except for name and signature, you do not have to repeat on the G-325A the information given on your I-130 petition.

B. **child and you are the mother,** give the child's birth certificate showing your name and the name of your child.

C. **child and you are the father or stepparent,** give the child's birth certificate showing both parents' names and your marriage certificate. **Child born out of wedlock and you are the father,** give proof that a parent/child relationship exists or existed. For example, the child's birth certificate showing your name and evidence that you have financially supported the child. (A blood test may be necessary).

D. **brother or sister,** your birth certificate and the birth certificate of your brother or sister showing both parents' names. If you do not have the same mother, you must also give the marriage certificates of your father to both mothers.

E. **mother,** give your birth certificate showing your name and the name of your mother.

F. **father,** give your birth certificate showing the names of both parents and your parents' marriage certificate.

G. **stepparent,** give your birth certificate showing the names of both natural parents and the marriage certificate of your parent to your stepparent.

H. **adoptive parent or adopted child,** give a certified copy of the adoption decree, the legal custody decree if you obtained custody of the child before adoption, and a statement showing the dates and places you have lived together with the child.

8. **What if a document is not available?**

   If the documents needed above are not available, you can give INS the following instead. (INS may require a statement from the appropriate civil authority certifying that the needed document is not available.)

   A. Church record: A certificate under the seal of the church where the baptism, dedication, or comparable rite occurred within two months after birth, showing the date and place of child's birth, date of the religious ceremony, and the names of the child's parents.

   B. School record: A letter from the authorities of the school attended (preferably the first school), showing the date of admission to the school, child's date and place of birth, and the names and places of birth parents, if shown in the school records.

   C. Census record: State or federal census record showing the names, place of birth, and date of birth or the age of the person listed.

   D. Affidavits: Written statements sworn to or affirmed by two persons who were living at the time and who have personal knowledge of the event you are trying to prove; for example, the date and place of birth, marriage, or death. The persons making the affidavits need not be citizens of the United States. Each affidavit should contain the following information regarding the person making the affidavit his or her full name, address, date and place of birth, and his or her relationship to you, if any; full information concerning the event; and complete details concerning how the person acquired knowledge of the event.

9. **How should you prepare this form?**
   A. Type or print legibly in ink.
   B. If you need extra space to complete any item, attach a continuation sheet, indicate the item number, and date and sign each sheet.
   C. Answer all questions fully and accurately. If any item does not apply, please write "N/A".

10. **Where should you file this form?**
    A. If you live in the United States, send or take the form to the INS office that has jurisdiction over where you live.
    B. If you live outside the United States, contact the nearest American Consulate to find out where to send or take the completed form.

11. **What is the fee?**
    You must pay one hundred ten dollars ($110.00) to file this form. **The fee will not be refunded, whether the petition is approved or not.** DO NOT MAIL CASH. All checks or money orders, whether U.S. or foreign, must be payable in U.S. currency at a financial institution in the United States. When a check is drawn on the account of a person other than yourself, write your name on the face of the check. If the check is not honored, INS will charge you $30.00.

    Pay by check or money order in the exact amount. Make the check Or money order payable to "Immigration and Naturalization Service". However,
    A. if you live in Guam: Make the check or money order payable to Treasurer, Guam", or
    B. if you live in the U.S. Virgin Islands: Make the check or money order payable to "Commissioner of Finance of the Virgin Islands".

12. **When will a visa become available?**
    When a petition is approved for the husband, wife, parent, or unmarried minor child of a United States citizen, these relatives do not have to wait for a visa number, as they are not subject to the immigrant visa limit. However, for a child to qualify for this category, all processing must be completed and the child must enter the United States before his or her 21st birthday.

    For all other alien relatives there are only a limited number of immigrant visas each year. The visas are given out in the order in which INS receives properly filed petitions. To be considered properly filed, a petition must be completed accurately and signed, the required documents must be attached, and the fee must be paid.

    For a monthly update on the dates for which immigrant visas are available, you may call (202) 647-0508.

13. **What are the penalties for committing marriage fraud or submitting false information or both?**
    Title 8, United States Code, Section 1325 states that any individual who knowingly enters into a marriage contract for the purpose of evading any provision of the immigration laws shall be imprisoned for not more than five years, or fined not more than $250,000.00 or both.

    Title 18, United States Code, Section 1001 states that whoever willfully and knowingly falsifies a material fact, makes a false statement, or makes use of a false document will be fined up to $10,000 or imprisoned up to five years, or both.

14. **What is our authority for collecting this information?**
    We request the information on the form to carry out the immigration laws contained in Title 8, United States Code, Section 1154(a). We need this information to determine whether a person is eligible for immigration benefits. The information you provide may also be disclosed to other federal, state, local, and foreign law enforcement and regulatory agencies during the course of the investigation required by this Service. You do not have to give this information. However, if you refuse to give some or all of it, your petition may be denied.

15. **Reporting Burden.**
    A person is not required to respond to a collection of information unless it displays a currently valid OMB control number. Public reporting burden for this collection of information is estimated to average 30 minutes per response, including the time for reviewing instructions, searching existing data sources, gathering and maintaining the data needed, and completing and reviewing the collection of information. Send comments regarding this burden estimate or any other aspect of this collection of information, including suggestions for reducing this burden, to: U.S. Department of Justice, Immigration and Naturalization Service (Room 5307),Washington, D.C. 20536; OMB No.1115-0054. **DO NOT MAIL YOUR COMPLETED APPLICATION TO THIS ADDRESS.**

It is not possible to cover all the conditions for eligibility or to give instructions for every situation. If you have carefully read all the instructions and still have questions, please contact your nearest INS office.

U.S. Department of Justice
Immigration and Naturalization Service (INS)

Petition for Alien Relative

OMB #1115-0054

DO NOT WRITE IN THIS BLOCK - FOR EXAMINING OFFICE ONLY

Case ID#	Action Stamp	Fee Stamp
A#		
G-28 or Volag #		

Section of Law:
- [ ] 201 (b) spouse
- [ ] 201 (b) child
- [ ] 201 (b) parent
- [ ] 203 (a)(1)
- [ ] 203 (a)(2)
- [ ] 203 (a)(4)
- [ ] 203 (a)(5)

AM CON: _____

Petition was filed on: _____ (priority date)
- [ ] Personal Interview
- [ ] Pet. [ ] Ben. "A" File Reviewed
- [ ] Field Investigations
- [ ] 204 (a)(2)(A) Resolved
- [ ] Previously Forwarded
- [ ] Stateside Criteria
- [ ] I-485 Simultaneously
- [ ] 204 (h) Resolved

Remarks:

A. Relationship

1. The alien relative is my
- [ ] Husband/Wife [ ] Parent [ ] Brother/Sister [ ] Child

2. Are you related by adoption?
- [ ] Yes [ ] No

3. Did you gain permanent residence through adoption?
- [ ] Yes [ ] No

B. Information about you

1. Name (Family name in CAPS)   (First)   (Middle)

2. Address (Number and Street)   (Apartment Number)

   (Town or City)   (State/Country)   (ZIP/Postal Code)

3. Place of Birth (Town or City)   (State/Country)

4. Date of Birth (Mo/Day/Yr)
5. Sex [ ] Male [ ] Female
6. Marital Status [ ] Married [ ] Widowed [ ] Single [ ] Divorced

7. Other Names Used (including maiden name)

8. Date and Place of Present Marriage (if married)

9. Social Security Number   10. Alien Registration Number (if any)

11. Names of Prior Husbands/Wives   12. Date(s) Marriages(s) Ended

13. If you are a U.S. citizen, complete the following:
   My citizenship was acquired through (check one)
   - [ ] Birth in the U.S.
   - [ ] Naturalization (Give number of certificate, date and place it was issued)
   - [ ] Parents
      Have you obtained a certificate of citizenship in your own name?
      [ ] Yes [ ] No
      If "Yes", give number of certificate, date and place it was issued

14a. If you are a lawful permanent resident alien, complete the following:
   Date and place of admission for, or adjustment to, lawful permanent residence, and class of admission:

14b. Did you gain permanent resident status through marriage to a United States citizen or lawful permanent resident? [ ] Yes [ ] No

C. Information about your alien relative

1. Name (Family name in CAPS)   (First)   (Middle)

2. Address (Number and Street)   (Apartment Number)

   (Town or City)   (State/Country)   (ZIP/Postal Code)

3. Place of Birth (Town or City)   (State/Country)

4. Date of Birth (Mo/Day/Yr)
5. Sex [ ] Male [ ] Female
6. Marital Status [ ] Married [ ] Widowed [ ] Single [ ] Divorced

7. Other Names Used (including maiden name)

8. Date and Place of Present Marriage (if married)

9. Social Security Number   10. Alien Registration Number (if any)

11. Names of Prior Husbands/Wives   12. Date(s) Marriages(s) Ended

13. Has your relative ever been in the U.S.?
   [ ] Yes [ ] No

14. If your relative is currently in the U.S., complete the following: He or she last arrived as a (visitor, student, stowaway, without inspection, etc.)

Arrival/Departure Record (I-94) Number   Date arrived (Month/Day/Year)

Date authorized stay expired, or will expire, as shown on Form I-94 or I-95

15. Name and address of present employer (if any)

Date this employment began (Month/Day/Year)

16. Has your relative ever been under immigration proceedings?
   [ ] Yes [ ] No Where _____ When _____
   [ ] Exclusion [ ] Deportation [ ] Recission [ ] Judicial Proceedings

INITIAL RECEIPT	RESUBMITTED	RELOCATED		COMPLETED		
		Rec'd	Sent	Approved	Denied	Returned

Form I-130 (Rev. 10/13/98)N

C. (continued) Information about your alien relative

16. List husband/wife and all children of your relative (if your relative is your husband/wife, list only his or her children).

(Name)	(Relationship)	(Date of Birth)	(Country of Birth)

17. Address in the United States where your relative intends to live

(Number and Street)	(Town or City)	(State)

18. Your relative's address abroad

(Number and Street)	(Town or City)	(Province)	(Country)	(Phone Number)

19. If your relative's native alphabet is other than Roman letters, write his or her name and address abroad in the native alphabet:

(Name)	(Number and Street)	Town or City	(Province)	(Country)

20. If filing for your husband/wife, give last address at which you both lived together:

(Name)	(Number and Street)	(Town or City)	(Province)	(Country)	From (Month) (Year)	To (Month) (Year)

21. Check the appropriate box below and give the information required for the box you checked:

☐ Your relative will apply for a visa abroad at the American Consulate in _____

                                          (City)   (Country)

☐ Your relative is in the United States and will apply for adjustment of status to that of a lawful permanent resident in the office of the Immigration and Naturalization Service at _____ . If your relative is not eligible for adjustment of status, he or she will

                           (City)   (State)

apply for a visa abroad at the American Consulate in _____ ,

                                 (City)   (Country)

(Designation of a consulate outside the country of your relative's last residence does not guarantee acceptance for processing by that consulate. Acceptance is at the discretion of the designated consulate.)

D. Other Information

1. If separate petitions are also being submitted for other relatives, give names of each and relationship.

2. Have you ever filed a petition for this or any other alien before?   ☐ Yes   ☐ No
If "Yes," give name, place and date of filing, and result.

Warning: The INS investigates claimed relationships and verifies the validity of documents. The INS seeks criminal prosecutions when family relationships are falsified to obtain visas.

Penalties: You may, by law be imprisoned for not more than five years, or fined $250,000, or both, for entering into a marriage contract for the purpose of evading any provision of the immigration laws and you may be fined up to $10,000 or imprisoned up to five years or both, for knowingly and willfully falsifying or concealing a material fact or using any false document in submitting this petition.

Your Certification: I certify, under penalty of perjury under the laws of the United States of America, that the foregoing is true and correct. Furthermore, I authorize the release of any information from my records which the Immigration and Naturalization Service needs to determine eligibility for the benefit that I am seeking.

Signature _____ Date _____ Phone Number _____

Signature of Person Preparing Form if Other than Above

I declare that I prepared this document at the request of the person above and that it is based on all information of which I have any knowledge.

Print Name _____ (Address) _____ (Signature) _____ (Date) _____

G-28 ID Number _____

Volag Number _____

Form I-130 (Rev. 10/13/98)N

NOTICE TO PERSONS FILING FOR SPOUSES IF MARRIED LESS THAN TWO YEARS

Pursuant to section 216 of the Immigration and Nationality Act, your alien spouse may be granted conditional permanent resident status in the United States as of the date he or she is admitted or adjusted to conditional status by an officer of the Immigration and Naturalization Service. Both you and your conditional permanent resident spouse are required to file a petition, Form I-751, Joint Petition to Remove Conditional Basis of Alien's Permanent Resident Status, during the ninety day period immediately before the second anniversary of the date your alien spouse was granted conditional permanent residence.

Otherwise, the rights, privileges, responsibilities and duties which apply to all other permanent residents apply equally to a conditional permanent resident. A conditional permanent resident is not limited to the right to apply for naturalization, to file petitions in behalf of qualifying relatives, or to reside permanently in the United States as an immigrant in accordance with the immigration laws.

> **Failure to file Form I-751, Joint Petition to Remove the Conditional Basis of Alien's Permanent Resident Status, will result in termination of permanent residence status and initiation of deportation proceedings.**

NOTE: You must complete Items 1 through 6 to assure that petition approval is recorded. Do not write in the section below item 6.

---

1. Name of relative (Family name in CAPS)   (First)   (Middle)

2. Other names used by relative (Including maiden name)

3. Country of relative's birth   4. Date of relative's birth (Month/Day/Year)

5. Your name (Last name in CAPS) (First) (Middle)   6. Your phone number

Action Stamp

SECTION
- ☐ 201 (b)(spouse)
- ☐ 201 (b)(child)
- ☐ 201 (b)(parent)
- ☐ 203 (a)(1)
- ☐ 203 (a)(2)
- ☐ 203 (a)(4)
- ☐ 203 (a)(5)

DATE PETITION FILED

☐ STATESIDE
CRITERIA GRANTED

SENT TO CONSUL AT;

CHECKLIST

Have you answered each question?

Have you signed the petition?

Have you enclosed:
- ☐ The filing fee for each petition?
- ☐ Proof of your citizenship or lawful permanent residence?
- ☐ All required supporting documents for each petition?

If you are filing for your husband or wife have you included:
- ☐ Your picture?
- ☐ His or her picture?
- ☐ Your G-325A?
- ☐ His or her G-325A?

Relative Petition Card
Form I-130 (Rev. 10/13/98)N

OMB No. 1115-0053

U.S. Department of Justice
Immigration and Naturalization Service

Form I-485, Application to Register Permanent Residence or Adjust Status

Purpose of This Form.
This form is used by a person who is in the United States to apply to the Immigration and Naturalization Service (INS) to adjust to permanent resident status or register for permanent residence. It may also be used by certain Cuban nationals to request a change in the date their permanent residence began.

Who May File.
Based on an immigrant petition. You may apply to adjust your status if:

- an immigrant visa number is immediately available to you based on an approved immigrant petition; or

- you are filing this application with a complete relative, special immigrant juvenile or special immigrant military petition, which if approved, would make an immigrant visa number immediately available to you.

Based on being the spouse or child (derivative) at the time another adjustment applicant (principal) files to adjust status or at the time a person is granted permanent resident status in an immigrant category that allows derivative status for spouses and children.

- **If the spouse or child is in the United States,** the individual derivatives may file their Form I-485 adjustment of status applications concurrently with the Form I-485 for the principal beneficiary, or file the Form I-485 at anytime after the principal is approved, if a visa number is available.

- **If the spouse or child is residing abroad,** the person adjusting status in the United States should file the **Form I-824, Application for Action on an Approved Application or Petition,** concurrently with the principal's adjustment of status application to allow the derivates to immigrate to the United States without delay, if the principal's adjustment of status application is approved. **No I-824 fee will be refunded if the principal's adjustment is not granted.**

Based on admission as the fiance(e) of a U. S. citizen and subsequent marriage to that citizen. You may apply to adjust status if you were admitted to the U. S. as the K-1 fiance(e) of a U. S. citizen and you married that citizen within 90 days of your entry. If you were admitted as the K-2 child of such a fiance(e), you may apply based on your parent's adjustment application.

Based on asylum status. You may apply to adjust status if you have been granted asylum in the U. S. after being physically present in the U. S. for one year after the grant of asylum, if you still qualify as an asylee or as the spouse or child of a refugee.

Based on Cuban citizenship or nationality. You may apply to adjust status if:

- you are a native or citizen of Cuba, were admitted or paroled into the U.S. after January 1, 1959, and thereafter have been physically present in the U.S. for at least one year; or
- you are the spouse or unmarried child of a Cuban described above, and regardless of your nationality, you were admitted or paroled after January 1, 1959, and thereafter have been physically present in the U.S. for at least one year.

Based on continuous residence since before January 1, 1972. You may apply for permanent residence if you have continuously resided in the U.S. since before January 1, 1972.

Applying to change the date your permanent residence began. If you were granted permanent residence in the U. S. prior to November 6, 1966, and are a native or citizen of Cuba, his or her spouse or unmarried minor child, you may ask to change the date your lawful permanent residence began to your date of arrival in the U. S. or May 2, 1964, whichever is later.

Other basis of eligibility. If you are not included in the above categories, but believe you may be eligible for adjustment or creation of record of permanent residence, contact your local INS office.

Persons Who Are Ineligible.
Unless you are applying for creation of record based on continuous residence since before January 1, 1972, or adjustment of status under a category in which special rules apply (such as asylum adjustment, Cuban adjustment, special immigrant juvenile adjustment or special immigrant military personnel adjustment), **you are not eligible for adjustment of status if any of the following apply to you:**

- you entered the U.S. in transit without a visa;
- you entered the U.S. as a nonimmigrant crewman;
- you were not admitted or paroled following inspection by an immigration officer;
- your authorized stay expired before you filed this application; you were employed in the U.S. prior to filing this application, without INS authorization; or you otherwise failed to maintain your nonimmigrant status, other than through no fault of your own or for technical reasons, unless you are applying because you are an immediate relative of a U.S. citizen (parent, spouse, widow, widower or unmarried child under 21 years old), a K-1 fiance(e) or K-2 fiance(e) dependent who married the U.S. petitioner within 90 days of admission or an "H" or "I" or special

immigrant (foreign medical graduates, international organization employees or their derivative family members);

- you are or were a J-1 or J-2 exchange visitor, are subject to the two-year foreign residence requirement and have not complied with or been granted a waiver of the requirement;

- you have an A, E or G nonimmigrant status, or have an occupation which would allow you to have this status, unless you complete Form I-508 (I-508F for French nationals) to wave diplomatic rights, privileges and immunities, and if you are an A or G nonimmigrant, unless you submit a complete Form I-566;
- you were admitted to Guam as a visitor under the Guam visa waiver program;
- you were admitted to the U.S. as a visitor under the Visa Waiver Pilot Program, unless you are applying because you are an immediate relative of a U.S. citizen (parent, spouse, widow, widower or unmarried child under 21 years old);
- you are already a conditional permanent resident;
- you were admitted as a K-1 fiance(e) but did not marry the U.S. citizen who filed the petition for you, or were admitted as the K-2 child of a fiance(e) and your parent did not marry the U.S. citizen who filed the petition.

General Filing Instructions.
Please answer all questions by typing or clearly printing in black ink. Indicate that an item is not applicable with **"N/A."** If the answer is **"none,"** write **"none."** If you need extra space to answer any item, attach a sheet of paper with your name and your alien registration number (A#), if any, and indicate the number of the item to which the answer refers. You must file your application with the required **Initial Evidence** described below, beginning on this page. Your application must be properly signed and filed with the correct fee. If you are under 14 years of age, your parent or guardian may sign your application.

Translations. Any foreign language document must be accompanied by a full English translation which the translator has certified as complete and correct, and by the translator's certification that he or she is competent to translate the foreign language into English.

Copies. If these instructions state that a copy of a document may be filed with this application, and you choose to send us the original, we may keep the original for our records.

Initial Evidence.
You must file your application with the following evidence:

- **Birth certificate.** Submit a copy of your foreign birth certificate or other record of your birth that meets the provisions of secondary evidence found in 8 CFR 103.2(b)(2).

- **Copy of passport page with nonimmigrant visa.** If you have obtained a nonimmigrant visa(s) from an American consulate abroad within the last year, submit a photocopy(ies) of the page(s) of your passport with the visa(s).

- **Photos.** Submit two (2) identical natural color photographs of yourself, taken within 30 days of the application. Photos must have a white background, be unmounted, printed on thin paper and be glossy and unretouched. They must show a three-quarter frontal profile showing the right side of your face, with your right ear visible and with your head bare. You may wear a headdress if required by a religious order of which you are a member. The photos must be no larger than 2 X 2 inches, with the distance from the top of the head to just below the chin about 1 and 1/4 inches. Lightly print your A# (or your name if you have no A#) on the back of each photo, using a pencil.

- **Fingerprints.** If you are between the ages of 14 and 75, you must be fingerprinted. After filing this application, INS will notify you in writing of the time and location where you must go to be fingerprinted. Failure to appear to be fingerprinted may result in denial of your application.

- **Police clearances.** If you are filing for adjustment of status as a member of a special class described in an I-485 supplement form, please read the instructions on the supplement form to see if you need to obtain and submit police clearances, in addition to the required fingerprints, with your application.

- **Medical examination (Section 232 of the Act).** When required, submit a medical examination report on the form you have obtained from INS.

-- **A. Individuals applying for adjustment of status through the INS Service Center: 1) General:** If you are filing your adjustment of status application with the INS Service Center, include your medical exam report with the application, unless you are a refugee or asylee. **2) Refugees:** If you are applying for adjustment of status one year after you were admitted as a refugee, you only need to submit a vaccination supplement with your adjustment of status application, not the entire medical report, **unless** there were medical grounds of inadmissibility that arose during the initial exam you had overseas.

-- **B. Individuals applying for adjustment of status through the local INS office and asylees applying for adjustment of status through the Service Center:** If you are filing your adjustment of status application with the local INS office, or if you are an asylee filing an adjustment of status application with the Service Center, one year after you were granted asylum, do not submit a medical report with your adjustment of status application. Wait for further instructions from INS about how and where to take the medical exam and submit the medical exam report.

-- **Fiance(e)s:** If you are a K-1 fiance(e) or K-2 dependent who had a medical exam within the past year as required for the nonimmigrant fiance (e) visa, you only need to submit a vaccination supplement, not the entire medical report. You may include the vaccination supplement with your adjustment of status application.

-- **Individuals not required to have a medical exam:** The medical report is not required if you are applying for creation of a record for admission as a lawful permanent resident under section 249 of the Act as someone who has continuously resided in the United States since January 1, 1972 (registry applicant).

● **Form G-325A, Biographic Information Sheet.** You must submit a completed G-325A if you are between 14 and 79 years of age.

● **Evidence of status.** Submit a copy of your Form I-94, Nonimmigrant Arrival/Departure Record, showing your admission to the U.S. and current status, or other evidence of your status.

● **Affidavit of Support/Employment Letter.**

-- **Affidavit of Support.** Submit the Affidavit of Support (Form I-864) if your adjustment of status application is based on your entry as a fiance(e), or a relative visa petition (Form I-130) filed by your relative or on an employment based visa petition (Form I-140) based on a business that is five percent or more owned by your family.

-- **Employment Letter.** If your adjustment of status application is based on an employment based visa petition (Form I-140), you must submit a letter on the letterhead of the petitioning employer which confirms that the job on which the visa petition is based is still available to you. The letter must also state the salary that will be paid.

(Note: The affidavit of support and/or employment letter are not required if you applying for creation of record based on continuous residence since before January 1, 1972, asylum adjustment, or a Cuban or a spouse or unmarried child of a Cuban who was admitted after January 1, 1959.)

● **Evidence of eligibility.**

-- **Based on an immigrant petition.** Attach a copy of the approval notice for an immigrant petition which makes a visa number immediately available to you, or submit a complete relative, special immigrant juvenile or special immigrant military petition which, if approved, will make a visa number immediately available to you.

-- **Based on admission as the K-1 fiance(e) of a U.S. citizen and subsequent marriage to that citizen.** Attach a copy of the fiance(e) petition approval notice, a copy of your marriage certificate and your Form I-94.

-- **Based on asylum status.** Attach a copy of the letter or Form I-94 which shows the date you were granted asylum.

-- **Based on continuous residence in the U.S. since before January 1, 1972.** Attach copies of evidence that shows continuous residence since before January 1, 1972.

-- **Based on Cuban citizenship or nationality.** Attach evidence of your citizenship or nationality, such as a copy of your passport, birth certificate or travel document.

-- **Based on derivative status as the spouse or child of another adjustment applicant or person granted permanent residence based on issuance of an immigrant visa.** File your application with the application of that other applicant, or with evidence that it is pending with the Service or has been approved, or evidence that your spouse or parent has been granted permanent residence based on an immigrant visa and:

● If you are applying as the spouse of that person, also attach a copy of your marriage certificate and copies of documents showing the legal termination of all other marriages by you and your spouse;

● If you are applying as the child of that person, also attach a copy of your birth certificate, and if the other person is not your natural mother, copies of evidence (such as a marriage certificate and documents showing the legal termination of all other marriages and an adoption decree) to demonstrate that you qualify as his or her child.

● **Other basis for eligibility.** Attach copies of documents proving that you are eligible for the classification.

Where to File.
File this application at the INS office having jurisdiction over your place of residence.

Fee. The fee for this application is **$220**, except that it is **$160** if you are less than 14 years old. There is no application fee if you are filing as a refugee under section 209(a) of the Act. If you are between the ages of 14 and 75, there is a $25 fingerprinting fee in addition to the application fee. For example, if your application fee is $220 and you are between the ages of 14 and 75, the total fee you must pay is $245. You may submit one check or money order for both the application and fingerprinting fees. Fees must be submitted in the exact amount. **DO NOT MAIL CASH.** Fees cannot be refunded. All checks and money orders must be drawn on a bank or other institution located in the United States and must be payable in United States currency. The check or money order should be made payable to the Immigration and Naturalization Service, except that:

-- if you live in Guam and are filing this application in Guam, make your check or money order payable to the "Treasurer, Guam."

-- if you live in the U.S. Virgin Islands and are filing this application in the U.S. Virgin Islands, make your check or money order payable to the "Commissioner of Finance of the Virgin Islands."

Checks are accepted subject to collection. An uncollected check in payment of an application fee will render the application and any document issued invalid. A charge of $30 will be imposed if a check in payment of a fee is not honored by the bank on which it is drawn.

Processing Information.

Acceptance. Any application that is not signed, or is not accompanied by the correct application fee, will be rejected with a notice that the application is deficient. You may correct the deficiency and resubmit the application. An application is not considered properly filed until accepted by the INS.

Initial Processing. Once an application has been accepted, it will be checked for completeness, including submission of the required initial evidence. If you do not completely fill out the form, or file it without required initial evidence, you will not establish a basis for eligibility, and we may deny your application.

Requests for More Information. We may request more information or evidence. We may also request that you submit the originals of any copy. We may return these originals when they are no longer required.

Interview. After you file your application you will be notified to appear at an INS office to answer questions about the application. You will be required to answer these questions under oath or affirmation. You must bring your Arrival-Departure Record (Form I-94) and any passport to the interview.

Decision. You will be notified in writing of the decision on your application.

Selective Service Registration. If you are a male at least 18 years old, but not yet 26 years old, and required according to the Military Selective Service Act to register with the Selective Service System, the INS will help you register. When your signed application is filed and accepted by the INS, we will transmit your name, current address, Social Security number, date of birth and the date you filed the application to the Selective Service to record your registration as of the filing date. If the INS does not accept your application, and if still so required, you are responsible to register with the Selective Service by other means, provided you are under 26 years of age. If you have already registered, the Selective Service will check its records to avoid any duplication. **(Note: men 18 through 25 years old, who are applying for student financial aid, government employment or job training benefits should register directly with the Selective Service or such benefits may be denied. Men can register at a local post office or on the Internet at http://www.sss.gov).**

Form I-485 (Rev. 02/07/00)N Page 2

Travel Outside the U.S. for Adjustment of Status Applicants Under Sections 209 and 245 of the Act and Registry Applicants Under Section 249 of the Act. Your departure from the U.S. (including brief visits to Canada or Mexico) constitutes an abandonment of your adjustment of status application, unless you are granted permission to depart and you are inspected upon your return to the U.S. Such permission to travel is called "advance parole." To request advance parole, you must file Form I-131, with fee, with the INS office where you applied for adjustment of status.

-- **Exceptions: 1) H and L nonimmigrants:** If you are an H or L nonimmigrant who continues to maintain his or her status, you may travel on a valid H or L visa without obtaining advance parole. **2) Refugees and Asylees:** If you are applying for adjustment of status one year after you were admitted as a refugee or one year after you were granted asylum, you may travel outside the United States on your valid refugee travel document, if you have one, without the need to obtain advance parole.

-- **WARNING:** Travel outside of the U.S. may trigger the 3-and 10-year bars to admission under section 212(a)(9)(B)(i) of the Act for adjustment applicants, but not registry applicants. This ground of inadmissibility is triggered if you were unlawfully present in the U.S. (i.e., you remained in the United States beyond the period of stay authorized by the Attorney General) for more than 180 days before you applied for adjustment of status, and you travel outside of the U.S. while your adjustment of status application is pending. (Note: Only unlawful presence that accrued on or after April 1, 1997, counts towards the 3-and 10-year bars under section 212 (a)(9) (B)(i) of the Act.)

-- If you become inadmissible under section 212(a)(9)(B)(i) of the Act while your adjustment of status application is pending, you will need a waiver of inadmissibility under section 212(a)(9)(B)(v) of the Act before your adjustment of status application can be approved. This waiver, however, is granted on a case-by-case basis and in the exercise of discretion. It requires a showing of extreme hardship to your U.S. citizen or lawful permanent resident spouse or parent, unless you are a refugee or asylee. For refugees and asylees, the waiver may be granted for humanitarian reasons, to assure family unity or if it is otherwise in the public interest.

Penalties. If you knowingly and willfully falsify or conceal a material fact or submit a false document with this request, we will deny the benefit you are filing for and may deny any other immigration benefit. In addition, you will face severe penalties provided by law and may be subject to criminal prosecution.

Privacy Act Notice. We ask for the information on this form and associated evidence to determine if you have established eligibility for the immigration benefit you are seeking. Our legal right to ask for this information is in 8 USC 1255 and 1259. We may provide this information to other government agencies, including the Selective Service System. Your failure to provide this information on this form and any requested evidence may delay a final decision or result in denial of your application.

Paperwork Reduction Act Notice. A person is not required to respond to a collection of information unless it displays a current valid OMB number. We try to create forms and instructions that are accurate, can be easily understood and which impose the least possible burden on you to provide us with information. Often this is difficult because some immigration laws are very complex. The estimated average time to complete and file this application is computed as follows: (1) 20 minutes to learn about the law and form; (2) 25 minutes to complete the form and (3) 270 minutes to assemble and file the application, including the required interview and travel time -- for a total estimated average of 5 hours and 15 minutes per application. If you have comments regarding the accuracy of this estimate or suggestions to make this form simpler, you should write to the Immigration and Naturalization Service, 425 I Street, N.W., Room 5307, Washington, D.C. 20536; OMB No. 1115-0053. **DO NOT MAIL YOUR COMPLETED APPLICATION TO THIS ADDRESS.**

OMB No. 1115-0053

U.S. Department of Justice
Immigration and Naturalization Service

Form I-485, Application to Register Permanent Resident or Adjust Status

START HERE - Please Type or Print

Part 1.   Information About You.

Family Name	Given Name	Middle Initial

Address - C/O

Street Number and Name	Apt. #

City

State	Zip Code

Date of Birth (month/day/year)	Country of Birth

Social Security #	A # (if any)

Date of Last Arrival (month/day/year)	I-94 #

Current INS Status	Expires on (month/day/year)

Part 2.   Application Type. *(check one)*

I am applying for an adjustment to permanent resident status because:

a. ☐ an immigrant petition giving me an immediately available immigrant visa number has been approved. (Atttach a copy of the approval notice-- or a relative, special immigrant juvenile or special immigrant military visa petition filed with this application that will give you an immediately available visa number, if approved.)

b. ☐ my spouse or parent applied for adjustment of status or was granted lawful permanent residence in an immigrant visa category that allows derivative status for spouses and children.

c. ☐ I entered as a K-1 fiance(e) of a U.S. citizen whom I married within 90 days of entry, or I am the K-2 child of such a fiance(e). [Attach a copy of the fiance(e) petition approval notice and the marriage certificate.]

d. ☐ I was granted asylum or derivative asylum status as the spouse or child of a person granted asylum and am eligible for adjustment.

e. ☐ I am a native or citizen of Cuba admitted or paroled into the U.S. after January 1, 1959, and thereafter have been physically present in the U.S. for at least one year.

f. ☐ I am the husband, wife or minor unmarried child of a Cuban described in (e) and am residing with that person, and was admitted or paroled into the U.S. after January 1, 1959, and thereafter have been physically present in the U.S. for at least one year.

g. ☐ I have continuously resided in the U.S. since before January 1, 1972.

h. ☐ Other basis of eligibility. Explain. (If additional space is needed, use a separate piece of paper.)

_____

I am already a permanent resident and am applying to have the date I was granted permanent residence adjusted to the date I originally arrived in the U.S. as a nonimmigrant or parolee, or as of May 2,1964, whichever date is later, and: *(Check one)*

i. ☐ I am a native or citizen of Cuba and meet the description in (e), above.

j. ☐ I am the husband, wife or minor unmarried child of a Cuban, and meet the description in (f), above.

FOR INS USE ONLY

Returned	Receipt
_____	
Resubmitted	
_____	
Reloc Sent	
_____	
Reloc Rec'd	
_____	
Applicant Interviewed	

Section of Law
☐ Sec. 209(b), INA
☐ Sec. 13, Act of 9/11/57
☐ Sec. 245, INA
☐ Sec. 249, INA
☐ Sec. 2 Act of 11/2/66
☐ Sec. 2 Act of 11/2/66
☐ Other _____

Country Chargeable

Eligibility Under Sec. 245
☐ Approved Visa Petition
☐ Dependent of Principal Alien
☐ Special Immigrant
☐ Other _____

Preference

Action Block

To be Completed by
Attorney or Representative, **if any**

☐ Fill in box if G-28 is attached to represent the applicant.
VOLAG #

ATTY State License #

Continued on back

Part 3. Processing Information.

A. City/Town/Village of Birth	Current Occupation
Your Mother's First Name	Your Father's First Name

Give your name exactly how it appears on your Arrival /Departure Record (Form 1-94)

Place of Last Entry Into the U.S. (City/State)	In what status did you last enter? *(Visitor, student, exchange alien, crewman, temporary worker, without inspection, etc.)*
Were you inspected by a U.S. Immigration Officer? ☐ Yes ☐ No	
Nonimmigrant Visa Number	Consulate Where Visa Was Issued
Date Visa Was Issued (month/day/year)	Sex: ☐ Male ☐ Female	Marital Status ☐ Married ☐ Single ☐ Divorced ☐ Widowed

Have you ever before applied for permanent resident status in the U.S.? ☐ No ☐ Yes If you checked "Yes," give date and place of filing and final disposition.

B. List your present husband/wife and all your sons and daughters. (If you have none, write "none." If additional space is needed, use a separate piece of paper.)

Family Name	Given Name	Middle Initial	Date of Birth (month/day/year)
Country of Birth	Relationship	A #	Applying with You? ☐ Yes ☐ No
Family Name	Given Name	Middle Initial	Date of Birth (month/day/year)
Country of Birth	Relationship	A #	Applying with You? ☐ Yes ☐ No
Family Name	Given Name	Middle Initial	Date of Birth (month/day/year)
Country of Birth	Relationship	A #	Applying with You? ☐ Yes ☐ No
Family Name	Given Name	Middle Initial	Date of Birth (month/day/year)
Country of Birth	Relationship	A #	Applying with You? ☐ Yes ☐ No
Family Name	Given Name	Middle Initial	Date of Birth (month/day/year)
Country of Birth	Relationship	A #	Applying with You? ☐ Yes ☐ No

C. List your present and past membership in or affiliation with every political organization, association, fund, foundation, party, club, society or similar group in the United States or in other places since your 16th birthday. Include any foreign military service in this part. If none, write "none." Include the name(s) of the organization(s), location(s), dates of membership from and to, and the nature of the organization (s). If additional space is needed, use a separate piece of paper.

Part 3. Processing Information. *(Continued)*

Please answer the following questions. (If your answer is "Yes" to any one of these questions, explain on a separate piece of paper. Answering "Yes" does not necessarily mean that you are not entitled to adjust your status or register for permanent residence.)

1. Have you ever, in or outside the U. S.:

   a. knowingly committed any crime of moral turpitude or a drug-related offense for which you have not been arrested? ☐ Yes ☐ No

   b. been arrested, cited, charged, indicted, fined or imprisoned for breaking or violating any law or ordinance, excluding traffic violations? ☐ Yes ☐ No

   c. been the beneficiary of a pardon, amnesty, rehabilitation decree, other act of clemency or similar action? ☐ Yes ☐ No

   d. exercised diplomatic immunity to avoid prosecution for a criminal offense in the U. S.? ☐ Yes ☐ No

2. Have you received public assistance in the U.S. from any source, including the U.S. government or any state, county, city or municipality (other than emergency medical treatment), or are you likely to receive public assistance in the future? ☐ Yes ☐ No

3. Have you ever:

   a. within the past ten years been a prostitute or procured anyone for prostitution, or intend to engage in such activities in the future? ☐ Yes ☐ No

   b. engaged in any unlawful commercialized vice, including, but not limited to, illegal gambling? ☐ Yes ☐ No

   c. knowingly encouraged, induced, assisted, abetted or aided any alien to try to enter the U.S. illegally? ☐ Yes ☐ No

   d. illicitly trafficked in any controlled substance, or knowingly assisted, abetted or colluded in the illicit trafficking of any controlled substance? ☐ Yes ☐ No

4. Have you ever engaged in, conspired to engage in, or do you intend to engage in, or have you ever solicited membership or funds for, or have you through any means ever assisted or provided any type of material support to, any person or organization that has ever engaged or conspired to engage, in sabotage, kidnapping, political assassination, hijacking or any other form of terrorist activity? ☐ Yes ☐ No

5. Do you intend to engage in the U.S. in:

   a. espionage? ☐ Yes ☐ No

   b. any activity a purpose of which is opposition to, or the control or overthrow of, the government of the United States, by force, violence or other unlawful means? ☐ Yes ☐ No

   c. any activity to violate or evade any law prohibiting the export from the United States of goods, technology or sensitive information? ☐ Yes ☐ No

6. Have you ever been a member of, or in any way affiliated with, the Communist Party or any other totalitarian party? ☐ Yes ☐ No

7. Did you, during the period from March 23, 1933 to May 8, 1945, in association with either the Nazi Government of Germany or any organization or government associated or allied with the Nazi Government of Germany, ever order, incite, assist or otherwise participate in the persecution of any person because of race, religion, national origin or political opinion? ☐ Yes ☐ No

8. Have you ever engaged in genocide, or otherwise ordered, incited, assisted or otherwise participated in the killing of any person because of race, religion, nationality, ethnic origin or political opinion? ☐ Yes ☐ No

9. Have you ever been deported from the U.S., or removed from the U.S. at government expense, excluded within the past year, or are you now in exclusion or deportation proceedings? ☐ Yes ☐ No

10. Are you under a final order of civil penalty for violating section 274C of the Immigration and Nationality Act for use of fradulent documents or have you, by fraud or willful misrepresentation of a material fact, ever sought to procure, or procured, a visa, other documentation, entry into the U.S. or any immigration benefit? ☐ Yes ☐ No

11. Have you ever left the U.S. to avoid being drafted into the U.S. Armed Forces? ☐ Yes ☐ No

12. Have you ever been a J nonimmigrant exchange visitor who was subject to the two-year foreign residence requirement and not yet complied with that requirement or obtained a waiver? ☐ Yes ☐ No

13. Are you now withholding custody of a U.S. citizen child outside the U.S. from a person granted custody of the child? ☐ Yes ☐ No

14. Do you plan to practice polygamy in the U.S.? ☐ Yes ☐ No

Continued on back

Part 4. Signature. *(Read the information on penalties in the instructions before completing this section. You must file this application while in the United States.)*

I certify, under penalty of perjury under the laws of the United States of America, that this application and the evidence submitted with it is all true and correct. I authorize the release of any information from my records which the INS needs to determine eligibility for the benefit I am seeking.

Selective Service Registration. The following applies to you if you are a man at least 18 years old, but not yet 26 years old, who is required to register with the Selective Service System: I understand that my filing this adjustment of status application with the Immigration and Naturalization Service authorizes the INS to provide certain registration information to the Selective Service System in accordance with the Military Selective Service Act. Upon INS acceptance of my application, I authorize INS to transmit to the Selective Service System my name, current address, Social Security number, date of birth and the date I filed the application for the purpose of recording my Selective Service registration as of the filing date. If, however, the INS does not accept my application, I further understand that, if so required, I am responsible for registering with the Selective Service by other means, provided I have not yet reached age 26.

Signature	*Print Your Name*	*Date*	*Daytime Phone Number*

Please Note: *If you do not completely fill out this form or fail to submit required documents listed in the instructions, you may not be found eligible for the requested benefit and this application may be denied.*

Part 5. Signature of Person Preparing Form, If Other Than Above. *(Sign Below)*

I declare that I prepared this application at the request of the above person and it is based on all information of which I have knowledge.

Signature	*Print Your Name*	*Date*	*Daytime Phone Number*

Firm Name and Address

U.S. Department of Justice
Immigration and Naturalization Service

FORM G-325A
BIOGRAPHIC INFORMATION

OMB No. 1115-0066

(Family name)	(First name)	(Middle name)	☐ MALE ☐ FEMALE	BIRTHDATE (Mo.-Day-Yr.)	NATIONALITY	FILE NUMBER A-

ALL OTHER NAMES USED (Including names by previous marriages)	CITY AND COUNTRY OF BIRTH	SOCIAL SECURITY NO. (If any)

	FAMILY NAME	FIRST NAME	DATE, CITY AND COUNTRY OF BIRTH (If known)	CITY AND COUNTRY OF RESIDENCE
FATHER				
MOTHER (Maiden name)				

HUSBAND (If none, so state) OR WIFE	FAMILY NAME (For wife, give maiden name)	FIRST NAME	BIRTHDATE	CITY & COUNTRY OF BIRTH	DATE OF MARRIAGE	PLACE OF MARRIAGE

FORMER HUSBANDS OR WIVES (if none, so state)

FAMILY NAME (For wife, give maiden name)	FIRST NAME	BIRTHDATE	DATE & PLACE OF MARRIAGE	DATE AND PLACE OF TERMINATION OF MARRIAGE

APPLICANT'S RESIDENCE LAST FIVE YEARS. LIST PRESENT ADDRESS FIRST.

STREET AND NUMBER	CITY	PROVINCE OR STATE	COUNTRY	FROM MONTH	FROM YEAR	TO MONTH	TO YEAR
						PRESENT TIME	

APPLICANT'S LAST ADDRESS OUTSIDE THE UNITED STATES OF MORE THAN ONE YEAR

STREET AND NUMBER	CITY	PROVINCE OR STATE	COUNTRY	FROM MONTH	FROM YEAR	TO MONTH	TO YEAR

APPLICANT'S EMPLOYMENT LAST FIVE YEARS. (IF NONE, SO STATE.) LIST PRESENT EMPLOYMENT FIRST

FULL NAME AND ADDRESS OF EMPLOYER	OCCUPATION (SPECIFY)	FROM MONTH	FROM YEAR	TO MONTH	TO YEAR
				PRESENT TIME	

Show below last occupation abroad if not shown above. (Include all information requested above.)

THIS FORM IS SUBMITTED IN CONNECTION WITH APPLICATION FOR: ☐ NATURALIZATION ☐ STATUS AS PERMANENT RESIDENT ☐ OTHER (SPECIFY):	SIGNATURE OF APPLICANT	DATE
Are all copies legible? ☐ Yes	IF YOUR NATIVE ALPHABET IS IN OTHER THAN ROMAN LETTERS, WRITE YOUR NAME IN YOUR NATIVE ALPHABET IN THIS SPACE:	

PENALTIES: SEVERE PENALTIES ARE PROVIDED BY LAW FOR KNOWINGLY AND WILLFULLY FALSIFYING OR CONCEALING A MATERIAL FACT.

APPLICANT: **BE SURE TO PUT YOUR NAME AND ALIEN REGISTRATION NUMBER IN THE BOX OUTLINED BY HEAVY BORDER BELOW.**

COMPLETE THIS BOX (Family name)	(Given name)	(Middle name)	(Alien registration number)

Form G-325 A (Rev. 10-1-82)   (1) Ident.

Form **9003** (October 1994)	Department of the Treasury — Internal Revenue Service **Additional Questions to be Completed by All Applicants for Permanent Residence in the United States**	OMB Clearance No. 1545-1065

This form must accompany your application for permanent residence in the United States

Privacy Act Notice: Your responses to the following questions will be provided to the Internal Revenue Service pursuant to Section 6039E of the Internal Revenue Code of 1986. Use of this information is limited to that needed for tax administration purposes. Failure to provide this information may result in a $500 penalty unless failure is due to reasonable cause.

On the date of issuance of the Alien Registration Receipt Card, the Immigration and Naturalization Service will send the following information to the Internal Revenue Service: your name, social security number, address, date of birth, alien identification number, occupation, class of admission, and answers to IRS Form 9003.

Name *(Last—Surname—Family)*   *(First—Given)*   *(Middle Initial)*

Taxpayer Identification Number. . . . . |___|___|___|___|___|___|___|___|___|

Enter your Social Security Number (SSN) if you have one. If you do not
have an SSN but have used a Taxpayer Identification Number issued to you
by the Internal Revenue Service, enter that number. Otherwise, write "NONE"
in the space provided; i.e., "|___|___|___| N.O.N.E.".

	Mark appropriate column	
	Yes	**No**
1. Are you self-employed? Mark "yes" if you own and actively operate a business in which you share in the profits other than as an investor.		
2. Have you been in the United States for 183 days or more during any one of the three calendar years immediately preceding the current calendar year? Mark "yes" if you spent 183 days or more (not necessarily consecutive) in the United States during any **one of the three prior** calendar years **whether or not you worked** in the United States.		
3. During the last three years did you receive income from sources in the United States? Mark "yes" if you received income paid by individuals or institutions located in the United States. Income includes, but is not limited to, compensation for services provided by you, interest, dividends, rents, and royalties.		
4. Did you file a United States Individual Income Tax Return (Forms 1040, 1040A, 1040EZ or 1040NR) in any of the last three years?		

If you answered yes to question 4, for which tax year was the last return filed? . . . . 19___ ___

Paperwork Reduction Act Notice—We ask for the information on this form to carry out the Internal Revenue laws of the United States. You are required to give us the information. We need it to ensure that you are complying with these laws and to allow us to figure and collect the right amount of tax.

The time needed to complete and file this form will vary depending on individual circumstances. The estimated average time is 5 minutes. If you have comments concerning the accuracy of this time estimate or suggestions for making this form more simple, we would be happy to hear from you. You can write to both the **Internal Revenue Service**, Attention: Reports Clearance Officer, PC:FP, Washington, DC 20224, and the **Office of Management and Budget**, Paperwork Reduction Project (1545-1065), Washington, DC 20503. **DO NOT send this form to either of these offices. Instead, return it to the appropriate office of the Department of State or the Immigration and Naturalization Service.**

Remarks

Cat. No. 10126D   Form **9003** (Rev. 10-94)

U. S. IMMIGRATION & NATURALIZATION SERVICE

COLOR PHOTOGRAPH SPECIFICATIONS

IDEAL PHOTOGRAPH ◄

IMAGE MUST FIT INSIDE THIS BOX ►

THE PICTURE AT LEFT IS IDEAL SIZE, COLOR, BACKGROUND, AND POSE. THE IMAGE SHOULD BE 30MM (1 3/16IN) FROM THE HAIR TO JUST BELOW THE CHIN, AND 26MM (1 IN) FROM LEFT CHEEK TO RIGHT EAR. THE IMAGE MUST FIT IN THE BOX AT RIGHT.

THE PHOTOGRAPH

* THE OVERALL SIZE OF THE PICTURE, INCLUDING THE BACKGROUND, MUST BE AT LEAST 40MM (1 9/16 INCHES) IN HEIGHT BY 35MM (1 3/8IN) IN WIDTH.

* PHOTOS MUST BE FREE OF SHADOWS AND CONTAIN NO MARKS, SPLOTCHES, OR DISCOLORATIONS.

* PHOTOS SHOULD BE HIGH QUALITY, WITH GOOD BACK LIGHTING OR WRAP AROUND LIGHTING, AND MUST HAVE A WHITE OR OFF-WHITE BACKGROUND.

* PHOTOS MUST BE A GLOSSY OR MATTE FINISH AND UN-RETOUCHED.

* POLAROID FILM HYBRID #5 IS ACCEPTABLE; HOWEVER SX-70 TYPE FILM OR ANY OTHER INSTANT PROCESSING TYPE FILM IS UNACCEPTABLE. NON-PEEL APART FILMS ARE EASILY RECOGNIZED BECAUSE THE BACK OF THE FILM IS BLACK. ACCEPTABLE INSTANT COLOR FILM HAS A GRAY-TONED BACKING.

THE IMAGE OF THE PERSON

* THE DIMENSIONS OF THE IMAGE SHOULD BE 30MM (1 3/16 INCHES) FROM THE HAIR TO THE NECK JUST BELOW THE CHIN, AND 26MM (1 INCH) FROM THE RIGHT EAR TO THE LEFT CHEEK. IMAGE CANNOT EXCEED 32MM BY 28MM (1 1/4IN X 1 1/16IN).

* IF THE IMAGE AREA ON THE PHOTOGRAPH IS TOO LARGE OR TOO SMALL, THE PHOTO CANNOT BE USED.

* PHOTOGRAPHS MUST SHOW THE ENTIRE FACE OF THE PERSON IN A 3/4 VIEW SHOWING THE RIGHT EAR AND LEFT EYE.

* FACIAL FEATURES MUST BE IDENTIFIABLE.

* CONTRAST BETWEEN THE IMAGE AND BACKGROUND IS ESSENTIAL. PHOTOS FOR VERY LIGHT SKINNED PEOPLE SHOULD BE SLIGHTLY UNDER-EXPOSED. PHOTOS FOR VERY DARK SKINNED PEOPLE SHOULD BE SLIGHTLY OVER-EXPOSED.

SAMPLES OF UNACCEPTABLE PHOTOGRAPHS

INCORRECT POSE

IMAGE TOO LARGE

IMAGE TOO SMALL

IMAGE TOO DARK UNDER-EXPOSED

IMAGE TOO LIGHT

DARK BACKGROUND

OVER-EXPOSED

SHADOWS ON PIC

Immigration & Naturalization Service
Form M-378 (6-92)

U.S. Department of Justice
Immigration and Naturalization Service

OMB NO. 1115-0214
Affidavit of Support Under Section 213A of the Act

INSTRUCTIONS

Purpose of this Form

This form is required to show that an intending immigrant has adequate means of financial support and is not likely to become a public charge.

Sponsor's Obligation

The person completing this affidavit is the sponsor. A sponsor's obligation continues until the sponsored immigrant becomes a U.S. citizen, can be credited with 40 qualifying quarters of work, departs the United States permanently, or dies. Divorce does not terminate the obligation. By executing this form, you, the sponsor, agree to support the intending immigrant and any spouse and/or children immigrating with him or her and to reimburse any government agency or private entity that provides these sponsored immigrants with Federal, State, or local means-tested public benefits.

General Filing Instructions

Please answer all questions by typing or clearly printing in black ink only. Indicate that an item is not applicable with "N/A". If an answer is "none," please so state. If you need extra space to answer any item, attach a sheet of paper with your name and Social Security number, and indicate the number of the item to which the answer refers.

You must submit an affidavit of support for each applicant for immigrant status. You may submit photocopies of this affidavit and all supporting documentation for any spouse or children immigrating with an immigrant you are sponsoring, but the signature on each photocopied affidavit must be original. For purposes of this form, a spouse or child is immigrating with an immigrant you are sponsoring if he or she is: 1) listed in Part 3 of this affidavit of support; and 2) applies for an immigrant visa or adjustment of status within 6 months of the date this affidavit of support is originally completed and signed. The signature on the affidavit, including the signature on photocopies, must be notarized by a notary public or signed before an Immigration or a Consular Officer.

You should give the completed affidavit of support with all required documentation to the sponsored immigrant for submission to either a Consular Officer with Form OF-230, Application for Immigrant Visa and Alien Registration, or an Immigration Officer with Form I-485, Application to Register Permanent Residence or Adjust Status. You may enclose the affidavit of support and accompanying documents in a sealed envelope to be opened only by the designated Government official. The sponsored immigrant must submit the affidavit of support to the Government within 6 months of its signature.

Who Needs an Affidavit of Support under Section 213A?

This affidavit must be filed at the time an intending immigrant is applying for an immigrant visa or adjustment of status. It is required for:

- All immediate relatives, including orphans, and family-based immigrants. (Self-petitioning widow/ers and battered spouses and children are exempt from this requirement); and

- Employment-based immigrants where a relative filed the immigrant visa petition or has a significant ownership interest (5 percent or more) in the entity that filed the petition.

Who Completes an Affidavit of Support under Section 213A?

- For immediate relatives and family-based immigrants, the family member petitioning for the intending immigrant must be the sponsor.

- For employment-based immigrants, the petitioning relative or a relative with a significant ownership interest (5 percent or more) in the petitioning entity must be the sponsor. The term "relative," for these purposes, is defined as husband, wife, father, mother, child, adult son or daughter, brother, or sister.

- If the petitioner cannot meet the income requirements, a joint sponsor may submit an additional affidavit of support.

A sponsor, or joint sponsor, must also be:

- A citizen or national of the United States or an alien lawfully admitted to the United States for permanent residence;

- At least 18 years of age; and

- Domiciled in the United States or its territories and possessions.

Sponsor's Income Requirement

As a sponsor, your household income must equal or exceed 125 percent of the Federal poverty line for your household size. For the purpose of the affidavit of support, household size includes yourself, all persons related to you by birth, marriage, or adoption living in your residence, your dependents, any immigrants you have previously sponsored using INS Form I-864 if that obligation has not terminated, and the intending immigrant(s) in Part 3 of this affidavit of support. The poverty guidelines are calculated and published annually by the Department of Health and Human Services. Sponsors who are on active duty in the U.S. Armed Forces other than for training need only demonstrate income at 100 percent of the poverty line *if* they are submitting this affidavit for the purpose of sponsoring their spouse or child.

If you are currently employed and have an *individual* income which meets or exceeds 125 percent of the Federal poverty line or (100 percent, if applicable) for your household size, you do not need to list the income of any other person. When determining your income, you may include the income generated by individuals related to you by birth, marriage, or adoption who are living in your residence, if they have lived in your residence for the previous 6 months, or who are listed as dependents on your most recent Federal income tax return whether or not they live in your residence. For their income to be considered, these household members or dependents must be willing to make their income available for the support of the sponsored immigrant(s) if necessary, and to complete and sign Form I-864A, Contract Between Sponsor and Household Member. However, a household member who is the immigrant you are sponsoring only need complete Form I-864A if his or her income will be used to determine your ability to support a spouse and/or children immigrating with him or her.

If in any of the most recent 3 tax years, you and your spouse each reported income on a joint income tax return, but you want to use only your own income to qualify (and your spouse is not submitting a Form I-864A), you may provide a separate breakout of your individual income for these years. Your individual income will be based on the earnings from your W-2 forms, Wage and Tax Statement, submitted to IRS for any such years. If necessary to meet the income requirement, you may also submit evidence of other income listed on your tax returns which can be attributed to you. You must provide documentation of such reported income, including Forms 1099 sent by the payer, which show your name and Social Security number.

You must calculate your household size and total household income as indicated in Parts 4.C. and 4.D. of this form. You must compare your total household income with the minimum income requirement for your household size using the poverty guidelines. For the purposes of the affidavit of support, determination of your ability to meet the income requirements will be based on the most recent income-poverty guidelines published in the Federal Register at the time the Consular or Immigration Officer makes a decision on the intending immigrant's application for an immigrant visa or adjustment of status. Immigration and Consular Officers will begin to use updated poverty guidelines on the first day of the second month after the date the guidelines are published in the Federal Register.

If your total household income is equal to or higher than the minimum income requirement for your household size, you do not need to provide information on your assets, and you may *not* have a joint sponsor unless you are requested to do so by a Consular or Immigration Officer. If your total household income does not meet the minimum income requirement, the intending immigrant will be ineligible for an immigrant visa or adjustment of status, unless:

- You provide evidence of assets that meet the requirements outlined under "Evidence of Assets" below; and/or

- The immigrant you are sponsoring provides evidence of assets that meet the requirements under "Evidence of Assets" below; or

- A joint sponsor assumes the liability of the intending immigrant with you. A joint sponsor must execute a separate affidavit of support on behalf of the intending

immigrant and any accompanying family members. A joint sponsor must individually meet the minimum requirement of 125 percent of the poverty line based on his or her household size and income and/or assets, including any assets of the sponsored immigrant.

The Government may pursue verification of any information provided on or in support of this form, including employment, income, or assets with the employer, financial or other institutions, the Internal Revenue Service, or the Social Security Administration.

Evidence of Income

In order to complete this form you must submit the following evidence of income:

- A copy of your complete Federal income tax return, as filed with the Internal Revenue Service, for each of the most recent 3 tax years. If you were not required to file a tax return in any of the most recent 3 tax years, you must provide an explanation. If you filed a joint income tax return and are using only your own income to qualify, you must also submit copies of your W-2s for each of the most recent 3 tax years, and *if* necessary to meet the income requirement, evidence of other income reported on your tax returns, such as Forms 1099.

- If you rely on income of any members of your household or dependents in order to reach the minimum income requirement, copies of their Federal income tax returns for the most recent 3 tax years. These persons must each complete and sign a Form I-864A, Contract Between Sponsor and Household Member.

- Evidence of current employment or self-employment, such as a recent pay statement, *or* a statement from your employer on business stationery, showing beginning date of employment, type of work performed, and salary or wages paid. You must also provide evidence of current employment for any person whose income is used to qualify.

Evidence of Assets

If you want to use your assets, the assets of your household members or dependents, and/or the assets of the immigrant you are sponsoring to meet the minimum income requirement, you must provide evidence of assets with a cash value that equals at least five times the difference between your total household income and the minimum income requirement. For the assets of a household member, other than the immigrant(s) you are sponsoring, to be considered, the household member must complete and sign Form I-864A, Contract Between Sponsor and Household Member.

All assets must be supported with evidence to verify location, ownership, and value of each asset. Any liens and liabilities relating to the assets must be documented. List only assets that can be readily converted into cash within 1 year. Evidence of assets includes, but is not limited to the following:

- Bank statements covering the last 12 months, *or a statement* from an officer of the bank or other financial institution in which you have deposits, including deposit/withdrawal history for the last 12 months, and current balance;

- Evidence of ownership and value of stocks, bonds, and certificates of deposit, and date(s) acquired;

- Evidence of ownership and value of other personal property, and date(s) acquired; and

- Evidence of ownership and value of any real estate, and date(s) acquired.

Change of Sponsor's Address

You are required by 8 U.S.C. 1183a(d) and 8 CFR 213a.3 to report every change of address to the Immigration and Naturalization Service and the State(s) in which the sponsored immigrant(s) reside(s). You must report changes of address to INS on Form I-865, Sponsor's Notice of Change of Address, within 30 days of any change of address. You must also report any change in your address to the State(s) in which the sponsored immigrant(s) live.

Penalties

If you include in this affidavit of support any material information that you know to be false, you may be liable for criminal prosecution under the laws of the United States.

If you fail to give notice of your change of address, as required by 8 U.S.C. 1183a(d) and 8 CFR 213a.3, you may be liable for the civil penalty established by 8 U.S.C. 1183a(d)(2). The amount of the civil penalty will depend on whether you failed to give this notice because you were aware that the immigrant(s) you sponsored had received Federal, State, or local means-tested public benefits.

Privacy Act Notice

Authority for the collection of the information requested on this form is contained in 8 U.S.C. 1182(a)(4), 1183a, 1184(a), and 1258. The information will be used principally by the INS or by any Consular Officer to whom it is furnished, to support an alien's application for benefits under the Immigration and Nationality Act and specifically the assertion that he or she has adequate means of financial support and will not become a public charge. Submission of the information is voluntary. Failure to provide the information will result in denial of the application for an immigrant visa or adjustment of status.

The information may also, as a matter of routine use, be disclosed to other Federal, State, and local agencies or private entities providing means-tested public benefits for use in civil action against the sponsor for breach of contract. It may also be disclosed as a matter of routine use to other Federal, State, local, and foreign law enforcement and regulatory agencies to enable these entities to carry out their law enforcement responsibilites.

Reporting Burden

A person is not required to respond to a collection of information unless it displays a currently valid OMB control number. We try to create forms and instructions that are accurate, can be easily understood, and which impose the least possible burden on you to provide us with information. Often this is difficult because some immigration laws are very complex. The reporting burden for this collection of information on Form I-864 is computed as follows: 1) learning about the form, 17 minutes; 2) completing the form, 22 minutes; and 3) assembling and filing the form, 30 minutes, for an estimated average of 69 minutes per response. The reporting burden for collection of information on Form I-864A is computed as: 1) learning about the form, 5 minutes; 2) completing the form, 8 minutes; 3) assembling and filing the form, 2 minutes, for an estimated average of 15 minutes per response. If you have comments regarding the accuracy of this estimates, or suggestions for making this form simpler, you can write to the Immigration and Naturalization Service, 425 I Street, N.W., Room 5307, Washington, D.C. 20536. **DO NOT MAIL YOUR COMPLETED AFFIDAVIT OF SUPPORT TO THIS ADDRESS.**

CHECK LIST

The following items must be submitted with Form I-864, Affidavit of Support Under Section 213A:

For *ALL* sponsors:

This form, the **I-864, completed and signed** before a notary public or a Consular or Immigration Officer.

Proof of **current employment** or self employment.

Your individual Federal **income tax returns for the most recent 3 tax years,** or an explanation if fewer are submitted. Your **W-2s** for any of the most recent 3 tax years for which you filed a joint tax return but are using only your own income to qualify. Forms 1099 or evidence of other reported income *if* necessary to qualify.

For *SOME* sponsors:

If the immigrant you are sponsoring is bringing a spouse or children, **photocopies of the immigrant's affidavit of support and all supporting documentation with original notarized signatures** *on each photocopy of the affidavit for each spouse and/or child immigrating with the immigrant you are sponsoring.*

If you are on active duty in the Armed Forces and are sponsoring a spouse or child using the 100 percent of poverty level exception, **proof of your active military status.**

If you are using the income of persons in your household or dependents to qualify,

A separate **Form I-864A** for each person whose income you will use other than a sponsored immigrant/household member who is not immigrating with a spouse and/or child.

Proof of their **residency** and **relationship** to you if they are not listed as dependents on your income tax return for the most recent tax year.

Proof of their **current employment** or self-employment.

☐ Copies of their individual Federal **income tax returns for the 3 most recent tax years,** or an explanation if fewer are submitted.

If you use your assets or the assets of the sponsored immigrant to qualify,

☐ **Documentation of assets** establishing location, ownership, date of acquisition, and value. Evidence of any liens or liabilities against these assets.

☐ A separate **Form I-864A** for each household member other than the sponsored immigrant/household member.

If you or a household member or dependent has used any type of means-tested public benefits in the last 3 years,

☐ **A list of the programs and dates.**

If you are a joint sponsor or the relative of an employment-based immigrant requiring an affidavit of support, **proof of your citizenship status.**

☐ For U.S. citizens or nationals, a copy of your birth certificate, passport, or certificate of naturalization or citizenship.

☐ For lawful permanent residents, a copy of both sides of your I-551, Alien Registration Receipt Card.

U.S. Department of Justice
Immigration and Naturalization Service

OMB #1115-0214

Affidavit of Support Under Section 213A of the Act

START HERE - Please Type or Print

Part 1. Information on Sponsor (You)

Last Name	First Name	Middle Name

Mailing Address *(Street Number and Name)*	Apt/Suite Number

City	State or Province

Country	ZIP/Postal Code	Telephone Number ( )

Place of Residence if different from above *(Street Number and Name)*	Apt/Suite Number

City	State or Province

Country	ZIP/Postal Code	Telephone Number ( )

Date of Birth *(Month, Day, Year)*	Place of Birth *(City, State, Country)*	Are you a U.S. Citizen? ☐ Yes ☐ No

Social Security Number	A-Number *(If any)*

FOR AGENCY USE ONLY

This Affidavit   Receipt

[ ] Meets

[ ] Does not meet

Requirements of Section 213A

Part 2. Basis for Filing Affidavit of Support

I am filing this affidavit of support because *(check one):*

a. ☐ I filed/am filing the alien relative petition.

b. ☐ I filed/am filing an alien worker petition on behalf of the intending immigrant, who is related to me as my _____ .
(relationship)

c. ☐ I have ownership interest of at least 5% of _____
(name of entity which filed visa petition)
which filed an alien worker petition on behalf of the intending immigrant, who is related to me as my _____
(relationship)

d. ☐ I am a joint sponsor willing to accept the legal obligations with any other sponsor(s).

Officer's Signature

Location

Date

Part 3. Information on the Immigrant(s) You Are Sponsoring

Last Name	First Name	Middle Name

Date of Birth *(Month, Day, Year)*	Sex: ☐ Male ☐ Female	Social Security Number *(If any)*

Country of Citizenship	A-Number *(If any)*

Current Address *(Street Number and Name)*	Apt/Suite Number	City

State/Province	Country	ZIP/Postal Code	Telephone Number ( )

List any spouse and/or children immigrating with the immigrant named above in this Part: *(Use additional sheet of paper if necessary.)*

Name	Relationship to Sponsored Immigrant			Date of Birth			A-Number *(If any)*	Social Security Number *(If any)*
	Spouse	Son	Daughter	Mo.	Day	Yr.		

Form I-864 (1/21/98)Y

Part 4.   Eligibility to Sponsor

To be a sponsor you must be a U.S. citizen or national or a lawful permanent resident. If you are not the petitioning relative, you must provide proof of status. To prove status, U.S. citizens or nationals must attach a copy of a document proving status, such as a U.S. passport, birth certificate, or certificate of naturalization, and lawful permanent residents must attach a copy of both sides of their Alien Registration Card (Form I-551).

The determination of your eligibility to sponsor an immigrant will be based on an evaluation of your demonstrated ability to maintain an annual income at or above 125 percent of the Federal poverty line (100 percent if you are a petitioner sponsoring your spouse or child and you are on active duty in the U.S. Armed Forces). The assessment of your ability to maintain an adequate income will include your current employment, household size, and household income as shown on the Federal income tax returns for the 3 most recent tax years. Assets that are readily converted to cash and that can be made available for the support of sponsored immigrants if necessary, including any such assets of the immigrant(s) you are sponsoring, may also be considered.

The greatest weight in determining eligibility will be placed on current employment and household income. If a petitioner is unable to demonstrate ability to meet the stated income and asset requirements, a joint sponsor who *can* meet the income and asset requirements is needed. Failure to provide adequate evidence of income and/or assets or an affidavit of support completed by a joint sponsor will result in denial of the immigrant's application for an immigrant visa or adjustment to permanent resident status.

A. Sponsor's Employment

I am: 1.   ☐   Employed by _____ *(Provide evidence of employment)*
Annual salary $ _____ *or* hourly wage $ _____ *(for _____ hours per week)*

2.   ☐   Self employed _____ *(Name of business)*
Nature of employment or business _____

3.   ☐   Unemployed or retired since _____

B. Use of Benefits

Have you or anyone related to you by birth, marriage, or adoption living in your household or listed as a dependent on your most recent income tax return received any type of means-tested public benefit in the past 3 years?
☐Yes   ☐   No *(If yes, provide details, including programs and dates, on a separate sheet of paper)*

C. Sponsor's Household Size   **Number**

1.   Number of persons (related to you by birth, marriage, or adoption) living in your residence, including yourself. *(Do NOT include persons being sponsored in this affidavit.)*
2.   Number of immigrants being sponsored in this affidavit *(Include all persons in Part 3.)*   _____
3.   Number of immigrants **NOT** living in your household whom you are still obligated to support under a previously signed affidavit of support using Form I-864.   _____
4.   Number of persons who are otherwise dependent on you, as claimed in your tax return for the most recent tax year.   _____
5.   Total household size.   *(Add lines 1 through 4.)*   **Total**   _____

List persons below who are included in lines 1 or 3 for whom you previously have submitted INS Form I-864, *if your support obligation has not terminated.*
(If additional space is needed, use additional paper)

Name	A-Number	Date Affidavit of Support Signed	Relationship

Form I-864 (1/21/98)Y **Page 2**

Part 4. Eligibility to Sponsor *(Continued)*

D. Sponsor's Annual Household Income

Enter total unadjusted income from your Federal income tax return for the most recent tax year below. If you last filed a joint income tax return but are using only your *own* income to qualify, list total earnings from your W-2 Forms, or, *if* necessary to reach the required income for your household size, include income from other sources listed on your tax return. If your *individual* income does not meet the income requirement for your household size, you may also list total income for anyone related to you by birth, marriage, or adoption currently living with you in your residence if they have lived in your residence for the previous 6 months, or any person shown as a dependent on your Federal income tax return for the most recent tax year, even if not living in the household. For their income to be considered, household members or dependents must be willing to make their income available for support of the sponsored immigrant(s) and to complete and sign Form I-864A, Contract Between Sponsor and Household Member. A sponsored immigrant/household member only need complete Form I-864A if his or her income will be used to determine your ability to support a spouse and/or children immigrating with him or her.

You must attach evidence of current employment and copies of income tax returns as filed with the IRS for the most recent 3 tax years for yourself and all persons whose income is listed below. See "Required Evidence" in Instructions. Income from all 3 years will be considered in determining your ability to support the immigrant(s) you are sponsoring.

☐ I filed a single/separate tax return for the most recent tax year.
☐ I filed a joint return for the most recent tax year which includes only my own income.
☐ I filed a joint return for the most recent tax year which includes income for my spouse and myself.
  ☐ I am submitting documentation of my individual income (Forms W-2 and 1099).
  ☐ I am qualifying using my spouse's income; my spouse is submitting a Form I-864A.

Indicate most recent tax year _____
(tax year)

Sponsor's individual income $_____

or

Sponsor and spouse's combined income $_____
(If joint tax return filed; spouse must submit Form I-864A.)

Income of other qualifying persons.
(List names; include spouse if applicable. Each person must complete Form I-864A.)

_____ $_____
_____ $_____
_____ $_____

Total Household Income $_____

Explain on separate sheet of paper if you or any of the above listed individuals are submitting Federal income tax returns for fewer than 3 years, or if other explanation of income, employment, or evidence is necessary.

E. Determination of Eligibility Based on Income

1. ☐ I am subject to the 125 percent of poverty line requirement for sponsors.
   ☐ I am subject to the 100 percent of poverty line requirement for sponsors on active duty in the U.S. Armed Forces sponsoring their spouse or child.
2. Sponsor's total household size, from Part 4.C., line 5 _____.
3. Minimum income requirement from the Poverty Guidelines chart for the year of _____ is $_____ for this household size. *(year)*

If you are currently employed and your household income for your household size is equal to or greater than the applicable poverty line requirement (from line E.3.), you do not need to list assets (Parts 4.F. and 5) or have a joint sponsor (Part 6) unless you are requested to do so by a Consular or Immigration Officer. You may skip to Part 7, Use of the Affidavit of Support to Overcome Public Charge Ground of Admissibility. Otherwise, you should continue with Part 4.F.

Part 4.   Eligibility to Sponsor   *(Continued)*

F. Sponsor's Assets and Liabilities

Your assets and those of your qualifying household members and dependents may be used to demonstrate ability to maintain an income at or above 125 percent (or 100 percent, if applicable) of the poverty line *if* they are available for the support of the sponsored immigrant(s) and can readily be converted into cash within 1 year.   The household member, other than the immigrant(s) you are sponsoring, must complete and sign Form I-864A, Contract Between Sponsor and Household Member.   List the cash value of each asset *after* any debts or liens are subtracted.   Supporting evidence must be attached to establish location, ownership, date of acquisition, and value of each asset listed, including any liens and liabilities related to each asset listed. See "Evidence of Assets" in Instructions.

Type of Asset	Cash Value of Assets *(Subtract any debts)*
Savings deposits	$
Stocks, bonds, certificates of deposit	$
Life insurance cash value	$
Real estate	$
Other *(specify)*	$
Total Cash Value of Assets	$

Part 5.   Immigrant's Assets and Offsetting Liabilities

The sponsored immigrant's assets may also be used in support of your ability to maintain income at or above 125 percent of the poverty line *if* the assets are or will be available in the United States for the support of the sponsored immigrant(s) and can readily be converted into cash within 1 year.

The sponsored immigrant should provide information on his or her assets in a format similar to part 4.F. above. Supporting evidence must be attached to establish location, ownership, and value of each asset listed, including any liens and liabilities for each asset listed. See "Evidence of Assets" in Instructions.

Part 6.   Joint Sponsors

If household income and assets do not meet the appropriate poverty line for your household size, a joint sponsor is required.   There may be more than one joint sponsor, but each joint sponsor must individually meet the 125 percent of poverty line requirement based on his or her household income and/or assets, including any assets of the sponsored immigrant. By submitting a separate Affidavit of Support under Section 213A of the Act (Form I-864), a joint sponsor accepts joint responsibility with the petitioner for the sponsored immigrant(s) until they become U.S. citizens, can be credited with 40 quarters of work, leave the United States permanently, or die.

Part 7.   Use of the Affidavit of Support to Overcome Public Charge Ground of Inadmissibility

Section 212(a)(4)(C) of the Immigration and Nationality Act provides that an alien seeking permanent residence as an immediate relative (including an orphan), as a family-sponsored immigrant, or as an alien who will accompany or follow to join another alien is considered to be likely to become a public charge and is inadmissible to the United States unless a sponsor submits a legally enforceable affidavit of support on behalf of the alien.   Section 212(a)(4)(D) imposes the same requirement on an employment-based immigrant, and those aliens who accompany or follow to join the employment-based immigrant, if the employment-based immigrant will be employed by a relative, or by a firm in which a relative owns a significant interest.   Separate affidavits of support are required for family members at the time they immigrate if they are not included on this affidavit of support or do not apply for an immigrant visa or adjustment of status within 6 months of the date this affidavit of support is originally signed.   The sponsor must provide the sponsored immigrant(s) whatever support is necessary to maintain them at an income that is at least 125 percent of the Federal poverty guidelines.

> *I submit this affidavit of support in consideration of the sponsored immigrant(s) not being found inadmissible to the United States under section 212(a)(4)(C) (or 212(a)(4)(D) for an employment-based immigrant) and to enable the sponsored immigrant(s) to overcome this ground of inadmissibility.   I agree to provide the sponsored immigrant(s) whatever support is necessary to maintain the sponsored immigrant(s) at an income that is at least 125 percent of the Federal poverty guidelines.   I understand that my obligation will continue until my death or the sponsored immigrant(s) have become U.S. citizens, can be credited with 40 quarters of work, depart the United States permanently, or die.*

Part 7. Use of the Affidavit of Support to Overcome Public Charge Grounds *(Continued)*

Notice of Change of Address.

Sponsors are required to provide written notice of any change of address within 30 days of the change in address until the sponsored immigrant(s) have become U.S. citizens, can be credited with 40 quarters of work, depart the United States permanently, or die. To comply with this requirement, the sponsor must complete INS Form I-865. Failure to give this notice may subject the sponsor to the civil penalty established under section 213A(d)(2) which ranges from $250 to $2,000, unless the failure to report occurred with the knowledge that the sponsored immigrant(s) had received means-tested public benefits, in which case the penalty ranges from $2,000 to $5,000.

> *If my address changes for any reason before my obligations under this affidavit of support terminate, I will complete and file INS Form I-865, Sponsor's Notice of Change of Address, within 30 days of the change of address. I understand that failure to give this notice may subject me to civil penalties.*

Means-tested Public Benefit Prohibitions and Exceptions.

Under section 403(a) of Public Law 104-193 (Welfare Reform Act), aliens lawfully admitted for permanent residence in the United States, with certain exceptions, are ineligible for most Federally-funded means-tested public benefits during their first 5 years in the United States. This provision does not apply to public benefits specified in section 403(c) of the Welfare Reform Act or to State public benefits, including emergency Medicaid; short-term, non-cash emergency relief; services provided under the National School Lunch and Child Nutrition Acts; immunizations and testing and treatment for communicable diseases; student assistance under the Higher Education Act and the Public Health Service Act; certain forms of foster-care or adoption assistance under the Social Security Act; Head Start programs; means-tested programs under the Elementary and Secondary Education Act; and Job Training Partnership Act programs.

Consideration of Sponsor's Income in Determining Eligibility for Benefits.

If a permanent resident alien is no longer statutorily barred from a Federally-funded means-tested public benefit program and applies for such a benefit, the income and resources of the sponsor and the sponsor's spouse will be considered (or deemed) to be the income and resources of the sponsored immigrant in determining the immigrant's eligibility for Federal means-tested public benefits. Any State or local government may also choose to consider (or deem) the income and resources of the sponsor and the sponsor's spouse to be the income and resources of the immigrant for the purposes of determining eligibility for their means-tested public benefits. The attribution of the income and resources of the sponsor and the sponsor's spouse to the immigrant will continue until the immigrant becomes a U.S. citizen or has worked or can be credited with 40 qualifying quarters of work, provided that the immigrant or the worker crediting the quarters to the immigrant has not received any Federal means-tested public benefit during any creditable quarter for any period after December 31, 1996.

> *I understand that, under section 213A of the Immigration and Nationality Act (the Act), as amended, this affidavit of support constitutes a contract between me and the U.S. Government. This contract is designed to protect the United States Government, and State and local government agencies or private entities that provide means-tested public benefits, from having to pay benefits to or on behalf of the sponsored immigrant(s), for as long as I am obligated to support them under this affidavit of support. I understand that the sponsored immigrants, or any Federal, State, local, or private entity that pays any means-tested benefit to or on behalf of the sponsored immigrant(s), are entitled to sue me if I fail to meet my obligations under this affidavit of support, as defined by section 213A and INS regulations.*

Civil Action to Enforce.

If the immigrant on whose behalf this affidavit of support is executed receives any Federal, State, or local means-tested public benefit before this obligation terminates, the Federal, State, or local agency or private entity may request reimbursement from the sponsor who signed this affidavit. If the sponsor fails to honor the request for reimbursement, the agency may sue the sponsor in any U.S. District Court or any State court with jurisdiction of civil actions for breach of contract. INS will provide names, addresses, and Social Security account numbers of sponsors to benefit-providing agencies for this purpose. Sponsors may also be liable for paying the costs of collection, including legal fees.

Part 7.   Use of the Affidavit of Support to Overcome Public Charge Grounds   *(Continued)*

I acknowledge that section 213A(a)(1)(B) of the Act grants the sponsored immigrant(s) and any Federal, State, local, or private agency that pays any means-tested public benefit to or on behalf of the sponsored immigrant(s) standing to sue me for failing to meet my obligations under this affidavit of support. I agree to submit to the personal jurisdiction of any court of the United States or of any State, territory, or possession of the United States if the court has subject matter jurisdiction of a civil lawsuit to enforce this affidavit of support. I agree that no lawsuit to enforce this affidavit of support shall be barred by any statute of limitations that might otherwise apply, so long as the plaintiff initiates the civil lawsuit no later than ten (10) years after the date on which a sponsored immigrant last received any means-tested public benefits.

Collection of Judgment.

I acknowledge that a plaintiff may seek specific performance of my support obligation. Furthermore, any money judgment against me based on this affidavit of support may be collected through the use of a judgment lien under 28 U.S.C. 3201, a writ of execution under 28 U.S.C. 3203, a judicial installment payment order under 28 U.S.C. 3204, garnishment under 28 U.S.C. 3205, or through the use of any corresponding remedy under State law. I may also be held liable for costs of collection, including attorney fees.

Concluding Provisions.

I, _____ , *certify under penalty of perjury under the laws of the United States that:*

(a) *I know the contents of this affidavit of support signed by me;*

(b) *All the statements in this affidavit of support are true and correct;*

(c) *I make this affidavit of support for the consideration stated in Part 7, freely, and without any mental reservation or purpose of evasion;*

(d) *Income tax returns submitted in support of this affidavit are true copies of the returns filed with the Internal Revenue Service; and*

(e) *Any other evidence submitted is true and correct.*

_____   _____
(Sponsor's Signature)   *(Date)*

Subscribed and sworn to *(or affirmed)* before me this

_____ day of _____ , _____
                              (Month)   *(Year)*

at _____ .

My commission expires on _____ .

_____
(Signature of Notary Public or Officer Administering Oath)

_____
(Title)

Part 8.   If someone other than the sponsor prepared this affidavit of support, that person must complete the following:

I certify under penalty of perjury under the laws of the United States that I prepared this affidavit of support at the sponsor's request, and that this affidavit of support is based on all information of which I have knowledge.

Signature	Print Your Name	Date	Daytime Telephone Number ( )

Firm Name and Address

OMB #1115-0214

U.S. Department of Justice
Immigration and Naturalization Service

Contract Between Sponsor and Household Member

Sponsor's Name *(Last, First, Middle)*	Social Security Number	A-Number (If any)

General Filing Instructions:

Form I-864A, Contract Between Sponsor and Household Member, is an attachment to Form I-864, Affidavit of Support Under Section 213A of the Immigration and Nationality Act (the Act). The sponsor enters the information above, completes Part 2 of this form, and signs in Part 5. The household member completes Parts 1 and 3 of this form and signs in Part 6. A household member who is also the sponsored immigrant completes Parts 1 and 4 (Instead of Part 3) of this form and signs in Part 6. The Privacy Act Notice and information on penalties for misrepresentation or fraud are included on the instructions to Form I-864.

The signatures on the I-864A must be notarized by a notary public or signed before an Immigration or Consular Officer. A separate form must be used for each household member whose income and/or assets are being used to qualify. This blank form may be photocopied for that purpose. A sponsored immigrant who qualifies as a household member is only required to complete this form if he or she has one or more family members immigrating with him or her and is making his or her *income* available for their support. Sponsored immigrants who are using their *assets* to qualify are not required to complete this form. This completed form is submitted with Form I-864 by the sponsored immigrant with an application for an immigrant visa or adjustment of status.

Purpose:

This contract is intended to benefit the sponsored immigrant(s) and any agency of the Federal Government, any agency of a State or local government, or any private entity to which the sponsor has an obligation under the affidavit of support to reimburse for benefits granted to the sponsored immigrant, and these parties will have the right to enforce this contract in any court with appropriate jurisdiction. This contract must be completed and signed by the sponsor and any household member, including the sponsor's spouse, whose income is included as household income by a person sponsoring one or more immigrants under Section 213A of Act. The contract must also be completed if a sponsor is relying on the assets of a household member who is not the sponsored immigrant to meet the income requirements. If the sponsored immigrant is a household member immigrating with a spouse or children, and is using his or her income to assist the sponsor in meeting the income requirement, he or she must complete and sign this contract as a "sponsored immigrant/household member."

By signing this form, a household member, who is not a sponsored immigrant, agrees to make his or her income and/or assets available to the sponsor to help support the immigrant(s) for whom the sponsor has filed an affidavit of support and to be responsible, along with the sponsor, to pay any debt incurred by the sponsor under the affidavit of support. A sponsored immigrant/household member who signs this contract agrees to make his or her income available to the sponsor to help support any spouse or children immigrating with him or her and to be responsible, along with the sponsor, to pay any debt incurred by the sponsor under the affidavit of support. The obligations of the household member and the sponsored immigrant/household member under this contract terminate when the obligations of the sponsor under the affidavit of support terminate. For additional information see section 213A of the Act, part 213a of title 8 of the Code of Federal Regulations, and Form I-864, Affidavit of Support Under Section 213A of the Act.

Definitions:

1) An "affidavit of support" refers to INS Form I-864, Affidavit of Support Under Section 213A of the Act, which is completed and filed by the sponsor;

2) A "sponsor" is a person, either the petitioning relative, the relative with a significant ownership interest in the petitioning entity, or another person accepting joint and several liability with the sponsor, who completes and files the Affidavit of Support under Section 213A of the Act on behalf of a sponsored immigrant;

3) A "household member" is any person (a) sharing a residence with the sponsor for at least the last 6 months who is related to the sponsor by birth, marriage, or adoption, *or* (b) whom the sponsor has lawfully claimed as a dependent on the sponsor's most recent Federal income tax return even if that person does not live at the same residence as the sponsor, *and* whose income and/or assets will be used to demonstrate the sponsor's ability to maintain the sponsored immigrant(s) at an annual income at the level specified in section 213A(f)(1)(E) or 213A(f)(3) of the Act;

4) A "sponsored immigrant" is a person listed on this form on whose behalf an affidavit of support will be completed and filed; and

5) A "sponsored immigrant/household member" is a sponsored immigrant who is also a household member.

Part 1. Information on Sponsor's Household Member or Sponsored Immigrant/Household Member

Last Name	First Name	Middle Name

Date of Birth *(Month, Day, Year)*	Social Security Number *(Mandatory for non-citizens; voluntary for U.S. citizens)*	A-Number *(If any)*

Address *(Street Number and Name)*	Apt Number	City	State/Province	ZIP/Postal Code

Telephone Number ( )	Relationship to Sponsor: _____ I am: ☐ The sponsor's household member. *(Complete Part 3.)* ☐ The sponsored immigrant/household member. *(Complete Part 4.)*	Length of residence with sponsor (_____ years, _____ months)

Part 2. Sponsor's Promise

I, THE SPONSOR, _____, in consideration of the household member's promise to support the
(Print name of sponsor)
sponsored immigrant(s) and to be jointly and severally liable for any obligations I incur under the affidavit of support, promise to complete and file an affidavit of support on behalf of the following_____ sponsored immigrant(s):
(Indicate number)

Name of Sponsored Immigrant *(First, Middle, Last)*	Date of Birth *(Month, Day, Year)*	Social Security Number *(If any)*	A-Number *(If any)*
_____	_____	_____	_____
_____	_____	_____	_____
_____	_____	_____	_____
_____	_____	_____	_____
_____	_____	_____	_____

Part 3. Household Member's Promise

I, THE HOUSEHOLD MEMBER, _____, in consideration of the sponsor's
(Print name of household member)
promise to complete and file the affidavit of support on behalf of the sponsored immigrant(s):

1) Promise to provide any and all financial support necessary to assist the sponsor in maintaining the sponsored immigrant(s) at or above the minimum income provided for in section 213A(a)(1)(A) of the Act (not less than 125 percent of the Federal poverty line) during the period in which the affidavit of support is enforceable;

2) Agree to be jointly and severally liable for payment of any and all obligations owed by the sponsor under the affidavit of support to the sponsored immigrant(s), to any agency of the Federal Government, to any agency of a State or local government, or to any private entity;

3) Agree to submit to the personal jurisdiction of any court of the United States or of any State, territory, or possession of the United States if the court has subject matter jurisdiction of a civil lawsuit to enforce this contract or the affidavit of support; and

4) Certify under penalty of perjury under the laws of the United States that all the information provided on this form is true and correct to the best of my knowledge and belief and that the income tax returns I submitted in support of the sponsor's affidavit are true copies of the returns filed with the Internal Revenue Service.

Part 4. Sponsored Immigrant/Household Member's Promise

I, THE SPONSORED IMMIGRANT/HOUSEHOLD MEMBER, _____

(Print name of sponsored immigrant)

in consideration of the sponsor's promise to complete and file the affidavit of support on behalf of the sponsored immigrant(s) accompanying me:

1) Promise to provide any and all financial support necessary to assist the sponsor in maintaining any sponsored immigrant(s) immigrating with me at or above the minimum income provided for in section 213A(a)(1)(A) of the Act (not less than 125 percent of the Federal poverty line) during the period in which the affidavit of support is enforceable;

2) Agree to be jointly and severally liable for payment of any and all obligations owed by the sponsor under the affidavit of support to any sponsored immigrant(s) immigrating with me, to any agency of the Federal Government, to any agency of a State or local government, or to any private entity;

3) Agree to submit to the personal jurisdiction of any court of the United States or of any State, territory, or possession of the United States if the court has subject matter jurisdiction of a civil lawsuit to enforce this contract or the affidavit of support; and

4) Certify under penalty of perjury under the laws of the United States that all the information provided on this form is true and correct to the best of my knowledge and belief and that the income tax returns I submitted in support of the sponsor's affidavit of support are true copies of the returns filed with the Internal Revenue Service.

Part 5. Sponsor's Signature

_____ Date: _____

Sponsor's Signature

Subscribed and sworn to *(or affirmed)* before me this _____ day of _____ , _____

(Month) *(Year)*

at _____ . My commission expires on _____ .

_____ _____

Signature of Notary Public or Officer Administering Oath *Title*

Part 6. Household Member's or Sponsored Immigrant/Household Member's Signature

_____ Date: _____

Household Member's or Sponsored Immigrant/Household Member's Signature

Subscribed and sworn to *(or affirmed)* before me this _____ day of _____ , _____

(Month) *(Year)*

at _____ . My commission expires on _____ .

_____ _____

Signature of Notary Public or Officer Administering Oath *Title*

Form I-864A (1/21/98)Y **Page 3**

U. S. Department of Justice
Immigration and Naturalization Service

OMB# 1115-0214
Poverty Guidelines

2000 Poverty Guidelines*
Minimum Income Requirement For Use in Completing Form I-864

For the 48 Contiguous States, the District of Columbia, Puerto Rico, the U.S. Virgin Islands, and Guam:

Sponsor's Household Size	100% of Poverty Line For sponsors on active duty in the U.S. Armed Forces who are petitioning for their spouse or child.	125% of Poverty Line For all other sponsors
2	$11.250	$14,062
3	14,150	17,687
4	17,050	21,312
5	19,950	24,937
6	22,850	28,562
7	25,750	32,187
8	28,650	35,812
	Add $2,900 for each additional person.	Add $3,625 for each additional person.

Sponsor's Household Size	For Alaska 100% of Poverty Line For sponsors on active duty in the U.S. Armed Forces who are petitioning for their spouse or child	125% of Poverty Line For all other sponsors	For Hawaii 100% of Poverty Line For sponsors on active duty in the U.S. Armed Forces who are petitioning for their spouse or child	125% of Poverty Line For all other sponsors
2	$14,060	$17,575	$12,930	$16,162
3	17,690	22,112	16,270	20,337
4	21,320	26,650	19,610	24,512
5	24,950	31,187	22,950	28,687
6	28,580	35,725	26,290	32,862
7	32,210	40,262	29,630	37,037
8	35,840	44,800	32,970	41,212
	Add $3,630 for each additional person.	Add $4,537 for each additional person.	Add $3,340 for each additional person.	Add $4,175 for each additional person.

Means-tested Public Benefits

Federal Means-tested Public Benefits. To date, Federal agencies administering benefit programs have determined that Federal means-tested public benefits include Food Stamps, Medicaid, Supplemental Security Income (SSI), Temporary Assistance for Needy Families (TANF), and the State Child Health Insurance Program (CHIP).

State Means-tested Public Benefits. Each State will determine which, if any, of its public benefits are means-tested. If a State determines that it has programs which meet this definition, it is encouraged to provide notice to the public on which programs are included. Check with the State public assistance office to determine which, if any, State assistance programs have been determined to be State means-tested public benefits.

Programs Not Included: The following Federal and State programs are *not* included as means-tested benefits: emergency Medicaid; short-term, non-cash emergency relief; services provided under the National School Lunch and Child Nutrition Acts; immunizations and testing and treatment for communicable diseases; student assistance under the Higher Education Act and the Public Health Service Act; certain forms of foster-care or adoption assistance under the Social Security Act; Head Start Programs; means-tested programs under the Elementary and Secondary Education Act; and Job Training Partnership Act programs.

* These poverty guidelines remain in effect for use with the Form I-864 Affidavit of Support from April 1, 2000 until new poverty guidelines go into effect in the Spring of 2001.

Form I-864P (Rev. 3/14/00)N

U. S. Department of Justice
Immigration and Naturalization Service

OMB # 1115-0163
Application for Employment Authorization

Do Not Write In This Block

Remarks	Action Stamp	Fee Stamp
A#		
Applicant is filing under 274a.12 _____		

☐ Application Approved. Employment Authorized / Extended (Circle One) _____ (Date).
until _____ (Date).
Subject to the following conditions: _____
☐ Application Denied.
    ☐ Failed to establish eligibility under 8 CFR 274a.12 (a) or (c).
    ☐ Failed to establish economic necessity as required in 8 CFR 274a.12(c) (14), (18) and 8 CFR 214.2(f)

I am applying for: ☐ Permission to accept employment
    ☐ Replacement (of lost employment authorization document).
    ☐ Renewal of my permission to accept employment (attach previous employment authorization document).

1. Name (Family Name in CAPS)   (First)   (Middle)

2. Other Names Used (Include Maiden Name)

3. Address in the United States (Number and Street)   (Apt. Number)

   (Town or City)   (State/Country)   (ZIP Code)

4. Country of Citizenship/Nationality

5. Place of Birth (Town or City) (State/Province)   (Country)

6. Date of Birth (Month/Day/Year)   7. Sex   ☐ Male ☐ Female

8. Marital Status   ☐ Married   ☐ Single   ☐ Widowed   ☐ Divorced

9. Social Security Number (Include all Numbers you have ever used)

10. Alien Registration Number (A-Number) or I-94 Number (if any)

11. Have you ever before applied for employment authorization from INS?
   ☐ Yes (If yes, complete below)   ☐ No
   Which INS Office?   Date(s)

   Results (Granted or Denied - attach all documentation)

12. Date of Last Entry into the U.S. (Month/Day/Year)

13. Place of Last Entry into the U.S.

14. Manner of Last Entry (Visitor, Student, etc.)

15. Current Immigration Status (Visitor, Student, etc.)

16. Go to Part 2 of the instructions, Eligibility Categories. In the space below, place the letter and number of the category you selected from the instructions (For example, (a)(8), (c)(17)(iii), etc.).

Eligibility under 8 CFR 274a.12

(   ) (   ) (   )

Certification

Your Certification: I certify, under penalty of perjury under the laws of the United States of America, that the foregoing is true and correct. Furthermore, I authorize the release of any information which the Immigration and Naturalization Service needs to determine eligibility for the benefit I am seeking. I have read the Instructions in Part 2 and have identified the appropriate eligibility category in Block 16.

Signature   Telephone Number   Date

Signature of Person Preparing Form If Other Than Above: I declare that this document was prepared by me at the request of the applicant and is based on all information of which I have any knowledge.

Print Name   Address   Signature   Date

Initial Receipt	Resubmitted	Relocated		Completed		
		Rec'd	Sent	Approved	Denied	Returned

Form I-765 (Rev. 10/13/98)N Page 7

U.S. Department of Justice
Immigration and Naturalization Service

OMB No. 1115-0145

Petition to Remove the Conditions on Residence

Purpose Of This Form.
This form is for a conditional resident who obtained such status through marriage to apply to remove the conditions on his or her residence.

Who May File.
If you were granted conditional resident status through marriage to a U.S. citizen or permanent resident, use this form to petition for the removal of those conditions. Your petition should be filed jointly by you and the spouse through whom you obtained conditional status if you are still married. However, you can apply for a waiver of this joint filing requirement on this form if:

- you entered into the marriage in good faith, but your spouse subsequently died;
- you entered into the marriage in good faith, but the marriage was later terminated due to divorce or annulment;
- you entered nto the marriage in good faith, and remain married, but have been battered or subjected to extreme mental cruelty by your U.S. citizen or permanent resident spouse; or
- the termination of your status, and deportation, would result in extreme hardship.

You may include your conditional resident children in your petition, or they can file separately.

General Filing Instructions.
Please answer all questions by typing or clearly printing in black ink. Indicate that an item is not applicable with "N/A". If an answer is "none," write "none". If you need extra space to answer any item, attach a sheet of paper with your name and your alien registration number (A#), and indicate the number of the item to which the answer refers. You must file your petition with the required Initial Evidence. Your petition must be properly signed and accompanied by the correct fee. If you are under 14 years of age, your parent or guardian may sign the petition in your behalf.

Translations. Any foreign language document must be accompanied by a full English translation which the translator has certified as complete and correct, and by the translator's certification that he or she is competent to translate from the foreign language into English.

Copies. If these instructions state that a copy of a document may be filed with this petition, and you choose to send us the original, we may keep that original for our records.

Initial Evidence.
Alien Registration Card. You must file your petition with a copy of your alien registration card, and with a copy of the alien registration card of any of your conditional resident children you are including in your petition.

Evidence of the relationship. Submit copies of documents indicating that the marriage upon which you were granted conditional status was entered into in "good faith", and was not for the purpose of circumventing immigration laws. You should submit copies of as many documents as you wish to establish this fact and to demonstrate the circumstances of the relationship from the date of the marriage to date, and to demonstrate any circumstances surrounding the end of the relationship, if it has ended. The documents should cover as much of the period since your marriage as possible. Examples of such documents are:

- Birth certificate(s) of child(ren) born to the marriage.
- Lease or mortgage contracts showing joint occupancy and/ or ownership of your communal residence.
- Financial records showing joint ownership of assets and joint responsibility for liabilities, such as joint savings and checking accounts, joint federal and state tax returns, insurance policies which show the other as the beneficiary, joint utility bills, joint installment or other loans.
- Other documents you consider relevant to establish that your marriage was not entered into in order to evade the immigration laws of the United States.

- Affidavits sworn to or affirmed by at least 2 people who have known both of you since your conditional residence was granted and have personal knowledge of your marriage and relationship. (Such persons may be required to testify before an immigration officer as to the information contained in the affidavit.) The original affidavit must be submitted, and it must also contain the following information regarding the person making the affidavit: his or her full name and address; date and place of birth; relationship to you or your spouse, if any; and full information and complete details explaining how the person acquired his or her knowledge. Affidavits must be supported by other types of evidence listed above.

If you are filing to waive the joint filing requirement due to the death of your spouse, also submit a copy of the death certificate with your petition.

If you are filing to waive the joint filing requirement because your marriage has been terminated, also submit a copy of the divorce decree or other document terminating or annulling the marriage with your petition.

If you are filing to waive the joint filing requirement because you and/or your conditional resident child were battered or subjected to extreme mental cruelty, also file your petition with the following.

- Evidence of the physical abuse, such as copies of reports or official records issued by police, judges, medical personnel, school officials, and representatives of social service agencies, and original affidavits as described under *Evidence of the Relationship*; or
- Evidence of the extreme mental cruelty, and an original evaluation by a professional recognized by the Service as an expert in the field. These experts include clinical social workers, psychologists and psychiatrists. A clinical social worker who is not licensed only because the State in which he or she practices does not provide for licensing is considered a licensed professional recognized by the Service if he or she is included by the National Association of Social Workers or is certified by the American Board of Examiners in Clinical Social Work. Each evaluation must contain the professional's full name, professional address and license number. It must also identify the licensing, certifying or registering authority.
- A copy of your divorce decree if your marriage was terminated by divorce on grounds of physical abuse or mental cruelty.

If you are filing for a waiver of the joint filing requirement because the termination of your status, and deportation would result in "extreme hardship", you must also file your petition with evidence your deportation would result in hardship significantly greater than the hardship encountered by other aliens who are deported from this country after extended stays. The evidence must relate only to those factors which arose since you became a conditional resident.

If you are a child filing separately from your parent, also file your petition with a full explanation as to why you are filing separately, along with copies of any supporting documentation.

When To File.
Filing jointly. If you are filing this petition jointly with your spouse, you must file it during the 90 days immediately before the second anniversary of the date you were accorded conditional resident status. This is the date your conditional residence expires. However, if you and your spouse are outside the United States on orders of the U.S. Government during the period in which the petition must be filed, you may file it within 90 days of your return to the U.S.

Form I-751 (Rev. 10/13/98)N

Filing with a request that the joint filing requirement be waived. You may file this petition at any time after you are granted conditional resident status and before you are deported.

Effect Of Not Filing. If this petition is not filed, you will automatically lose your permanent resident status as of the second anniversary of the date on which you were granted this status. You will then become deportable from the United States. If your failure to file was through no fault of your own, you may file your petition late with a written explanation and request that INS excuse the late filing. Failure to file before the expiration date may be excused if you demonstrate when you file the application that the delay was due to extraordinary circumstances beyond your control and that the length of the delay was reasonable.

Effect of Filing.
Filing this petition extends your conditional residence for six months. You will receive a filing receipt which you should carry with your alien registration card (Form I-551). If you travel outside the U.S. during this period, you may present your card and the filing receipt to be readmitted.

Where To File.
If you live in Connecticut, Delaware, District of Columbia, Maine, Maryland, Massachusetts, New Hampshire, New Jersey, New York, Pennsylvania, Puerto Rico, Rhode Island, Vermont, Virgin Islands, Virginia, or West Virginia, mail your petition to: USINS Eastern Service Center, 75 Lower Welden Street, St. Albans, VT 05479-0001.

If you live in Alabama, Arkansas, Florida, Georgia, Kentucky, Louisiana, Mississippi, New Mexico, North Carolina, Oklahoma, South Carolina, Tennessee, or Texas, mail your petition to: USINS Southern Service Center, P.O. Box 152122, Dept. A, Irving, TX 75015-2122.

If you live in Arizona, California, Guam, Hawaii, or Nevada, mail your petition to: USINS Western Service Center, P.O. Box 30111, Laguna Niguel, CA 92607-0111.

If you live in elsewhere in the U.S., mail your petition to: USINS Northern Service Center, 100 Centennial Mall North, Room B-26, Lincoln, NE 68508.

Fee.
The fee for this petition is $125.00. The fee must be submitted in the exact amount. It cannot be refunded. **DO NOT MAIL CASH.**

All checks and money orders must be drawn on a bank or other institution located in the United States and must be payable in United States currency. The check or money order should be made payable to the Immigration and Naturalization Service, except that:

- If you live in Guam, and are filing this petition in Guam, make your check or money order payable to the "Treasurer, Guam".
- If you are living in the Virgin Islands, and are filing this application in the Virgin Islands, make your check or money order payable to the "Commissioner of Finance of the Virgin Islands".

Checks are accepted subject to collection. An uncollected check will render the application and any document issued invalid. A charge of $30.00 will be imposed if a check in payment of a fee is not honored by the bank on which it is drawn.

Processing Information.
Acceptance. Any petition that is not signed, or is not accompanied by the correct fee, will be rejected with a notice that the petition is deficient. You may correct the deficiency and resubmit the petition. A petition is not considered properly filed until accepted by the Service.

Initial processing. Once a petition has been accepted, it will be checked for completeness, including submission of the required initial evidence. If you do not completely fill out the form, or file if without required initial evidence, you will not establish a basis for eligibility, and we may deny your petition.

Requests for more information or interview. We may request more information or evidence, or we may request that you appear at an INS office for an interview. We may also request that you submit the originals of any copy. We will return these originals when they are no longer required.

Decision. You will be advised in writing of the decision on your petition.

Penalties.
If you knowingly and willfully falsify or conceal a material fact or submit a false document with this request, we will deny the benefit you are filing for, and may deny any other immigration benefit. In addition, you will face severe penalties provided by law, and may be subject to criminal prosecution.

Privacy Act Notice.
We ask for the information on this form, and associated evidence, to determine if you have established eligibility for the immigration benefit you are filing for. Our legal right to ask for this information is in 8 USC 1184, 1255 and 1258. Failure to provide this information, and any requested evidence, may delay a final decision or result in denial of your request.

All the information provided on this form, including addresses, are protected by the Privacy Act and the Freedom of Information Act. This information will not be released in any form whatsoever to a third party, other than another government agency, who requests it without a court order, or without your written consent, or, in the case of a child, the written consent of the parent or legal guardian who filed the form on the child's behalf.

Paperwork Reduction Act Notice.
A person is not required to respond to a collection of information unless it displays a currently valid OMB control number. We try to create forms and instructions that are accurate, can be easily understood, and which impose the least possible burden on you to provide us with information. Often this is difficult because some immigration laws are very complex. The estimated average time to complete and file this application is as follows: (1) 15 minutes to learn about the law and form; (2) 15 minutes to complete the form; and (3) 50 minutes to assemble and file the petition; for a total estimated average of 1 hour and 20 minutes per petition. If you have comments regarding the accuracy of this estimate, or suggestions for making this form simpler, you can write to the Immigration and Naturalization Service, 425 I Street, N.W., Room 5307, Washington, D.C. 20536; OMB No. 1115-0145. **DO NOT MAIL YOUR COMPLETED APPLICATION TO THIS ADDRESS.**

Form I-751 (Rev. 10/13/98)N

U.S. Department of Justice
Immigration and Naturalization Service

Petition to Remove the Conditions on Residence

OMB No. 1115-0145

START HERE - Please Type or Print

Part 1. Information about you.

Family Name	Given Name	Middle Initial

Address - C/O:

Street Number and Name		Apt. #
City	State or Province	
Country	ZIP/Postal Code	

Date of Birth (month/day/year)	Country of Birth
Social Security #	A #

Conditional residence expires on (month/day/year)

Mailing address if different from residence in C/O:

Street Number and Name		Apt #
City	State or Province	
Country	ZIP/Postal Code	

Part 2. Basis for petition *(check one)*.

a. ☐ My conditional residence is based on my marriage to a U.S. citizen or permanent resident, and we are filing this petition together.

b. ☐ I am a child who entered as a conditional permanent resident and I am unable to be included in a Joint Petition to Remove the Conditional Basis of Alien's Permanent Residence (Form I-751) filed by my parent(s).

My conditional residence is based on my marriage to a U.S. citizen or permanent resident, but I am unable to file a joint petition and I request a waiver because: (check one)

c. ☐ My spouse is deceased.

d. ☐ I entered into the marriage in good faith, but the marriage was terminated though divorce/annulment.

e. ☐ I am a conditional resident spouse who entered in to the marriage in good faith, or I am a conditional resident child, who has been battered or subjected to extreme mental cruelty by my citizen or permanent resident spouse or parent.

f. ☐ The termination of my status and deportation from the United States would result in an extreme hardship.

Part 3. Additional information about you.

Other names used *(including maiden name)*:	Telephone #
Date of Marriage	Place of Marriage

If your spouse is deceased, give the date of death (month/day/year)

Are you in deportation or exclusion proceedings?   ☐ Yes ☐ No

Was a fee paid to anyone other than an attorney in connection with this petition?   ☐ Yes ☐ No

Continued on back.

FOR INS USE ONLY

Returned	Receipt

Resubmitted

Reloc Sent

Reloc Rec'd

☐ Applicant Interviewed

Remarks

Action

To Be Completed by Attorney or Representative, if any
☐ Fill in box if G-28 is attached to represent the applicant

VOLAG#

ATTY State License #

Form I-751 (Rev. 10/13/98)N

Part 3. Additional Information about you. (con't)

Since becoming a conditional resident, have you ever been arrested, cited, charged, indicted, convicted, fined or imprisoned for breaking or violating any law or ordinace (excluding traffic regulations), or committed any crime for which you were not arrested? □ Yes □ No

If you are married, is this a different marriage than the one through which conditional residence status was obtained? □ Yes □ No

Have you resided at any other address since you became a permanent resident? □ Yes □ No *(If yes, attach a list of all addresses and dates.)*

Is your spouse currently serving employed by the U. S. government and serving outside the U.S.? □ Yes □ No

Part 4. Information about the spouse or parent through whom you gained your conditional residence.

Family Name	Given Name	Middle Initial	Phone Number ( )
Address			

Date of Birth *(month/day/year)*	Social Security #	A#

Part 5. Information about your children. List all your children. Attach another sheet if necessary

	Name	Date of Birth *(month/day/year)*	If in U.S., give A#, current immigration status and U.S. Address	Living with you?
1				□ Yes □ No
2				□ Yes □ No
3				□ Yes □ No
4				□ Yes □ No

Part 6. Complete if you are requesting a waiver of the joint filing petition requirement based on extreme mental cruelty.

Evaluator's ID Number: State: [ ] Number: [ ][ ][ ][ ][ ][ ][ ][ ]	Expires on *(month/day/year)*	Occupation
Last Name	First Name	Address

Part 7. Signature. Read the information on penalties in the instructions before completing this section. If you checked block "a" in Part 2 your spouse must also sign below.

I certify, under penalty of perjury under the laws of the United States of America, that this petition, and the evidence submitted with it, is all true and correct. If conditional residence was based on a marriage, I further certify that the marriage was entered into in accordance with the laws of the place where the marriage took place, and was not for the purpose of procuring an immigration benefit. I also authorize the release of any information from my records which the Immigration and Naturalization Service needs to determine eligibility for the benefit being sought.

Signature	Print Name	Date
Signature of Spouse	Print Name	Date

Please note: If you do not completely fill out this form, or fail to submit any required documents listed in the instructions, then you cannot be found eligible for the requested benefit, and this petition may be denied.

Part 8. Signature of person preparing form if other than above.

I declare that I prepared this petition at the request of the above person and it is based on all information of which I have knowledge.

Signature	Print Name	Date

Firm Name and Address

Form I-751 (Rev. 10/13/98)N

U.S. Department of Justice

Immigration and Naturalization Service

OMB #1115-0009

Application   for Naturalization

INSTRUCTIONS

Purpose of This Form.
This form is for use to apply to become a naturalized citizen of the United States.

Who May File.
You may apply for naturalization if:
- you have been a lawful permanent resident for five years;
- you have been a lawful permanent resident for three years, have been married to a United States citizen for those three years, and continue to be married to that U.S. citizen;
- you are the lawful permanent resident child of United States citizen parents; or
- you have qualifying military service.

Children under 18 may automatically become citizens when their parents naturalize. You may inquire at your local Service office for further information. If you do not meet the qualifications listed above but believe that you are eligible for naturalization, you may inquire at your local Service office for additional information.

General Instructions.
Please answer all questions by typing or clearly printing in black ink. Indicate that an item is not applicable with "N/A". If an answer is "none," write "none". If you need extra space to answer any item, attach a sheet of paper with your name and your alien registration number (A#), if any, and indicate the number of the item.

Every application must be properly signed and filed with the correct fee. If you are under 18 years of age, your parent or guardian must sign the application.

If you wish to be called for your examination at the same time as another person who is also applying for naturalization, make your request on a separate cover sheet. Be sure to give the name and alien registration number of that person.

Initial Evidence Requirements.
You must file your application with the following evidence:

A copy of your alien registration card.

Photographs. You must submit two color photographs of yourself taken within 30 days of this application. These photos must be glossy, unretouched and unmounted, and have a white background. Dimension of the face should be about 1 inch from chin to top of hair. Face should be 3/4 frontal view of right side with right ear visible. Using pencil or felt pen, lightly print name and A#, if any, on the back of each photo. This requirement may be waived by the Service if you can establish that you are confined because of age or physical infirmity.

Fingerprints. If you are between the ages of 14 and 75years of age, you must be fingerprinted in connection with this application. *Applications residing in the United States.* After filing the application, INS will notify you in writing of the time and location where you must go to be fingerprinted. Failure to appear to be fingerprinted may result in denial of the application. *Applicants residing Abroad.* A completed fingerprint card (Form FD-258) must be submitted with the application. Do not bend, fold, or crease the fingerprint card. Fingerprint cards must be prepared by a United States consular office or United States military installation.

U.S. Military Service. If you have ever served in the Armed Forces of the United States at any time, you must submit a completed Form G-325B. If your application is based on your military service you must also submit Form N-426, "Request for Certification of Military or Naval Service."

Application for Child. If this application is for a permanent resident child of U.S. citizen parents, you must also submit copies of the child's birth certificate, the parents' marriage certificate, and evidence of the parents' U.S. citizenship. If the parents are divorced, you must also submit the divorce decree and evidence that the citizen parent has legal custody of the child.

Where to File.
File this application at the local Service office having jurisdiction over your place of residence.

Fee.
The fee for this application is $225. If you are between the ages of 14 and 75 and residing in the United States, there is a $25 fingerprinting fee in addition to the application fee, for a total fee of $250. You may submit one check or money order for both the application and fingerprinting fees. Fees must be submitted in the exact amount. Fees cannot be refunded. **DO NOT MAIL CASH.**

All checks and money orders must be drawn on a bank or other institution located in the United States and must be payable in United States currency. The check or money order should be made payable to the Immigration and Naturalization Service, except that:
- If you live in Guam, and are filing this application in Guam, make your check or money order payable to the "Treasurer, Guam."
- If you live in the Virgin Islands, and are filing this application in the Virgin Islands, make your check or money order payable to the "Commissioner of Finance of the Virgin Islands."

Checks are accepted subject to collection. An uncollected check will render the application and any document issued invalid. A charge of $30.00 will be imposed if a check in payment of a fee is not honored by the bank on which it is drawn.

Form N-400 (Rev. 01/15/99)

Processing information.

Rejection. Any application that is not signed or is not accompanied by the proper fee will be rejected with a notice that the application is deficient. You may correct the deficiency and resubmit the application. However, an application is not considered properly filed until it is accepted by the Service.

Requests for more information. We may request more information or evidence. We may also request that you submit the originals of any copy. We will return these originals when they are no longer required.

Interview. After you file your application, you will be notified to appear at a Service office to be examined under oath or affirmation. This interview may not be waived. If you are an adult, you must show that you have a knowledge and understanding of the history, principles, and form of government of the United States. There is no exemption from this requirement.

You will also be examined on your ability to read, write, and speak English. If on the date of your examination you are more than 50 years of age and have been a lawful permanent resident for 20 years or more, or you are 55 years of age and have been a lawful permanent resident for at least 15 years, you will be exempt from the English language requirements of the law. If you are exempt, you may take the examination in any language you wish.

Oath of Allegiance. If your application is approved, you will be required to take the following oath of allegiance to the United States in order to become a citizen:

"I hereby declare, on oath, that I absolutely and entirely renounce and abjure all allegiance and fidelity to any foreign prince, potentate, state or sovereignty, of whom or which I have heretofore been a subject or citizen; that I will support and defend the Constitution and laws of the United States of America against all enemies, foreign and domestic; that I will bear true faith and allegiance to the same; that I will bear arms on behalf of the United States when required by the law; that I will perform noncombatant service in the armed forces of the United States when required by the law; that I will perform work of national importance under civilian direction when required by the law; and that I take this obligation freely without any mental reservation or purpose of evasion; so help me God."

If you cannot promise to bear arms or perform noncombatant service because of religious training and belief, you may omit those statements when taking the oath. "Religious training and belief" means a person's belief in relation to a Supreme Being involving duties

superior to those arising from any human relation, but does not include essentially political, sociological, or philosophical views or merely a personal moral code.

Oath ceremony. You may choose to have the oath of allegiance administered in a ceremony conducted by the Service or request to be scheduled for an oath ceremony in a court that has jurisdiction over the applicant's place of residence. At the time of your examination you will be asked to elect either form of ceremony. You will become a citizen on the date of the oath ceremony and the Attorney General will issue a Certificate of Naturalization as evidence of United States citizenship.

If you wish to change your name as part of the naturalization process, you will have to take the oath in court.

Penalties.
If you knowingly and willfully falsify or conceal a material fact or submit a false document with this request, we will deny the benefit you are filing for, and may deny any other immigration benefit. In addition, you will face severe penalties provided by law, and may be subject to criminal prosecution.

Privacy Act Notice.
We ask for the information on this form, and associated evidence, to determine if you have established eligibility for the immigration benefit you are filing for. Our legal right to ask for this information is in 8 USC 1439, 1440, 1443, 1445, 1446, and 1452. We may provide this information to other government agencies. Failure to provide this information, and any requested evidence, may delay a final decision or result in denial of your request.

Paperwork Reduction Act Notice.
We try to create forms and instructions that are accurate, can be easily understood, and which impose the least possible burden on you to provide us with information. Often this is difficult because some immigration laws are very complex. Accordingly, the reporting burden for this collection of information is computed as follows: (1) learning about the law and form, 20 minutes; (2) completing the form, 25 minutes; and (3) assembling and filing the application (includes statutory required interview and travel time, after filing of application), 3 hours and 35 minutes, for an estimated average of 4 hours and 20 minutes per response. If you have comments regarding the accuracy of this estimate, or suggestions for making this form simpler, you can write to both the Immigration and Naturalization Service, 425 I Street, N.W., Room 5307, Washington, D.C. 20536; OMB No. 1115-0009, **DO NOT MAIL YOUR COMPLETED APPLICATION TO THIS ADDRESS.**

U.S. Department of Justice
Immigration and Naturalization Service

OMB #1115-0009
Application for Naturalization

START HERE - Please Type or Print

Part 1. Information about you.

Family Name	Given Name	Middle Initial

U.S. Mailing Address - Care of

Street Number and Name		Apt. #

City	County

State	ZIP Code

Date of Birth (month/day/year)	Country of Birth

Social Security #	A #

Part 2. Basis for Eligibility *(check one)*.

a.   I have been a permanent resident for at least five (5) years .

b.   I have been a permanent resident for at least three (3) years and have been married to a United States Citizen for those three years.

c.   I am a permanent resident child of United States citizen parent(s) .

d.   I am applying on the basis of qualifying military service in the Armed Forces of the U.S. and have attached completed Forms N-426 and G-325B

e.   Other. (Please specify section of law)_____ .

Part 3. Additional information about you.

Date you became a permanent resident (month/day/year)	Port admitted with an immmigrant visa or INS Office where granted adjustment of status.

Citizenship

Name on alien registration card (if different than in Part 1)

Other names used since you became a permanent resident (including maiden name)

Sex Male Female	Height	Marital Status: Single Married	Divorced Widowed

Can you speak, read and write English ?   No   Yes.

Absences from the U.S.:

Have you been absent from the U.S. since becoming a permanent resident?   No   Yes.

If you answered **"Yes"** , complete the following, Begin with your most recent absence. If you need more room to explain the reason for an absence or to list more trips, continue on separate paper.

Date left U.S.	Date returned	Did absence last 6 months or more?	Destination	Reason for trip
		☐Yes ☐No		
		☐Yes ☐No		
		☐Yes ☐No		
		☐Yes ☐No		
		☐Yes ☐No		
		☐Yes ☐No		

Continued on back.

FOR INS USE ONLY

Returned	Receipt

Resubmitted

Reloc Sent

Reloc Rec'd

Applicant Interviewed

At interview
request naturalization ceremony at court

Remarks

Action

To Be Completed by
Attorney or *Representative*, if any
☐ Fill in box if G-28 is attached to represent the applicant

VOLAG#

ATTY State License #

Form N-400 (Rev. 01/15/99)N

Part 4.   Information about your residences and employment.

List your addresses during the last five (5) years or since you became a permanent resident, whichever is less. Begin with your current address. If you need more space, continue on separate paper:

Street Number and Name, City, State, Country, and Zip Code	Dates (month/day/year)	
	From	To

List your employers during the last five (5) years. List your present or most recent employer first. If none, write "None". If you need more space, continue on separate paper.

Employer's Name	Employer's Address	Dates Employed (month/day/year)		Occupation/position
	Street Name and Number - City, State and ZIP Code	From	To	

Part 5.   Information about your marital history.

A.   Total number of times you have been married _____ . If you are now married, complete the following regarding your husband or wife.

Family name	Given name	Middle initial

Address

Date of birth (month/day/year)	Country of birth	Citizenship
Social Security#	A# *(if applicable)*	Immigration status (If not a U.S. citizen)

Naturalization (If applicable)
(month/day/year)   Place   (City, State)

If you have ever previously been married or if your current spouse has been previously married, please provide the following on separate paper: Name of prior spouse, date of marriage, date marriage ended, how marriage ended and immigration status of prior spouse.

Part 6.   Information about your children.

Total Number of Children _____ .   Complete the following information for each of your children. If the child lives with you, state "with me" in the address column; otherwise give city/state/country of child's current residence. If deceased, write "deceased" in the address column.   If you need more space, continue on separate paper.

Full name of child	Date of birth	Country of birth	Citizenship	A - Number	Address

Continued on next page   Form N-400 (Rev. 01/15/99)N

Continued on back

Part 7.   Additional eligibility factors.

Please answer each of the following questions. If your answer is **"Yes"**, explain on a separate paper.

1.   Are you now, or have you ever been a member of, or in any way connected or associated with the Communist Party, or ever
       knowingly aided or supported the Communist Party directly, or indirectly through another organization, group or person, or ever
       advocated, taught, believed in, or knowingly supported or furthered the interests of communism?   ☐ Yes ☐ No
2.   During the period March 23, 1933 to May 8, 1945, did you serve in, or were you in any way affiliated with, either directly or
       indirectly, any military unit, paramilitary unit, police unit, self-defense unit, vigilante unit, citizen unit of the Nazi party or SS,
       government agency or office, extermination camp, concentration camp, prisoner of war camp, prison, labor camp, detention camp
       or transit camp, under the control or affiliated with:
       a.   The Nazi Government of Germany?   ☐ Yes ☐ No
       b.   Any government in any area occupied by, allied with, or established with the assistance or cooperation of, the Nazi
              Government of Germany?   ☐ Yes ☐ No
3.   Have you at any time, anywhere, ever ordered, incited, assisted, or otherwise participated in the persecution of any person
       because of race, religion, national origin, or political opinion?   ☐ Yes ☐ No
4.   Have you ever left the United States to avoid being drafted into the U.S. Armed Forces?   ☐ Yes ☐ No
5.   Have you ever failed to comply with Selective Service laws?   ☐ Yes ☐ No
       If you have registered under the Selective Service laws, complete the following information:
                  Selective Service Number:_____   Date Registered:_____
       If you registered before 1978, also provide the following:
                  Local Board Number:_____   Classification:_____
6.   Did you ever apply for exemption from military service because of alienage, conscientious objections or other reasons?   ☐ Yes ☐ No
7.   Have you ever deserted from the military, air or naval forces of the United States?   ☐ Yes ☐ No
8.   Since becoming a permanent resident , have you ever failed to file a federal income tax return ?   ☐ Yes ☐ No
9.   Since becoming a permanent resident , have you filed a federal income tax return as a nonresident or failed to file a federal return
       because you considered yourself to be a nonresident?   ☐ Yes ☐ No
10   Are deportation proceedings pending against you, or have you ever been deported, or ordered deported, or have you ever applied
       for suspension of deportation?   ☐ Yes ☐ No
11. Have you ever claimed in writing, or in any way, to be a United States citizen?   ☐ Yes ☐ No
12. Have you ever:
       a.   been a habitual drunkard?   ☐ Yes ☐ No
       b.   advocated or practiced polygamy?   ☐ Yes ☐ No
       c.   been a prostitute or procured anyone for prostitution?   ☐ Yes ☐ No
       d.   knowingly and for gain helped any alien to enter the U.S. illegally?   ☐ Yes ☐ No
       e.   been an illicit trafficker in narcotic drugs or marijuana?   ☐ Yes ☐ No
       f.   received income from illegal gambling?   ☐ Yes ☐ No
       g.   given false testimony for the purpose of obtaining any immigration benefit?   ☐ Yes ☐ No
13. Have you ever been declared legally incompetent or have you ever been confined as a patient in a mental institution?   ☐ Yes ☐ No
14. Were you born with, or have you acquired in same way, any title or order of nobility in any foreign State?   ☐ Yes ☐ No
15. Have you ever:
       a.   knowingly committed any crime for which you have not been arrested?   ☐ Yes ☐ No
       b.   been arrested, cited, charged, indicted, convicted, fined or imprisoned for breaking or violating any law or ordinance
              excluding traffic regulations?   ☐ Yes ☐ No
(If you answer yes to 15 , in your explanation give the following information for each incident or occurrence the **city**, **state**, and
country, where the offense took place, the **date** and **nature** of the offense, and the **outcome** or **disposition** of the case).

Part 8.   Allegiance to the U.S.

If your answer to any of the following questions is **"NO"**, attach a full explanation:
   1.   Do you believe in the Constitution and form of government of the U.S.?   ☐ Yes ☐ No
   2.   Are you willing to take the full Oath of Allegiance to the U.S.? (see instructions)   ☐ Yes ☐ No
   3.   If the law requires it, are you willing to bear arms on behalf of the U.S.?   ☐ Yes ☐ No
   4.   If the law requires it, are you willing to perform noncombatant services in the Armed Forces of the U.S.?   ☐ Yes ☐ No
   5.   If the law requires it, are you willing to perform work of national importance under civilian direction?   ☐ Yes ☐ No

Continued on back   Form N-400 (Rev. 01/15/99)N

Part 9. Memberships and organizations.

A. List your present and past membership in or affiliation with every organization, association, fund, foundation, party, club, society, or similar group in the United States or in any other place. Include any military service in this part. If none, write "none". Include the name of organization, location, dates of membership and the nature of the organization. If additional space is needed, use separate paper.

_____

_____

_____

_____

Part 10. Complete only if you checked block " C " in Part 2.

How many of your parents are U.S. citizens? ☐ One ☐ Both (Give the following about one U.S. citizen parent:)

Family Name	Given Name	Middle Name

Address

Basis for citizenship:
☐ Birth
☐ Naturalization Cert. No.

Relationship to you (check one): ☐ natural parent ☐ adoptive parent
☐ parent of child legitimated after birth

If adopted or legitimated after birth, give date of adoption or, legitimation: *(month/day/year)*_____.

Does this parent have legal custody of you? ☐ Yes ☐ No

Attach a copy of relating evidence to establish that you are the child of this U.S. citizen and evidence of this parent's citizenship.)

Part 11. Signature. *(Read the information on penalties in the instructions before completing this section).*

I certify or, if outside the United States, I swear or affirm, under penalty of perjury under the laws of the United States of America that this application, and the evidence submitted with it, is all true and correct. I authorize the release of any information from my records which the Immigration and Naturalization Service needs to determine eligibility for the benefit I am seeking.

Signature   *Date*

Please Note: *If you do not completely fill out this form, or fail to submit required documents listed in the instructions, you may not be found eligible for naturalization and this application may be denied.*

Part 12. Signature of person preparing form if other than above. *(Sign below)*

I declare that I prepared this application at the request of the above person and it is based on all information of which I have knowledge.

Signature   **Print Your Name**   *Date*

Firm Name
and Address

DO NOT COMPLETE THE FOLLOWING UNTIL INSTRUCTED TO DO SO AT THE INTERVIEW

I swear that I know the contents of this application, and supplemental pages 1 through____, that the corrections , numbered 1 through____, were made at my request, and that this amended application, is true to the best of my knowledge and belief.

_____
(Complete and true signature of applicant)

Subscribed and sworn to before me by the applicant.

_____
(Examiner's Signature)   *Date*

Form N-400 (Rev. 01/15/99)N

U.S. Department of Justice
Immigration and Naturalization Service

OMB No. 1115-0009

N-400, Application for Naturalization
Supplement A

PART A. INSTRUCTIONS

Please complete this supplement and file it with your application *(Form N-400)* to help us better process your request. If you have already filed your application, you may complete and submit this supplement to the Office where your application is pending.

If you are submitting this supplement with your application, sign your name in ink on the side of your photographs, but **DO NOT** write over your face. Sign your name as show on your green card unless you are seeking to change your name, in which case please sign your full name as you indicated it in question 7.

Public Report Burden for this supplement is estimated to average 6 minutes per response. *(See Form N-400 for more information on reporting burden hours.)*

This supplement is considered part of your application for naturalization. All the information provided must be true and correct.

PART B. ADDITIONAL INFORMATION ABOUT YOU. *(The applicant for naturalization.)*

Last Name	First Name	Middle Name
Daytime Phone# ( ) _____ - _____	Alien Registration #	Date of Birth *(Month/Day/Year)*	Date you became a permanent resident (Month/Day/Year)

1. A. Did you graduate from an accredited college in the U.S.?
        Yes   No

    B. Did you graduate from college outside the U.S.?
        Yes   No

    •If Yes to either question, check the highest level of college degree you received:

    (Attach a copy of your highest degree to this supplement.)

    Associate's   Bachelor's   Master's   Doctorate

2. Did you graduate from High school in the U.S.?
    Yes   No

    •If Yes, how many years of high school did you attend in the U.S.?
    Less than 1   One   Two   Three   Four or more

    (Attach a copy of your high school degree to this supplement or complete the following.)

    Name of School _____ Year Graduated _____

    Location *(City, State)* _____

3. Did you already passed an INS approved citizenship test?
    Yes   No

    (If Yes, attach a copy of the test results.)

4. Have you completed an INS approved Adult Education Course?   Yes   No

    (If Yes, attach a copy of the certificate of completion.)

5. Within the past 5 years have you been required to pay child support through a separation agreement, divorce decree or other court order?   Yes   No   *(If No, skip to question 6)*

    If YES:
    •   At any time during the past 5 years were you more than 2 weeks behind in these payments?   Yes   No
    •   Are you currently more than 2 weeks behind?   Yes   No

6. Naturalization involves a formal ceremony. This ceremony can be conducted by INS or by certain courts. In many parts of the country both conduct ceremonies. However, you may request that you only be naturalized in a court ceremony. This would mean you would not be scheduled for an INS ceremony even if one were available.
    •   Would you like to only be scheduled for a court ceremony?   Yes   I have no preference

7. Your name as shown on your green card will normally be used when you naturalize. However, if you have changed your name through divorce or marriage since receiving your last green card we will update our records and issue your certificate in your current name. Any applicant also has the option of requesting a change of name when naturalizing; however, if you do we will schedule you for a court ceremony since only the court can grant a change of name.

    •   Do you want to change your name as a result of your marriage or divorce?   Yes   No
        (If Yes, attach a copy of the marriage or divorce decree.)
    •   Do you otherwise want to change your name when you naturalize?   Yes   No

    If you want to use a name other than the one on your current green card, Clearly Write it below:

Last Name	First Name	Middle Name

Form N-400 Supplement A (01-15-99)